To Donald —
With fondest fext
— wishes

Edward Villella

with

LARRY KAPLAN

SIMON & SCHUSTER

NEW YORK · LONDON
TORONTO · SYDNEY
TOKYO · SINGAPORE

Prodigal Son

DANCING
FOR
BALANCHINE
IN
A WORLD
OF PAIN
AND MAGIC

SIMON & SCHUSTER
Simon & Schuster Building
Rockefeller Center
1230 Avenue of the Americas
New York, New York 10020

Copyright © 1992 by Edward Villella
All rights reserved
including the right of reproduction
in whole or in part in any form.
SIMON & SCHUSTER and colophon are
registered trademarks of Simon & Schuster Inc.
Designed by Edith Fowler
Manufactured in the United States of America

10   9   8   7   6   5   4   3   2   1

Library of Congress Cataloging-in-Publication Data
Villella, Edward, 1937–
    Prodigal son/Edward Villella with Larry Kaplan.
        p.   cm.
    Includes index.
    1. Villella, Edward, 1937–   . 2. Ballet dancers—
United States—Biography.   I. Kaplan, Larry.
II. Title.
GV1785.V56A3   1992
792.8′028′92—dc20
[B]   91-39937
                                                          CIP
ISBN 0-671-72370-7

Every effort has been made to identify the source of material used in the picture section. Should additional information be supplied, the appropriate correction will be made
in any future printings.

ACKNOWLEDGMENTS

By my count, this is at least the fifth book written by a New York City Ballet dancer about George Balanchine. Balanchine was such a multifaceted individual that each person who stood before him and worked with him has his or her own sense of the man, based on their relationship. I think the reading public must be aware by now of the many different aspects of this extraordinary figure. I can't say that the definitive George Balanchine will be found on these pages, but this is my version of Mr. B.

I want to thank Lincoln Kirstein, Jerome Robbins, Betty Cage, the School of American Ballet, and the New York City Ballet for the influence they've had on my life; and I also want to acknowledge Stanley Williams, Janet Roberts, Marcia Preiss, and Buddy Monasch. These are people who have sustained me. They have been pivotal in my development as an artist and as a human being. I want to acknowledge my sister, Carolyn, who now runs a very successful ballet school in upstate New York, and my parents for the values they imparted to me and the love they always gave me.

I'd like to thank all the ballerinas I danced with during my career but haven't mentioned in the text; and also David Eden, Tony Randall, and the late Harry Reasoner.

I'd like to express my gratitude to Arlene Croce, whose *New Yorker* profile prompted my literary agent, Faith Hamlin, to contact me. This book has benefited from the projected one Arlene and I talked about but never wrote.

I'd like to thank my collaborator, Larry Kaplan. I'm a talker not a writer, and I think he's captured as near as possible the essence of my voice. This was a wonderful professional relationship, and it has evolved into a friendship.

And I'd like to thank Faith Hamlin for initiating the project and for working on it devotedly every step of the way.

I'd especially like to thank our editor, Alice Mayhew, for her vision of the book, her invaluable editorial guidance, and her enthusiasm throughout.

Thanks also to Marcia Preiss for her commitment to this project and for assembling the photographs for this book; to George Hodgman for his insight into the manuscript; to Eric Steel for his help; and to Charles Hayward, Dan Farley, Edith Fowler, Victoria Meyer, Mike Keller, Linda Hetzer, Joseph Spadafora, Frosene Sonderling, David Martin, and Bill Eppridge.

E.V.

6

To my loving family—my wife, Linda, who showed me the human side of life, and my children, Roddy, Lauren, and Crista, who taught me so much.

PROLOGUE: JUNE 1990

Standing center stage at the New York City Ballet, I felt I had made a pact with the devil. I was an addict returning to his old delicious poison. A decade after my retirement I was dancing a role created for me nineteen years before, and loving it. The whole thing, from the actual dancing to the feeling of the lights on my body, was a turn-on, a reminder of what my life had been about. After more than twenty years as a leading dancer with the New York City Ballet, I had been forced to quit without a proper finale. Now, I finally had the chance to say good-bye.

When Jerome Robbins first asked me to return to the stage, I howled. I hadn't danced onstage for nine years, and as head of the Miami City Ballet my schedule was already a disaster. How could I find time to rehearse and perform for Jerry Robbins, the perfectionist of perfectionists? His rehearsals never ended. There was something else, too: the pain. Throughout my career I had been in constant pain. But I had just kept pushing my poor battered body. I had punished myself for years, and even though the movement in *Watermill* was limited, I didn't know if I still had the energy or desire to dance. But I knew that if I *did* do it, I wanted to do it right. I didn't want to be a pale imitation of myself in my prime.

The role meant wearing a dance belt and absolutely nothing else 98 percent of the time, and at fifty-three I didn't think

I wanted to take off my clothes for people who'd seen me in my younger days. I was vain, embarrassed to have gotten older. I didn't relish the idea of being compared to younger dancers.

"My ego would love to do it," I told Jerry. "But I have to deal with reality. Let me consult my body and think about it for a while."

We agreed, or so I thought. But the next day Jerry announced in a *New York Times* interview that I would be returning to the stage. Typical Jerry move; he doesn't take no for an answer. I was half mad at him, but knew I would have done it anyway. And I realized he knew me well enough to know that.

It was cold in New York when I flew in to begin rehearsals for *Watermill*. I was nervous. What if my body just gave out? What if I just fell flat? At one point during an early rehearsal I grimaced and Jerry came on as if I were dying.

"Oh, baby," he said. "I hope I'm not pushing you too hard or too fast. Is this too much?"

"No, Jerry," I said. "But I will ask you one thing. Please respect my age."

Rehearsals were cake. I had a good time, got comfortable, got psyched. No surprise I suppose, but I found I couldn't wait to get back onstage. I realized how desperately I missed the rush of performing, the high of being around all the crazy, driven people, and the wild thrill of leaping high in the charged-up air. My life had been all about being onstage and being perfect. I was driven, and there are people who would tell you that during my years as a performer, I didn't care about much else. Ballet was my obsession—doing it and doing it right. Being the best. The first half of my life is the story of someone who sacrificed pretty much everything else to become the greatest dancer he could be.

Maybe I sacrificed too much, but as a member of the New York City Ballet in the late 1950s, '60s, and '70s, I had witnessed a golden age of ballet, an amazing era in which George Balanchine single-handedly transformed the art. I watched him do it. I was part of it all. He showed me what he wanted me to do in such ballets as *Apollo* and *Bugaku* by demonstrating the choreography. I imitated his movements and was able to grasp the roles. I often felt he was not only the greatest choreographer

10

I'd ever seen but also the greatest dancer. That doesn't mean we didn't argue. No artist worth anything doesn't argue.

When I was growing up, a red-blooded American boy from an Italian working-class family in Queens didn't choose to become a ballet dancer. But I fought people's prejudices about male dancers—and other battles. I even stood up to Balanchine, something that wasn't done. I tried every way I knew how to force him to see me as a real classical dancer. A complete artist, not just a technical spitfire.

Now everything was different. Balanchine was dead. The New York State Theater seemed haunted. The stage, the backstage corridors, the stairways, the studios, were empty and cold. I missed Balanchine and treasured his legacy more than ever. It had always seemed as if we never knew what it was to be without him. Now we did. Maybe he didn't choose me as his inheritor. Maybe he didn't think of me as the one who would keep his genius alive. But I will do what I can to preserve the work as it was.

11

EDWARD VILLELLA

ONE

I was a nine-year-old boy from Bayside, Queens, the block bully fast on my feet. Growing up in a tough neighborhood, I had to contend with friends who made fun because I studied classical ballet. But the best defense was a quick offense. The kids who jeered never got a chance to finish their sentences. I just whacked them and left a string of bloody noses in my wake. There were times I was bloodied and bruised myself, but I was too proud to tell my parents about the reason for my scuffles.

I come from a hardworking Catholic clan. My parents were first-generation Italian Americans, believers in the American dream, and in 1945 what did ballet have to do with the American dream, especially for a boy?

My mother was born Mildred Di Giovanni. She was raised in an orphanage after her mother died of a botched abortion, and she was bitter about her childhood. She never completed grammar school; she was forced to go to work when she was twelve. She had two dresses. One she washed and pressed every night for work. Another she saved for special occasions.

She was tough, small, and intense, so full of fire that she gave the impression of being taller than she really was. Growing up, she had wanted to become a dancer but never had an opportunity or money enough for lessons. But she was a great social dancer. On Saturday nights she went to a ballroom in 13

Corona, Queens, where she met my father, who played the piano and led the band. Between dances, she sat with him at the bandstand.

My father, Joseph Villella, was eight years older than Mom. Born in 1899, he was the son of a master tailor, one of eleven children. Nine survived. As a kid in Corona, my father walked the railroad tracks, picking up pieces of coal to burn in the family stove. But he wasn't just diligent. He was very musical and he played the jazz piano. He had no pretensions and didn't see himself becoming some sort of virtuoso, but at the time he met my mother he had his own radio show.

A short man, slight, tight, and muscly, he had an easy grace and gruff charm. He had lived in the shadow of his father, Dominick, a stiff, old-world Italian patriarch whose sense of authority he envied. My father was easygoing.

After their marriage, my mother reluctantly agreed to live in a small apartment at the back of my father's family house in Corona. My grandfather had built the house himself before the turn of the century. All of his children had been born here, and some of his grandchildren, too. I was born in Elmhurst Hospital on October 1, 1936, but spent the first years of my life in that house.

My grandfather was indomitable, but charming when he wanted to be. He was proud to have come from a small village in Calabria. His background made him feel important. I can still see his full head of close-cropped gray hair, bushy black eyebrows, and dark eyes. He had strong white teeth, every one his own. He brushed them with soot from the fireplace.

On weekends, family and neighbors dutifully gathered in his house at a table that practically ran the length of the basement. Everyone paid homage to my grandfather after Mass, feasting on food that took him two days to prepare—pasta, meatballs, sausages, and fresh vegetables from his garden. Desserts of peaches and figs were washed down with homemade wine. My grandfather regularly trimmed his fig trees in the backyard, and to simulate the climate of southern Italy, he covered them during the chilly season. He also buried his bottles of wine in an inaccessible corner of the cellar alongside jars of preserved fruits and pickled vegetables. This was Italian-style refrigeration. It made the basement clammy and dank, and I hated being sent down there.

14

My mother respected her Italian heritage, but she had her own ideas. After her marriage she did whatever she could to take control of her life. Eventually she pressured my father into buying a house in Bayside. It was far from my grandfather's, and more money than my father could afford, but we moved there when I was five. I remember Sunday evenings listening to the radio with my parents and my sister in our new house, my mother knitting, and my father with his paper and his pipe. "Duffy's Tavern" was a favorite show, and so were "Amos 'n' Andy" and "The Shadow." Civil defense wardens roamed the streets during blackouts the first few years we lived there. One night, one knocked on our door because our blackout curtains hadn't been fully drawn. It was wartime, and in those days the top half of automobile headlights had to be painted black.

My father was a truck driver in Manhattan's garment center and no longer had time for his band. Driving a truck was a hard way to earn a living in the Depression, and during the Second World War gasoline rationing made it even tougher to support a family. Dad doted on my sister, Carolyn, whom I called Carol, and was proud of her piano playing. He had long given up on me; I couldn't sit still long enough to play and showed no aptitude for music at all.

My father's closest friends were two former prizefighters who visited Friday nights. Their names were Willie, nicknamed Beanzie, and Phil, who had a nonsense nickname for me: Eddie Jabeeb. I loved watching them play penny-ante poker. And when it was time for the "Pabst Blue Ribbon Friday Night Fights," they'd let me go upstairs with them to watch. Hearing their conversations about their trainers, the gyms they worked in, and their bouts, I felt like a real tough guy.

My father was somewhat remote and preferred to be alone. Often he went fishing by himself. But he was a loving parent and I liked seeing his warm side. He had integrity and was no flirt. He was devoted to his wife and kids.

Ma was a tyrant. Because she had been brought up without parents and didn't express more tender feelings easily, she showed her love by doing everything in her power to give her kids what she never had. A first-rate seamstress, she knitted beautiful, intricately designed sweaters and scarves that looked like designer fashions. Being frugal, she saved everything, and I grew up knowing that nothing was disposable—everything

15

was to be recycled, used over and over. If we bought a pair of shoes or a new bicycle, it was an occasion, and I knew they had to last.

My mother was a devoted housewife, but in many ways she was unconventional. A health food fanatic in the 1940s, she had already discovered the books of Adelle Davis, the art of chiropractors, and the value of organic cooking. She was instrumental in curing my father's stomach pains, and her own arthritis, through diet and chiropractic treatment. Our family rarely consulted medical doctors. As a matter of course, my mother served blackstrap molasses and wheat germ, and she made her own pasta and tomato sauce and even her own yogurt. She used brown sugar and honey as sweeteners, and we never had white sugar on the table.

My mother was determined to raise us to the next social level. My father accused her of living vicariously, pushing Carol and me into ice-skating, horseback-riding, tennis, piano lessons. But nothing he or anyone else could say could stop her.

By the time my sister was nine, she was a student at the Anne Garrison School of Dance in Bayside. My mother took her to lessons, and I was left on my own. I was a strictly physical kid, a dynamo. My prizes were my baseball glove, my spikes, and the bicycle bought with my dad's hard-earned cash. Because I was constantly in motion in sneakers or on my bike, cuts and bruises were constant. Some required stitches. Whenever I could be forced into them, I wore shoes with special supports. The arches of both my feet had fallen, perhaps because of the running and the jumping I did from walls and roofs.

Always the quickest and strongest kid, I was a competitor, an achiever—and a fighter. I was also stubborn and hated to lose. I was often invited to play with older boys because I was scrappy and tough. In my neighborhood a boy was respected for his athletic ability and his daring.

One afternoon during a street game called running bases I was hit in the head by a fast-pitched hardball thrown by my friend Johnny Rocco. Wow! I felt a sharp pain at the back of my skull. Everything started to spin and grow dark. I can't remember anything else because it knocked me out.

16

My buddies carried me home, dropped me on the door-step, rang the bell, and ran like hell. I felt okay when I came to, but my mother went wild. She felt guilty because she had been with my sister at ballet school when I was brought back in a heap. She decided that I needed more supervision. The next week, I went to ballet class, too.

The Anne Garrison School of Dance smelled musty and the piano sounded creepy and out of tune. What a turnoff! Picture forty giggling girls, their moms, and me. There was no one for me to talk to, let alone tangle with. At first, I was forced to sit and watch. Boring. The floor was warped and splintery and the tap-dancing was a joke.

Fidgeting in my chair, I couldn't wait to lose the place. I had the distinct feeling that the wide-hipped instructor was eying me. When she then whispered something to my mother, I smelled trouble. I was right. "Edward," she called, "to keep you from distracting the girls, I'm going to have you join the class."

I had no say in the matter at all and I was steaming! I had to change in the head; there was no dressing room for boys. And I hated the slippers and tights. How was I going to explain this to the guys?

On lesson days, I wore my baseball uniform and cap and brought along my mitt and bat. I entered the ballet school by walking backward up the two flights of stairs so that it would look as if I were leaving the building to play baseball.

I told my mother that my ballet lessons had to be the best-kept secret on the block and begged her not to tell anyone. But she hung my dripping dance belts and tights on the clothesline and word got out. Walking to school, my friends tried to make fun of me, and I'd swing at them like mad. We'd show up in the classroom with bloody noses and shiners. Everyone noticed that I'd become better at baseball and at fighting.

I got better at ballet, too, better than the girls in my class including my sister, though she had more technique. I had raw talent, however, and energy. The barre work was dull, but the last half hour, the jumps, was fantastic. It was a great feeling to be sweating, flying across the room in the air.

My mother made my sister and me perform at the local Episcopalian church. She harbored secret plans for her two

17

EDWARD VILLELLA

children, plans centered on the School of American Ballet in Manhattan. Bayside was adequate for ballet basics, but not for what my mother had in mind. She had investigated all the options and knew about George Balanchine, his school, and his company. This was what she wanted for my sister. She had already looked into Ballet Theater and the Ballet Russe and decided they were passé. Balanchine was the wave of the future.

My sister was accepted at SAB after an audition and was awarded a partial scholarship. As my mother was leaving, she casually mentioned to Natalie Molostwoff, one of the school administrators, that she had a ten-year-old boy at home who also studied dancing. Madame Molostwoff opened her eyes wide.

"He's a boy?" she asked. "Can he walk? Bring him!"

The contrast between SAB and the Anne Garrison School of Dance was enormous. The School of American Ballet was located in an imposing building on Madison Avenue in the East Fifties, and the elevator opened on the fourth floor to a suite of offices, dressing rooms for boys and girls, and three big studios. The studio floors were clean and smooth. Shiny mirrors lined the walls, and bright overhead lights were suspended from very high ceilings.

The grand piano was in perfect tune and the accompanist chose her selections carefully, according to the kind of work we were doing. Muriel Stuart, an Englishwoman who had once danced in Anna Pavlova's company, taught the class. I knew at once this was the real thing.

On my first day, the school began to buzz about the boy who could dance. Two or three other teachers came in to observe, followed by some older students and members of Ballet Society, Balanchine's company, the forerunner of the New York City Ballet. By the time the class turned to jumps, the doorway was jammed. Without preparation, I was performing for an audience, a new kind of audience. I liked it. I mean, I *really* liked it. At the end of the afternoon, the school had informed my mother that I'd been granted a full scholarship.

At first I was worried. I thought the place would be loaded with snobs, but I was wrong. I was happy. The work had a purpose, a goal, and even very young, I wanted to work for

18

something. The movements required a degree of coordination that few people could even attempt, and I felt exhilarated when I mastered them. I was only ten, but being able to dance made me feel out of the ordinary and it was a comfort to me. I felt I had scaled some new level of accomplishment and I quickly fell in love with everyone—the dancers, teachers, administrators, and choreographers.

Seeing such stars as Maria Tallchief, Diana Adams, Igor Youskevitch, André Eglevsky, and Jerome Robbins thrilled me. I wasn't really sure who they were, but they had a physical confidence and dignity I'd never seen before. Their manner and their style impressed me. Just the way they moved and talked to each other made them seem special, more alive. They seemed like members of an exclusive, private club that was closed to outsiders. Suddenly, I was on the inside, but I knew I didn't belong. I was a rough kid, and I felt like an intruder.

My teachers intimidated me at first. They seemed like creatures from another world. One of them, Felia Doubrovska, wore flowing scarves and long skirts, and she pranced around on half-toe, scurrying—she didn't really walk. Tall and painfully thin, she was the prototype of the long-legged Balanchine ballerina and had created the role of the Siren in *Prodigal Son,* which Balanchine choreographed for the original Ballets Russes. She always gave us down-to-earth advice. "Rest well," she'd say. "Don't overwork. Take care of yourself."

Doubrovska was married to one of the other teachers, Pierre Vladimiroff. A leading dancer at the Imperial Theater in St. Petersburg when Balanchine was boy, he had been Anna Pavlova's regular partner when she had her own company. Years later, Balanchine said he thought that Vladimiroff was one of the greatest dancers in history. But unlike many of the greats, the man was very mild-mannered. He never displayed any temperament and was very sweet to all his students.

On the other hand, Anatole Oboukoff scared me to death. A gruff, flamboyant Russian, he'd grab me by my shoulders, press his face against mine, and growl, "Are you strong man today?" He'd make me prove it in the studio. He smelled of liquor and was always sucking peppermints to disguise his breath. In class he often whacked our legs, arms, heads, and backsides when we didn't do exactly what he wanted. These

19

were real blows and sent us reeling. Oboukoff lived with a former Russian ballerina and teacher, Vera Nemtchinova, and it was said she liked to drink, too. Everyone knew they weren't married. I didn't exactly understand the setup, but my mother thought it was scandalous.

Natalie Molostwoff and Eugenie Ouroussow were the chief administrators. Ouroussow was a Russian aristocrat. She and Molostwoff were cordial, but remote and aloof, and they set the school's tone. I feared them in a way, but I respected them.

In those days, there were only three young boys (including me) enrolled at SAB, so I was something of an oddity. All the other guys were older. Many, such as Robert Joffrey and Gerald Arpino, were World War II vets who were studying on the G.I. Bill of Rights. During my first week, the door kept opening as people came in to take a look at me. Sometimes dancers from the company—I remember Melissa Hayden, Beatrice Tompkins, Mary Ellen Moylan—came in twos and threes to watch and whisper. I felt I was being noticed and I didn't mind. "That door keeps opening," I remember thinking.

One afternoon it seemed as if the door flew open by some invisible force, and a lone figure stood in our midst. Electricity charged through the studio, and the atmosphere changed. I knew the man had to be George Balanchine. It had to be him! Even to a child he had an aura. I remember his looks, his elegance, his distinctive profile. But I was so brash that I wasn't at all nervous. I was delighted to show off.

Balanchine stayed that day for about fifteen or twenty minutes and then just disappeared. I was entranced.

A short time later, I spent more time with Balanchine in the studio of the renowned photographer George Platt Lynes. He was taking shots of Balanchine and some SAB students to be included in a book. My sister and I were part of this group. Balanchine wore a suit and tie for the occasion. We were in our practice clothes and stood on a raised platform. Balanchine removed his jacket and made an elaborate attempt to put us into position. He was gentle and kind, but he didn't make any small talk. He told us where to stand and how to pose. We were young students, but he expected us to do exactly what he said. Whether a dancer was ten, twenty, or thirty, he expected absolute professionalism.

20

This photo session was the extent of my dealings with him at that time because he didn't teach children's classes. But most of us used to sneak into SAB studios and watch him teach company class. I could already tell he was a very great man. I knew he was someone with a lot of power whom I had to please.

I also saw Lincoln Kirstein around the school, and I knew that he, too, was a great man. Lincoln had gone to Harvard, and he had the reputation of being an intellectual. He was also a poet and an art collector. He was rich and powerful and had rich and powerful friends. I knew he was responsible for bringing Balanchine to America and had founded SAB with him, and, later, the New York City Ballet.

Lincoln was a towering figure, nearly six feet four. He loomed like a massive, upright black silk vessel, always dressed in a suit and a white shirt and tie. He often stood with his hands behind his back, head jutting forward. In profile he looked like an eagle—like a figurehead on a ship's bow. He moved along the SAB corridor with a deliberate gait and he always seemed to be scowling. But the scowl was really a front. He laughed quickly and easily, and the impression I formed of him as an austere, forbidding character wasn't really accurate.

Just before my twelfth birthday, after I had completed two years at SAB, I started working summers as an assistant on my father's truck in the garment center. Up to that point my awareness of New York City had been restricted to SAB. I never ventured far from that neighborhood. Despite the fact that I attended the school, my parents were not comfortable in Manhattan. It glittered in the distance.

Seventh Avenue was a far cry from the realm of George Balanchine, Lincoln Kirstein, and Jerome Robbins. There was nothing refined about it. The streets were littered with dirt, people were brash and aggressive, and the hustle never let up. I replaced my uncle Ed, who was on vacation. I made twenty dollars a week, far less than my uncle earned, but a lot for a kid. My father thought the experience would be good for me. And indeed, it was an eye-opener.

I pushed hand trucks filled with hundreds of pounds of dresses, blouses, skirts, and huge bolts of fabric. One afternoon, my hand truck toppled over onto a pedestrian. The man

21

EDWARD VILLELLA

wasn't injured, but he made a great fuss. He wanted my license number and he threatened to sue me. I was scared but it turned out okay.

I had to vie with older, hard-boiled characters for freight elevators. They were always beating me out of a place. To test my strength, I'd often load my arms with batches of dresses, or large bolts of fabric, to see how much I could carry, and then walk up three flights of stairs. My biggest worry those summers was that someone from SAB or the company would see me and ask what in the world I was doing working on a truck instead of studying ballet. I was embarrassed to be doing such menial work. To be seen by anyone from the world of ballet would have been tremendously humiliating to me.

I was hypersensitive about who I was, maybe because I felt so out of place in both worlds. I felt I couldn't be a ballet dancer in the garment center, and that I couldn't be a trucker at SAB. During one summer the incident I most dreaded occurred when my father's truck was parked outside the Metropolitan Opera House on Thirty-ninth Street. A dancer I knew came out of the stage door and was headed toward me. Luckily, I saw him first. Hiding in the shadow of the truck, I turned my head and avoided his eye, and he passed without seeing me.

On the whole in those days, my sister and I were making great progress at SAB. My impatience to work on the higher levels made me sloppy in some areas, overlooking the finer points of technique and musicality, and my mother inferred from this that I wasn't really serious about what I was doing. She was fixated on my sister and grilled her intensely about every little detail of the class. It wasn't only young dance students who competed with one another; competition was fierce among ballet mothers. Mothers worried about the attention their daughters received in class and how their "line" was developing. This word was a really a euphemism for whether or not these girls were gaining weight. Invariably my mother and sister ended up quarreling about my sister's weight, and my sister would wind up in tears.

After some time, my mother took a job in a Lofts candy factory. She wanted to earn money so that my sister and I could attend a prep school in Manhattan from which she hoped we might graduate early and begin careers as professional dancers.

22

She also needed the extra cash to pay for biochemists and special diets for my sister as her weight problem continued.

Rhodes Prep, located in a mansion on West Fifty-fourth Street behind the Museum of Modern Art, was essentially for spoiled, rich kids, and a number of the students had been expelled from other schools. Once more as the son of a truck driver, I felt like an outsider. Members of the student body used to eat in expensive local restaurants during breaks, but I ate sandwiches I brought with me in brown paper bags. One of my Rhodes classmates was a young dancer, Allegra Kent. We would meet again in a few years as members of the New York City Ballet.

At the time, my father was dead set against my mother working. He never believed it was necessary for my sister and me to attend private school. In those days, only a woman whose husband couldn't provide for the family took a job, and my father was humiliated. He wanted my mother to be a typical Italian housewife, taking care of the children, keeping house, and cooking. My mother couldn't tolerate this reactionary attitude. Tensions increased. I think the conflict between my parents undermined my sister's will to dance, and relations between my sister and my mother degenerated into anger and bitterness. Carol didn't have the drive to compete against hundreds of other girls her age who were really committed to dancing.

My mother was always berating her for being overweight and for her lack of ambition. She accused her of not working hard enough. But it wasn't true. My sister was a good dancer. Once in a while, Carol answered back, but most of the time she sat silently. My sister was more like my father. He had often been on the receiving end of my mother's wrath, and he didn't like seeing his daughter bear the brunt of it now. He adored my sister and it was painful for him to see her unhappy. He often took her side. "Stop forcing her to do what *you* want her to do!" he'd shout at my mother. "Let her do what she wants!"

These quarrels were making me physically ill. I'd twitch and find myself unable to sit still. As a teenager I was allowed to drink beer. One evening when the bickering at the dinner table ruined my appetite, I drank two or three glasses of beer

23

instead of eating and lost control of my temper. I turned on my mother.

"All you ever do is harp and criticize," I screamed. "You only want to fight—it's making me crazy."

I'd never spoken to her like that and she began to cry. I felt guilty, and of course, my outburst didn't improve a thing. My parents argued more and more, and Carol became more and more estranged from them. The distance that sprang up between them was never closed during my parents' lifetime.

On the other hand, I was having success at dancing. I seemed to have a natural talent and didn't have to work hard at what other students struggled years to attain. At thirteen I could do triple air turns and all sorts of daring feats. Technique came easily to me. I went for the large gesture and liked the sensation of pulling it off. What was hard were subtleties. I lacked finesse, but my teachers didn't make an issue of it. People made fun of me for my lack of musicality, however. But since I could do all the pyrotechnical turns and jumps, I focused on that, and that was all anybody demanded of me.

By now I felt more at home at the school and thought a lot about Balanchine and Lincoln. They both personified the special new world I wanted to be part of. Although at that age I had no real understanding of its true nature, it seemed European and provocative, certainly far removed from anything I had grown up with. For one thing, I knew that Balanchine had had several wives. At the time he was married to Maria Tallchief, who was his leading ballerina. Not long after I enrolled in the school, she danced the lead in his production of the *Firebird*. I was part of the opening-night audience and was thrilled by her performance. It was said that Balanchine had given her an expensive diamond bracelet after the premiere, but I was also aware of rumors about his relationship with another dancer in the company, the seventeen-year-old Tanaquil Le Clercq. One day I saw Balanchine sipping a drink with Tanny in the Schrafft's restaurant on Madison and Fifty-ninth Street. He was oblivious of everyone but her. By then everyone knew he was in love with her. He was casting her in many new roles and wanted to marry her. Watching them together, I felt as if I were getting a glimpse of something I wasn't supposed to see.

24   I was thirteen, and just then beginning to understand Bal-

anchine's relationships with his dancers. There was always a ballerina who inspired him. He'd fall in love with her and then usually marry her. I was fascinated. So was everyone else. I had the feeling all the ballet mothers sitting in the hall would have gladly thrown their twelve-year-old daughters at him on the chance he'd become entranced with one of them and make her a star. After all, people said that in the 1930s in Europe, he had choreographed ballets for Tamara Toumanova when she was thirteen years old and Alicia Markova when she was sixteen.

The atmosphere at SAB intrigued me. The place reeked of elegance and sophistication. It couldn't have been less like the blue-collar world I came from. My father claimed that he had no interest in this world, but I think he was intimidated by it. My mother had no fear, however. The old-world Italian attitude of never going beyond one's predetermined station in life was unacceptable to her. From her perspective we didn't have to be excluded from this life. We could reach it by working hard.

That year, 1950, Balanchine choreographed selections to music by Mozart and Delibes for a program called "Music and Dance," presented at Carnegie Hall by the National Orchestra Society conducted by Leon Barzin. Maria Tallchief, Tanaquil Le Clercq, Patricia Wilde, and Nicholas Magallanes and other New York City Ballet dancers appeared on the program, which also included several SAB students. I was one of them. I wasn't concerned about appearing onstage or before an audience; what worried me was that I wasn't sure how to behave in the company of professional dancers. I was only thirteen, and I was shy. Men and women shared the same dressing room, and changing clothes in front of everyone embarrassed me. I also felt inadequate because I couldn't keep up with the general conversation. Everybody talked about painting and art galleries, and they all seemed to have vast knowledge about classical music. I thought, how can I ever belong?

Balanchine created a small solo variation on me in one of the works he choreographed. In it I had to wear a turban that had been created by the fashion designer Mr. John. As a matter of fact, Balanchine wanted me to dance a second variation, but a mix-up occurred in rehearsals and I never got to do the second piece. I was amazed at how quickly Balanchine worked. It only

25

took him two two-hour sessions to create the dances. He seemed controlled and calm, and I began to get a sense just how accomplished he was.

As time went by, it became obvious to me now that it was just a matter of time before I was going to be asked to join the New York City Ballet. Madame Molostwoff and Madame Ouroussow would each often say when I complained about something or other, "When you get into the company, things will be different. Maybe you'll move into the city."

Sometime after my fifteenth birthday I was riding in an elevator with Jerome Robbins. I was very much aware of who he was and I admired him. I'd seem him in class and knew that he was talented and widely respected—famous. Alone with him I was tongue-tied. I didn't really know what to say, and I wasn't really sure what he thought of my dancing. But he turned to me and smiled warmly. "You know, Eddie, everyone's waiting for the day you'll be able to join the company."

After that there was never a question in my mind that I'd be accepted. There weren't many young men around, and I had shown exceptional ability. I couldn't have been happier at the prospect of a dancing career. I hadn't taken into consideration that, in that era, dancers worked for only half a year at most and had to struggle financially. I had heard that Tallchief and Eglevsky, New York City Ballet's top stars, earned only $125 a week. Even at that time it didn't seem like a hell of a lot of money, considering who they were and what they could do.

Furthermore, even though I'd been the butt of some jokes and was aware of the stigma attached to ballet dancing for a man, it didn't really worry me that most people in this country were suspicious of a male ballet dancer's sexual orientation. I was confident in myself because I liked girls. I knew that my association with ballet made my sexuality suspect, and I built my defenses against it by basically denying that it bothered me.

My mother had warned me that I would come into contact with men at SAB who were interested in other men sexually. She said to me, "Beware of this, and be careful. And if you have a problem, kick 'em!"

In those days dancers were thought of as bohemians, members of the avant-garde, the kind of people who raised 26 eyebrows in my neighborhood. I had a Catholic upbringing and was taught that sex without marriage was strictly forbidden. Divorce was entirely unacceptable, and people could burn in hell for all eternity simply by eating meat on Friday. SAB's modern, liberal attitudes were a revelation to me. I met men and women living together who weren't married, and people who viewed middle-class values with disdain.

Of course it took time for me to adjust completely to this scene. There were, to be sure, many prim, young middle-class girls from Westchester and Connecticut escorted to classes by well-dressed mothers. But I also met men who wore long, flowing scarves and loose-fitting, billowing sweaters, men who camped around and called each other by drag names. Many of them used long, tapering cigarette holders when they smoked and were heavily perfumed. This eccentricity just seemed like another example of their worldly experience. No one ever accosted me, but soon enough I was comfortable in this environment. But an obstacle sprang from a quarter where I least expected it.

At the end of her senior year in high school, my sister announced to my parents that she was going to quit dancing. It was devastating news. At first my mother refused to believe it. Then she was heartbroken. After all, in order to pay for ballet lessons and private-school tuition, she had taken a job at the candy factory in Long Island City where she worked hard all day. Every morning she'd walk seven blocks to the bus stop, ride to the end of the line, get off at the Fifty-ninth Street Bridge, and still have a long walk to work. These were the sacrifices she made for my sister's career, and now she felt betrayed.

"I can't help it," Carol said. "I have to stop dancing. I won't do it. It's *my* life, not *yours.*"

My sister was her father's daughter with his values. And he stood behind her. He felt she'd endured enough abuse from my mother and that she had the right to choose the kind of life she wanted for herself. But it galled my mother to have an ungrateful daughter, and she cried and carried on. When she couldn't talk my sister out of her decision, my mother turned her back on ballet entirely and wanted it out of her life once and for all—and that meant my life as well.

My mother had a sense of my talent, but it was never as

27

important to her as what she wanted for my sister. I was always an afterthought as far as ballet was concerned. She'd made the sacrifices for my sister, and my sister's refusal to continue studying broke her spirit. She couldn't think rationally. She was thrashing about, striking out. I had to give up ballet— that's all there was to it.

At first I refused to believe that she was serious. Then I realized that she meant what she said. I was frantic. My mother, in this, had a great ally in my father, and my appeals to him fell on deaf ears. Neither one of them would budge. He said I had to quit, too. He had always thought ballet was frivolous, and that running two children into Manhattan on a daily basis was a waste of time and energy, a drain on the family resources. He'd been humoring my mother all along.

But I felt shattered. It was 1952. I was sixteen, and I knew that classical dancing was the only thing I wanted. I had been forced into studying ballet only to be seduced by it. Now it was all I thought about. The thought of giving it up was too painful. It wasn't only dancing I was giving up; I had to relinquish a whole new identity I was projecting for myself. And I felt guilty. I was a scholarship student at SAB who'd never paid a penny. It seemed to me that I owed it to them to explain the situation. But I never had a chance to say good-bye and no one ever called to ask where I was or what had happened.

I was enraged at my parents. My identity was being torn away from me. Bitter quarrels erupted, and mealtimes brought the most heated arguments. I stopped talking to them. Family ties were being broken, and my father decided to take charge. He insisted I give up dancing to go to college. Since he had never had the opportunity, he wanted me to be the first in the family to earn a college degree. But I vowed to myself that I wouldn't go. I planned to run away.

I remember making a list of how many pairs of socks and what kind of underwear I would need, and where I could get a job. I felt exhilarated, excited, anxious to make a new life for myself, but I was at a loss. What options did I have? I wasn't even sure. Most of the guys from my neighborhood went to work immediately after high school. People didn't often hear of a young man going to college. Two of my street-corner friends were now working as office boys for a firm in the

28

Chandler Building in Manhattan, and my intention was to get a job as an office boy there. I even made a budget, figuring out how much I'd need to earn a week to live on.

As the days went by, I clung to the idea of running away to become a dancer. But at least where my parents were concerned, I didn't really have the strength to rebel. A part of me was crushed, and I gave in.

I applied to Maritime College to study marine transportation because the brother of my best friend happened to be a student there. If my friend's brother had been going to Queens College, I would have applied there. I traveled to the Bronx to look at the school. They had a dress parade and admiral's inspection every Saturday afternoon, and the spectacle of it— phalanxes of bright cadets in spanking clean uniforms—was impressive. I thought this place as good as any. I didn't know what marine transportation was and didn't care.

As the start of the school semester approached, my gloom increased. I was being asked to start all over. I had been acquiring tools to build a good foundation for something that gave me great pleasure, and now I had to study subjects I had no feeling for—mechanics, mathematics, naval science, and navigation. One good thing about the school was that the curriculum included European cruises every summer, but the college was a part of the State University of New York, and regular academic subjects had to be added to an already extensive array of commercial courses, half again the load of most schools.

My father drove me to the school, which was located in Throgs Neck, and I stood at the entrance weighed down, a suitcase in each hand. Walking through the arches of what was a converted Civil War fort, I still couldn't believe what was happening. I felt confined by the walls of the school the moment I entered the gates. It was a college, but it felt like a prison.

29

EDWARD VILLELLA

TWO

Fort Schuyler, home of Maritime College, was shaped like a pentagon and stood on the tip of a peninsula that jutted out into Long Island Sound. During the Civil War, it had been used to defend Northern shipping en route to New York harbor. First-year students or fourth classmen were called Mugs, and all upperclassmen and military staff had authority over them. Mugs were required to live in "compartments" inside the Fort. Each housed twenty-four cadets in six double bunks on either side of the room.

Reveille sounded at six-fifteen, and we had to be up on our feet by the time the last notes sounded or we were put on report and given demerits. As soon as we were up, we had to shower, shave, dress, spit-polish our shoes, and brush off our uniforms. Work uniforms consisted of navy blue caps and woolen tops and trousers. They attracted lint and dust like a magnet.

Once we were dressed, we mustered into formation and stood in line at attention waiting to get into the mess deck. After breakfast came janitor duty. Brass polish, rags, mops, and brooms were issued. Later, the chores completed, we mustered again for inspection and headed for class. Among the other indignities, we were also subject to hazing.

Cadet/midshipmen were on base from Sunday night to Saturday afternoon of every week. Every fourth weekend we had to stand watch. The only time we had to ourselves was a

30

day and a half three out of four weekends. If a student received demerits, liberty privileges were denied, and disciplinary problems often led to months at the fort without a break.

Each summer, cadet/midshipmen departed on a three-month European training cruise in ships from the mothball fleet, broken-down vessels of World War II vintage. Worst was when the freshwater supply got scarce; baths, shaves, and laundry were drastically limited.

Neither the rigid structure of ship life nor the college disturbed me. The purpose of the discipline was to teach us to function as part of a greater operation. Discipline was something I was used to: ballet was much more rigorous than anything I encountered here.

I threw myself into athletic programs. Word had gotten out that I had studied ballet. So instead of waiting for the taunts, I acted first, pounding out my frustrations on the heavy bag every chance I got. They'd all see what they'd have to deal with if they crossed me. Soon enough, the boxing coach invited me to join the team, and I also went out for other athletics, as I had in high school. The year I became welterweight boxing champion of Maritime College, I also won my letter on the varsity baseball team.

My studies were going well, too. I was in the top ten in the class and had made a number of good friends. I had other reasons to be happy. My father bought me a secondhand car for my birthday, and when I traveled home to Queens for a visit, my mother loaded me up with leftovers. Outwardly, things were good. But I was just going through the motions. My father sensed my unhappiness, but he was convinced that in time ballet would become a dim memory.

No way. I became more and more obsessed with the idea of becoming a classical dancer. I wasn't sure what to do about it. How could I quit school? It meant turning my back on the sacrifices my parents had made on my behalf, and the goals they had set out for me. But I had to do something. I had to choose my own life.

Tension built as time passed. I worried I would never be able to get myself back into the proper condition to dance again. I talked about it all the time. I was trying to talk myself into going back, and people got tired of hearing me complain. 31

EDWARD VILLELLA

They started to make fun of me in a good-natured way. One morning I came flying down a corridor late for a class. My classmates saw me coming and quickly organized a prank. They jumped up out of their seats, formed a line that ringed the room, and were standing in their version of first position. The moment I charged in out of breath, they all did a grand plié. We all burst out laughing and then scurried back to our seats as the teacher arrived. He'd been late, too.

Dance continued to eat away at me. By the start of my senior year, my frustration had mounted to a breaking point. I complained all the time. "Do something about it," a friend said, "or just shut up!"

Then I started to twitch, a nervous habit from childhood that surfaced when I felt pressure I couldn't handle. I literally couldn't control my own body. I decided to take action. I talked a friend into traveling into Manhattan with me to look into a dancing school in Carnegie Hall. I knew that City Ballet dancers didn't go there. I wanted to see if I could get myself into shape and eventually present myself again at SAB.

My friend and I arrived at Carnegie Hall, entered the dingy Ballet Arts studio, took a place in the back, and audited a class. We stood out—two cadets in starchy white, brass-buttoned uniforms. I purchased a card for ten lessons, the first class scheduled for the following week.

Two problems remained. Where was I going to get the money for the classes, and how was I going to get off the base three nights a week to take them? Both problems taxed my ingenuity. Leaving the school without a pass was tantamount to jumping ship and was punishable by expulsion. I managed to sneak out at night by walking along a seawall on the beach and climbing over an unguarded fence. Some evenings in order to make my escape, I hid in the trunk or under a blanket on the backseat of a car of a buddy who had a special liberty. I also volunteered for any detail that gave me an opportunity for liberty. When I was desperate, I even forged a pass. As I look back now, it's hard to believe how rigidly the rules were enforced at the school in the 1950s. It was very much a reflection of the times.

To earn the extra money I needed, I bought cases of beer and hid them in my laundry bag. During study periods, I sold

32

six-packs to thirsty cadets. I'd knock on dorm doors in the evenings, drumming up sales. I had to be careful. I was committing another infraction that could get me expelled from the school. To add to my ill-gotten gains, I also worked in the post office during the Christmas and Easter breaks.

The night of my class at Ballet Arts, my first in nearly four years, found me extremely agitated and anxious. I was trembling, frightened. But as soon as I entered the studio, I knew that I was going to be all right. My body was still supple and pliant. My muscles remembered how to turn out, my knees how to straighten, my feet how to point. I could still turn and spin. Best of all, my powerful jump was still intact. After the class I felt exhilarated. My racing blood and the energy in my muscles felt familiar. A four-year burden had been lifted.

The next morning, however, found me in a complete state of physical shock. I could barely stand up, let alone move. Every muscle was cramped and knotted up. Even my bones were sore, and I had bruised both my big toenails. I lost both within a week. It was nearly two weeks before I could walk normally. But I was determined not to stop. That year during our annual European cruise, I had a friend, a naval engineer, hook up a DC transformer in the stateroom I shared with three other cadets. I put an LP, *Music Recorded for Ballet Class Under the Supervision of Alexandra Danilova,* on my record player and gave myself class. I locked everyone out of the cabin, closed the portholes, and worked two hours every day at sea. My roommates returned to the cabin when I was finished and complained about the odor in graphic terms.

In each port, I'd call the local embassies and use the telephone directory to track down the most professional-sounding ballet schools. In Paris I went to Studio Wacker, floor after floor of ballet studios in an old nineteenth-century building. Amenities were few, but Studio Wacker was the place to go, and such eminent teachers as Olga Preobrajenskaya taught there on a daily basis. She had been Pavlova's rival at the Imperial Ballet. I studied with a woman called Madame Nora. The pianist began playing music for pliés before Madame herself had arrived, so I simply followed what everyone else was doing. The ballerinas seemed extremely accomplished, and I assumed they were from the Paris Opéra Ballet. Niels Kehlet

33

from the Royal Danish Ballet was in the class and so was André Prokovsky, who was to become a colleague of mine at the New York City Ballet in the 1960s.

When Madame Nora finally showed up, she didn't pay too much attention to the exercises at the barre but spent time gossiping with various dancers. A faint, dark mustache lined her upper lip.

My ballet regimen continued full force the following semester at school, and it was the happiest period of my Maritime College life. I was doing what my parents wanted, but I was also taking control of my destiny, working toward becoming a dancer. But when it looked as if everything was running smoothly, during the Christmas break I was nearly killed in a brawl.

I had been drinking with my friends in a local hangout, a bar in Bayside, when six drunken and disorderly paratroopers tried to pick a fight with us. These guys had disrupted the place and were looking for trouble. Taunts were flung back and forth, and punches were almost exchanged. But the manager of the bar stepped in and threw the troublemakers out. He'd thrown them out earlier in the evening, too. The incident was soon forgotten inside the tavern. When the evening broke up, however, I settled the check and was the last of my friends to leave. Most of my buddies were already en route to their cars.

As soon as I stepped into the street, I could see the paratroopers were waiting for me. I wished them a merry Christmas and started to walk away. I only took two steps before someone came at me from behind. I was spun around, and my arms were pinned at my back. The biggest of the soldiers, who was now facing me, grabbed the back of my neck with one hand and shoved his fingers into my eyes with the other, hemorrhaging them. I was then viciously and professionally beaten and left unconscious in the street as they fled.

I woke up the next day in the hospital with a concussion, a broken nose, and multiple bruises and cuts. For a time I suffered loss of memory, speech, and even my eyesight. My face was so battered, my parents were only able to identify me by the bloody clothing lying in a heap by the bed.

It took me months to recover, and then another crisis occurred. My parents, angry and indignant, informed me that

34

they had discovered my Ballet Arts class card in the pocket of my jacket the night they took my clothes home from the hospital. They were furious and carried on as if I were trying to destroy them. There were constant quarrels, and I was further demoralized by the slow, painful pace of my recovery. My schoolwork was affected, too, because of the memory lapses I suffered. One day in the hospital I was visited by my college roommate, who was also my sister's fiancé. When my mother saw that I didn't recognize him, she burst into tears. I have never recovered full use of my memory.

The worst part was that I had missed two more crucial months of ballet training, but this only fortified my decision to continue dancing. And that in turn enraged my parents. During one of our more bitter arguments, I calmly agreed to finish college and get my degree, but what I did with my life after that would be my decision alone. After graduation, they were going to have to deal with their son the ballet dancer—or throw him out. My sister told me later that she was sorry for me but relieved for herself. For once she wasn't the one caught in a stormy battle.

It took a while for me to get back on my feet. I felt physically drained. My swollen joints and tendons refused to assume their normal size and shape, and my body was out of alignment. I was disoriented a lot of the time. I suffered from occasional blackouts and what seemed like a permanent headache. One day I was riding in an elevator and became completely disoriented. I didn't know who I was or where I was going, and it took me a half hour to regain my senses.

But after a few months my strength returned and the headache subsided, and I went right back to Ballet Arts. In order to present myself again at SAB, I drove myself mercilessly. In hardly any time at all, the improvement I'd made was clear to me. I was ready to go back to George Balanchine.

During my absence the School of American Ballet had moved from Madison Avenue to new quarters on Broadway and Eighty-second Street, a two-floor walk-up. Inside the entrance I stood at the bottom of the stairs and experienced déjà vu. The Anne Garrison School of Dance in Bayside had also been a two-flight walk-up, and climbing these stairs at SAB I felt a rush of memory. In my mind I could see the late-day sun

35

pouring in through the window at the top of the stairs in Queens, but here above me it was dark and foreboding.

There was a tremendous pounding in my chest. I had never said good-bye to anyone. I just vanished—after five years of tuition-free study. For all this time I had harbored the idea that everyone thought I was ungrateful. I didn't know if the pounding was a fear of rejection or if I was wondering whether I could really master this now. It had taken me four years to climb that staircase. This was the moment of truth. I had worn my brass-buttoned uniform and white cap for the occasion and had my battle bag in hand. I opened the plain blue security door. It was twenty-five past five. There had always been a five-thirty class.

I looked around, and to my amazement, I saw several familiar faces. The first person I spoke to when I entered was Natalie Molostwoff—"Natasha Molo."

I sheepishly said, "Hello. Do you remember me? I'm Eddie Villella."

She said, "Yes, of course."

"I'd like to take class," I said. "Can I take class?"

And in her typically Russian, School of American Ballet manner she said, "There's one starting in five minutes." There was no emotion or surprise on her part at all. Had she even noticed my absence? I thought about the cool behavior of the SAB staff, the way they kept their distance. I had always sensed an invisible line beyond which I couldn't pass. Did it reflect the Russian character, Balanchine's personality, or the way things had been done at the Imperial School and the Maryinsky Theatre in St. Petersburg? Maybe it was a combination of all three.

I went into the dressing room, my spirits rising every second. I took off my uniform and put on my dance clothes. I was back, and I went to class every day.

I had missed the start of my final college semester; there was nothing else to do but drop out. I was living at home in Bayside for the first time since I had gone away to college, and relations with my parents had completely soured. They knew I'd returned to SAB, and the atmosphere at home was filled with tension. But I didn't let it get to me. All I thought about was dancing.

36   I remember a Saturday about a week after I returned to

SAB. The company was rehearsing at the school, and there Balanchine and an attractive young ballerina were sitting together on a bench. I went over to them and asked him if he remembered me.

"Yeah, sure, sure. I do. Sure I do." He extended his hand. "How do you like new studios? It's very nice place to work," he said, using charming Russian syntax.

Somehow I got out the words, "Yes, yes, it's nice—it's absolutely the best—the only—place for me to work."

"Good," he said.

37

EDWARD VILLELLA

THREE

One afternoon at SAB, Barbara Horgan, Balanchine's personal assistant, asked if I was going to participate in a New York City Ballet audition. I thought about it and decided to as an opportunity to be seen, a chance to make myself visible. After the audition, I felt that I had shown myself technically superior to most of the other dancers. I felt powerful propelling myself into the air, in complete control of my body, and knew I had impressed the ballet masters. But before anyone offered me a job, I sought Horgan out. I needed to speak to her.

"I can't really join the company until I finish college," I said. "I still have one more semester to complete."

A look of disappointment crossed her face. "You're just teasing us, aren't you? You're not really interested."

"No," I protested. "I'd be happy to join the company, but I can only do it at a certain time."

She huddled for a moment with her colleagues. Then she returned to my side. "Okay," she said. "When you're ready to join us, let us know. It'll be fine."

My physical strength was now completely normal, and my progress at SAB was rapid. After inquiring at Maritime College, I learned that, in order to get my degree, I was going to have to wait over six months to make up the semester I lost. Forget it; the time had come: I was going to join the New York

38

City Ballet, and I spoke again to Barbara Horgan. There was a hitch, however. It was May 1957, and the company was about to embark on tour to Chicago. There was no place for me, no money in the budget to hire a dancer who wasn't going away with them—and how would I have learned the ballets in time? They were all leaving! I felt as if I were being left high and dry.

But Lincoln Kirstein heard about my problem, and he took the matter into his hands. He approached me and asked for the details of my situation.

"Things are very difficult for me," I answered. I didn't know exactly what to say, but I explained the state of affairs with my family.

By nature Lincoln is brusque. His direct, no-nonsense manner cuts through everything, and he got right down to business.

"We can take you into the company in ten weeks when we return," he said. "Until then I'll be able to help you out."

I looked at him blankly. What did he mean "help me out"?

How much money will you need a week to live?" he asked.

"Thirty-five dollars," I replied. The sum just popped out of my mouth. It was the amount my friends were earning a week as office boys.

On the spot Lincoln wrote out a check for three hundred and fifty dollars and handed it to me. Then he turned and walked away. I was rattled but delighted, and I remember thinking, what do you know? It's just as if I've been given a signing bonus by a baseball club or football team!

For the time being, I had completely forgotten about returning to Maritime College; in fact, it would be over two years before I was able to get my degree. My parents refused to speak to me at all when they learned that I planned to join the New York City Ballet. They deplored what they called my deceitfulness and they didn't like my throwing away a college education they had paid for. They wondered about the kind of life I would lead as a dancer and how I would make a decent living. I had other concerns. All I thought about was dancing. Every day I went to class, working hard to get myself in peak condition for the company's return.

To make use of the time, I landed a role at the Phoenix

39

EDWARD VILLELLA

Theater on Second Avenue in an off-Broadway musical based on *Tom Sawyer* called *Livin' the Life*. It was a way to pick up some stage experience and earn some money. The musical, which had a limited run, was choreographed by John Butler.

It was fall 1957 when I joined the New York City Ballet. Besides staging a major revival of his 1928 masterpiece *Apollo* for Jacques D'Amboise and Maria Tallchief, Balanchine was choreographing four new ballets, *Square Dance, Agon, Gounod Symphony,* and *Stars and Stripes*. The company was burning with energy.

There was no honeymoon period, no initiation week. A new dancer at City Ballet is thrown in and has to make his way. As a corps de ballet member, I had to learn fourteen roles in two weeks, and I was totally overwhelmed. I didn't know the basics. I had no background or experience, no idea at all how a dancer learned a repertory, or what he might use as memory aids.

Some dancers can pick up a ballet cold. Some just need music. Others need music and have to take notes. Still others need fellow dancers to learn from. I wasn't even sure of the kind of dancer I was. The first day of rehearsals I was totally terrorized, and I learned nothing. I was astounded that everything went by so fast. Nothing was broken down and hand-fed. We had to pick it up while it was in the air, so to speak, and those who didn't fell further and further behind. I needed time to analyze and digest what I was doing. I couldn't sleep that night. I thought to myself, I'll go in there tomorrow and find that everyone has the same problem I do. But no, everyone in the company already knew the ballets. They were long past analyzing and digesting. They just did the steps. The only other new dancer that season was Conrad Ludlow, and he had already had experience with the San Francisco Ballet. I was virtually alone. And lost. I had no process, no way of knowing how to do anything myself. But I watched what was being demonstrated by the ballet mistresses and imitated the movements of the other dancers. Soon enough I began to catch on.

The corps de ballet roles I had to learn that season included *Symphony in C* (second movement), *Western Symphony* (fourth movement), *Allegro Brillante, Orpheus* (lost soul), *Firebird* (mon-

40

ster), *Swan Lake* (hunter), and *Pas de Dix*. Learning the choreography was very tough. I thought I'd never get through it. But I was also part of the raw material Balanchine was using to create two of his new works; I was going to dance in the corps of *Square Dance,* and in the boys' regiment in *Stars and Stripes*.

The first time I worked with Balanchine personally was when he was choreographing *Square Dance*. I was a complete neophyte and knew nothing about the choreographic process, but seeing the steps pour out of this man was a revelation. He could just walk into a studio and begin choreographing the way most people begin to talk. It seemed that easy for him.

Balanchine was in his early fifties, but he moved like a man twenty years younger. He had vitality. He wore loose-fitting denim cowboy shirts with the sleeves rolled up, and soft trousers and jazz shoes. He wore a silver and turquoise bracelet sometimes and rolled the bottoms of his trousers up. Often his shoelaces were untied, but he always looked elegant.

Watching him work, I thought he was making everything up on the spot, but I later realized he had thought it all through beforehand. To see him go from one studio to the next, change gears without effort for each of the four new ballets he was creating, was extraordinary. After a rehearsal, he'd say, "Okay. Where do I go now?" Somebody would point him in the right direction; he'd move into a studio and start working on another of the new ballets. Each became a masterwork, a breakthrough. All remain in the repertory today.

Although Balanchine's behavior gave no hint of a problem, I heard he was going through hell. In 1951, his marriage to Maria Tallchief was annulled and he married Tanaquil Le Clercq. Tanny was his muse, and she had been one of the company's most glamorous stars. But in 1956 she was stricken with polio in Copenhagen where the company was on tour, and she nearly lost her life. She was left paralyzed from the waist down.

Balanchine's relations with women were complex. He had married his first wife, Tamara Geva, when he and she were young dancers in the Soviet Union. After they parted, he became involved with another Russian ballerina, Alexandra Danilova. He and Danilova never formalized their union, but they

41

lived together as man and wife in Paris when Balanchine was the ballet master for Serge Diaghilev's Ballets Russes and she was one of its leading dancers. He created roles for her in several ballets, including *Apollo*. In America in the 1930s, he was married to Vera Zorina, and he choreographed dances for her on Broadway and in Hollywood films.

Balanchine always said, Ballet is Woman, and each of his wives became an integral part of his art. Male dancers were secondary. It was Woman that inspired him and challenged him. "In politics it's Eisenhower, in sports it's Mickey Mantle, in ballet it's Woman," he would say.

"Women are more flexible," he explained to an interviewer. "They have more ideal body for ballet for technique, for speed, for fine technique. Boys made to jump, to lift the girl, support the girl. But boys don't have speedy legs because they are not built that way. I learned how to teach women. Almost nobody know, I think only Petipa and I. Male dancer is like prince consort. He's not the king, but she's the queen."

So I was to learn. I learned other things, too: everything in the New York City Ballet existed to serve Balanchine. All his other dancers, and everyone else, were part of his predetermined structure. No one was allowed to violate or disrupt it. Balanchine could clearly make his displeasure felt when some other dancer detracted from the Chosen ballerina. He chose who got the spotlight, and as a rule he didn't like it at all when a dancer wanted to exert control over his own career.

No one could do anything about the situation, and it seemed that no one wanted to. To everyone in the New York City Ballet, Balanchine was the holder of all knowledge, the provider, and he sheltered us. He was a genius. We all wanted to give ourselves to him, and everyone wanted to be the primary object of his interest. We were all always striving to be number one, but the men knew they could never be.

At the time I joined the company, there were several young dancers who were inspiring Balanchine. Diana Adams was one. She was tall with long limbs, beautiful proportions, and a good technique. Balanchine admired her dancing and was choreographing an important role for her in *Agon*. And Allegra Kent, whom I had first met at Rhodes Prep, was another he was clearly becoming obsessed with.

42

Balanchine flirted constantly with the girls as he worked, and for the most part he ignored the men. He'd play up his European manner and lay on the charm with the girls, talking about perfume and jewelry, Fabergé and Van Cleef and Arpels. They would respond. He seemed interested in all of them.

He said, "I remember perfume very well. I see girls, I give them some perfume . . . because I like to know where they are. I come to the theater, I recognize scent and I already know who's here."

I noticed that when Balanchine spoke, he sometimes sniffed. It was a nervous tic, a kind of twitch, and as a youngster in Russia it earned him the nickname Rat.

The atmosphere in Balanchine's rehearsals was relaxed. I watched his feet to pick up the movements. Nothing was described or discussed. He'd work intensely for twenty minutes, then take a break and tell stories and anecdotes. He was a charming raconteur. He talked once about the time he was a young man in France in the 1920s, living with Danilova. He told about a quarrel they'd had over a convertible he had purchased, his first car, which he drove to a seaport town and abandoned on a pier. Even as a young man he had little use for material things.

Balanchine was open and friendly with all his dancers and company staff members, including the stagehands, who called him George (the dancers called him Mr. B). But I also saw that he had the ability to keep people at a certain distance, which seemed appropriate. I didn't take it personally if he seemed aloof. I didn't expect that he'd have much to say to me.

During *Square Dance* rehearsals, I began to experience my first severe muscle cramps. I simply didn't know how to pace myself. Company class was held in the morning, and rehearsals continued through the early afternoon. There was a four-hour break from three P.M. to seven when SAB had exclusive use of the studios. By the time we were ready to work again, my muscles had completely cooled down. I didn't know that I could easily adjust to this cooling-down period by warming up again with a brief barre. Instead, when rehearsal started, I just plunged right in.

Square Dance wasn't as hard to learn as some of the other ballets; I was picking it up along with everyone else as it was

43

being created. But *Square Dance* had intricacies that I had difficulty mastering. Set to music by Antonio Vivaldi and Arcan-
gelo Corelli, it was full of syncopated combinations, shifting
balances, and sophisticated rhythms recalling eighteenth-
century dance forms as well as nineteenth-century classical
technique. It was danced with a full-out, energetic, neoclassical
attack that evoked the American West and the high spirits of
American social dancing. When he was first choreographing
Square Dance, Balanchine worked only with the dancers and a
pianist. We had no indication that it was going to be performed
with the orchestra on the stage and include a genuine square-
dance caller reciting calls he had made up himself. The caller
and the string orchestra were on a platform stage right, over
which a huge wagon wheel was suspended from the flies as if it
were a chandelier. In rehearsals I picked up the ballet quickly,
and that was satisfying; it was as if I were finally catching on.

Stars and Stripes, choreographed to music by John Philip
Sousa, reminded me of a spectacle at Radio City Music Hall,
and I was sure Balanchine had been inspired by some of these
images. *Stars* showed me what fun dancing could be. It gave
me a false sense of confidence, a sense that I could be brash and
bash my way through a role. This misapprehension didn't last
very long. Looking in on the *Agon* rehearsals brought me up
short. Here I formed an impression of what serious art could
be. *Stars* was all fun and wit. *Agon* was much more complicated, and its music by Igor Stravinsky was absolutely unset-
tling. I'd never heard a score like that, and it took me a very
long time to understand it.

Before this, I had worked only with scores that had a
simple and regulated beat. My SAB training hadn't prepared
me for musical challenges or given me a complete sense of
musicality.

Musicality is the relation of the attack within the dance
movement to the music. Moving to music in a Balanchine
ballet can be difficult because of the rhythmic complexity of the
scores he used. At that time, I didn't know about angularity or
syncopation, or about falling off and passing through balances.

Even Sousa's music in *Stars and Stripes* was something of a
strain for me. Sousa's marches themselves are straightforward,
foursquare, and not hard to hear or count. But Balanchine used

44

an orchestration that would allow him to make his own comments on the music as he had done in *Western Symphony* and would do again later with *Tarantella*. Because the Hershy Kay orchestrations reflected Balanchine ideas, dancing *Stars and Stripes* became a challenge.

I could see immediately that such sophisticated, highly developed musicality was going to be a problem for me. When Balanchine worked with eighteenth- and nineteenth-century music, his choreography supplemented the music. It may have made a comment on the score, but it also reflected the framework and the melody of the piece. Twentieth-century music by composers such as Stravinsky, Webern, and Hindemith, however, was another story. The dancer had to know the structure and architecture of these scores. We had to acquire the higher mathematics of twentieth-century music, make order of what at first sounded chaotic. Since this music can't be hummed, the scores themselves had to be studied. If a dancer didn't read music, and I didn't, this meant listening to recordings, which weren't always available. We didn't have cassettes in those days. I had to lug around a thirty-five-pound Tannenberg reel-to-reel tape recorder, on which I taped a recording when I was lucky enough to find one. Some of these scores still didn't make sense to me even after listening to them many times.

I had never had confidence in my musical ability and had repeatedly been told as a child that I was unmusical. My mother and her friend Jean Kresa, a singing teacher, used to laugh at me because I couldn't carry a tune. Unpleasant memories of being forced to take piano lessons as a boy lingered with me. Balanchine never commented on my musical aptitude one way or the other. But now that I was aware of the crucial position music played in the New York City Ballet, I saw myself at a tremendous disadvantage.

My main concern during the rehearsal period for the season was the corps de ballet roles I was learning. I wanted to be noticed but didn't want to call undue attention to myself, and I worried about making mistakes. But my relative anonymity didn't last long. In a matter of weeks after joining the company, which had actually occurred on my twenty-first birthday, I was

45

told by Jerome Robbins to learn the male role in *Afternoon of a Faun*. I was scheduled to perform it during the second week of the season. This was completely unexpected. I knew next to nothing about the ballet, and being chosen by Jerry kind of mystified me. I had taken class with him years before and had certainly been aware of him and his work, but we didn't really have a relationship. Robbins had been away for a while from New York City Ballet and was coming back to look after his ballets.

I was flattered and excited. *Faun* is a pas de deux set in a ballet studio, a fleeting encounter between a young man absorbed with his image in a mirror and a woman who enters the studio and interrupts his reverie. It's set to music by Debussy, the same score that Nijinsky used for his ballet for Diaghilev's Ballets Russes in 1912. That choreography caused a scandal.

The thing that concerned me most was that I was going to have to partner a ballerina. I had no background whatsoever in partnering, none, no ability at all. I was fifteen years old when I left SAB, and the adagio training that would have prepared me for the task was not a part of my education. I thought to myself, well, you were an athlete in college. You used to knock people out in the ring. You're stronger for your size than anyone you ever met. Just rely on your strength. This is how I reasoned. But I soon learned that using strength alone in partnering is like fighting a guerrilla war with tanks.

Partnering was to become a continuing problem for me during the first years of my career; it would take me a few years to master the art. Allegra Kent, the young NYCB principal who was going to dance opposite me in *Faun*, could tell right away I was incompetent, and worse, might sabotage her performance. During rehearsals, I overpartnered her, clutched at her, and held her hand with every ounce of strength I had. But gracious lady that she is, she still consented to dance with me. I can only imagine what she might have asked Robbins and Balanchine: "Are you sure this is the right moment for this guy to be dancing this role?"

The two master choreographers prevailed. I was cast for the part, and Nicholas Magallanes, an experienced principal dancer, came to the rehearsal to give me some pointers on partnering. Later, I realized that Allegra must have asked him to help out.

46

Another challenge in *Afternoon of a Faun* was that I had to create a character, reach the audience dramatically as well as show off my technical capabilities in this role. The ballet depicted a brief sensual encounter between two dancers in a studio. I danced with my shirt off. I was very young and felt that I looked good in the part. Jerry Robbins gave me a lot of visual imagery to use.

"You've just come out of the shower," he'd say. "You've put on cologne. It's summer, late afternoon, and you're lying in a shaft of sunlight."

In those first few weeks, no one else had worked with me individually in any other ballet. In Europe, roles are prepared six months in advance, and people who danced them previously coach new dancers in parts. At the Bolshoi, for example, a great prima ballerina such as Galina Ulanova might teach a young ballerina the role of Juliet. This wasn't the policy at City Ballet, and I soon found out that sometimes only six days to learn and dance a role was a lot of notice.

I thought all went well at my first performance of *Faun,* but after the curtain fell, Jerry came rushing backstage. He was agitated and didn't say a word about my dancing.

"That makeup, that makeup!" he cried. "We couldn't see your face out there. All those wonderful things you'd been doing in rehearsal were lost. We couldn't see your face."

Not knowing anything about makeup, nor being taught anything about it by anyone in the company, I had just streaked on Pan-Cake, lipstick, and eye shadow in the dressing room, convinced I looked presentable. I must have looked a sight. It was assumed that I was a professional simply because I was in the company, but I was an amateur. Today New York City Ballet has a makeup artist and a hair artist. In those days, no one was hired to look after such things. Dancers were expected to work it out themselves. Quite frankly, I wasn't too concerned about makeup. My body was my primary articulator, and throughout my career makeup was never a major concern unless I was doing a role such as Oberon or a ballet such as *Bugaku.* We corrected the makeup in subsequent performances of *Faun,* and Jerry eventually said complimentary things about my dancing.

A number of years later, I learned that I had actually been Jerry's inspiration for *Afternoon of a Faun* when he had seen me

47

as a teenage student work at SAB on Madison Avenue. Studios there had huge windows, and sunlight often poured in through them. One afternoon, I was standing in the fading light daydreaming and leaned against the barre, yawning and stretching absentmindedly. Watching me, Jerry was struck with an idea for the ballet. Although I was very flattered by that story, I was glad that I had been unaware of it when I first danced the role.

There were other surprises that season. One day Balanchine stopped me and matter-of-factly told me that I was going to be the understudy for Todd Bolender in *Agon*. I thought this was terrible news. *Agon* was probably the single most complicated work in the history of classical dance up to then. I was still trying to adjust to the sounds of the music. It was the first time I had been exposed to such a stark neoclassic style, an almost total abstraction of classical technique. Even an experienced dancer would have had his problems trying to follow *Agon;* for me it was a nightmare. Having been away for four years, I didn't know about the developments Balanchine had been making in the art, and I was completely out of my depth.

I didn't really have the confidence then to perform the remarkable gestures the ballet called for, gestures that I had not only never done but had never seen before. The first time I performed them they felt unnatural, and I was as uncomfortable with them as I was later on in my career when I had to do mime. But Balanchine said, "Ballet dancers make the unnatural natural," and I kept on working until these movements came more easily. One factor worked in my favor, almost subconsciously. *Agon* was a wholly American work, a representation of the new classicism, and as an American the style of the movements readily, almost instinctively, suited me.

During that first season, no matter where, rehearsal studio or backstage, I'd badger everyone into helping me. When a person learns badly, no one wants to be around him, and I had to seek help. I'd constantly corner Richard Rapp or Arthur Mitchell and ask them to reexplain something to me about the steps and the counts in various ballets that I hadn't picked up in rehearsal. Richard Rapp was exceptionally musical and gifted, and a great source of inspiration to me. But I felt his dancing only further exposed my ineptitude. I'd also go to Richard

48

Thomas because I'd forget what Arthur and Richard Rapp had told me. I'd corner them when they were working or rehearsing or just sitting around and hanging out, and I'd beg them to go over sections of ballets so I could master the steps and the counts. I shared a dressing room with Rapp, Thomas, and Arthur, and at Christmastime I gave each man a leather belt because I had hassled them every spare moment all season.

In the long run, however, it was satisfying to have been present at the creation of *Agon*. I was dazzled by it all, by the way our attention was intensely focused on Balanchine in the studio. Everyone waited, still and quiet, while he pondered a problem staring blankly at his index finger. Suddenly he'd come to, clap his hands, and say, "Okay," and he'd start working again.

One day when Balanchine was choreographing, the session was unexpectedly interrupted by a visit from a man whom everyone treated as royalty. In each of the huge studios at the school, a door opened onto a platform, and a staircase descended into the room. On this particular afternoon, everyone in the studio was intent on the ballet—the rehearsal was generating a great deal of energy and vitality, and no one paid any attention to who was coming in or out. All at once, activity came to a standstill. The door had opened, and everyone's eyes turned to an unusual-looking figure who was standing on the platform. I felt a change in the air, but didn't realize what was going on. What was happening? I wondered. I stopped what I was doing and looked up.

The tiny little man at the top of the stairs was wearing a huge camel's-hair coat that fell well below his knees and practically hid even his hands. Only a joint or two of his fingers, covered in gray suede gloves, peeked out from the sleeves. On his head was a homburg that came down over his forehead to his eyebrows. I noticed glasses and a mustache, and that he was carrying a cane. He didn't move a muscle, but the entire room paid reverence.

The rehearsal pianist, Kopakeine, was the first to rush up. Then Balanchine climbed the stairs, and together they escorted the visitor down the staircase into the studio. I could see that he commanded the greatest respect. Everyone hovered around him.

"Who is that?" I asked the dancer alongside me.

"It's Igor Stravinsky," she whispered. The famous composer, of course, who had written the score for the ballet.

Inside the room, Stravinsky moved to a chair, took off his hat, and handed it to his companion. Then he put his cane aside and removed his muffler, his coat, and finally his jacket. This tiny man grew even smaller as he shed his outer garments one by one. But once he got down to his shirtsleeves, he looked enormous. It was incredible: he assumed the proportions of a giant.

Stravinsky and Balanchine pored over the score together. They stood around the piano, talking in Russian and English. Sparks were flying. We all felt exhilarated in the presence of these two witty geniuses. They seemed to fill the space in the studio. Energy had doubled since Stravinsky's arrival, and now everything in the room was orbiting slowly around the startling vitality Stravinsky and Balanchine were generating.

In a few moments, Balanchine went to work again with the dancers. Occasionally, he'd stop and turn to the composer, and the two of them would savor the moment. What a thrill to see them collaborate. The pleasure they took in the work, their compatibility, not only as Russians and colleagues but as artists, was palpable. We even shared in their laughter. After a step or a gesture had been done to their satisfaction, they would stop the pianist and beam—they were so pleased with what they had created. It was remarkable to have the composer on hand, but of course the civilized atmosphere in which the work was being done was typical of the way Balanchine worked. Stravinsky was so relaxed he even conducted a little. He was so polite, so gracious, that it might have been patronizing if it hadn't been clear that he was absolutely sincere.

On that afternoon we were all aware—at least I know I was—of the significance of what was happening. It isn't often a person can say that he is witnessing an event that's going to change a country, a world, an art form, whatever. But we all felt that *Agon* was a ballet that was going to alter ballet history. And it did. I have never, *ever,* heard such screams and shouts of approval in a theater before or after. It was truly unbelievable.

50   Winter 1957–1958 was a landmark season for the com-

pany. I thought I had danced well and knew that Balanchine was aware of me, satisfied with what I was doing. But no specific acknowledgment was made of my presence. I already saw that Balanchine didn't personally interact with anyone until a particular situation presented itself. But I wanted to prove to him—to everyone—that I was worthy of being there.

I sometimes felt, however, that I didn't fit in. I had heard that the City Center was planning to revive the Irving Berlin musical *Annie Get Your Gun* for a brief run at the end of the ballet season. I thought that many of the dancers would take part in the show and mentioned that I intended to go to the audition. Everyone I told was aghast. They acted as if I'd made a real gaffe by even mentioning it. They were New York City Ballet dancers, not Broadway hoofers, and no one had any intention of becoming involved with the musical. I went ahead anyway and landed a place in the ensemble. I guess I was just a different kind of guy.

EDWARD VILLELLA

FOUR

I didn't have very many male friends in New York City Ballet. Most of my pals were women. I gravitated toward them naturally because I liked women a lot, and I was surrounded by ballerinas who didn't have any male colleagues interested in them as sexual beings. I *was* interested in them sexually, and I was unmarried. I got asked out to a lot of parties, but I usually turned down these invitations. I didn't want to lose sleep I needed for work. Nothing kept me from work. Maybe I thought my parents would forgive me if I became a star.

One night after a performance, however, I was asked to a party by someone who had come backstage to visit Herbert Bliss, a principal dancer in the company. I was free, my schedule was light the next day, and I needed to get out and relax. Like many principal men, Bliss was a real pro. He had been very helpful, watching out for me during performances, making sure I didn't make mistakes. He was up-front sincere. Since he was going to the party, I knew there'd be someone there I knew, so I decided to go. I showed up at the address on my own.

It was a luxurious town house. As soon as I arrived, I saw a dancer I knew, but the look on his face puzzled me. He seemed surprised to see me and somewhat embarrassed, too. I greeted a few other dancers and they also looked at me oddly. Going up the stairs, I tried to figure out what was wrong, and

52

when I got to the landing and looked into the main room, I saw the problem. There were no women at all at the party, only men. In my naïveté, I'd accepted an invitation to a gay party. Now it was my turn to feel awkward and unsure of what to do. I assumed that Bliss had been too embarrassed to tell me the kind of party it was—he probably thought I'd never show up. I didn't want to hurt anyone's feelings and didn't think it was right just to turn around and bolt. I didn't want to humiliate myself or anyone else for that matter, so I figured I would stand around unobtrusively for a few minutes and then make my good-byes.

The main room was dominated by a huge armchair in which Cecil Beaton, the famous photographer and theatrical designer was seated, holding court. The room kept filling up with faces I knew, most of whom were visibly surprised to see me. I started searching about for a telephone and headed for what I thought was an empty bedroom. Someone I knew stopped me as I was about to go inside and said, "I wouldn't go in there if I were you, Eddie. That's the 'cha-cha' room."

I finally found a phone and called Carole Fields, a dancer in the company I'd been seeing. It was pretty late, but I asked if I could visit her that night.

Carole said, "Come over right now."

I hung up the phone, let myself out without ever seeing my host, and was at Carole's within minutes.

My relationship with Carole had begun almost as soon as I entered the New York City Ballet, and she was my first serious romantic involvement. A member of the corps de ballet, she was tall, blond, beautiful—and I was tremendously attracted to her. But emotionally, I was still a kid. I had gone from a strict Catholic household to military college and ballet school without ever having much romantic experience or anyone to really explore my deeper feelings with. I lived strictly for work. But I was wild about Carole. She lived in a studio apartment on West Fifty-seventh Street, and instead of going back to Queens after performances I often spent the night with her.

And life was good. I was a dancer, I was earning a living, and I was growing up. But the New York City Ballet season was already taking its toll on my muscles and tendons, even on

53

my bones. Not only did I know next to nothing then about warming up and prepping myself to dance, I didn't know how to care for my body after a performance. In fact, my body was in a precarious state because of the four-year break in my training. I didn't know that this was the start of problems that would plague my entire career. Instead I gloried in every ache. The pain was satisfying. I thought it meant I was working full out and was well on my way to greatness. It was wonderful to go home each night practically unable to walk.

At the end of the winter 1958 season, the company departed for a six-month tour of Japan, the Philippines, and Australia. The trip had one fantastic consequence in that it enforced an extended separation between my parents and me. Both had been suffering over their relationships with their children. My sister had married and left home and my mother was disappointed all over again. She let me know it quite clearly that I had doubled her pain by becoming a dancer. I don't know what upset her more: the unorthodox career choice or the fact that I had defied her.

My father was also wounded; it was as if he had lost his son. Both my parents believed I had a new life they could never be part of. I was concerned that they didn't understand what I was trying to do with my life.

The Pacific tour was an ordeal. In 1958, it took forty-four hours with three stopovers to fly to Tokyo. We had to adjust not only to the time change but to the exotic food, the customs, and the language. I was nervous, scared of the strangeness. Japan was utterly intimidating to me. I couldn't read signs in restaurants or in our theater, couldn't ask directions on the street or communicate with most of the people. Our hotel resembled an army barracks with prisonlike cells.

In Australia, conditions improved a little, but the weather was cold and damp for much of our stay, and the chill permeated everything. Dancers always try to stay warm, and it was impossible. People wore woolen gloves in class. I was disoriented by all the changing time zones.

During one performance in Australia I had an accident. Doing a double air turn, landing on one leg and sliding the other along the floor, I broke a bone in my big toe, the first of many fractures I would suffer as a dancer. I was told to stay off

54

it for two weeks. But I disregarded the doctor's advice and continued to dance, slitting open a section of my ballet slipper. It was stupid.

After Australia, the weather was hot and humid in the Philippines, and we performed in an enormous Quonset hut that seated five thousand people. The floor didn't rise away from the stage on a slight incline as it does in most theaters; the seats were all on one level. When we looked out into the audience, we saw a flat sea of heads. There was no air-conditioning, and my sympathy went out to the dancers in *Scotch Symphony* in their velvet jackets, hats, and woolen kilts. Backstage conditions were primitive. There was no place to rehearse or warm up; we'd use the stage for this purpose while the stagehands and technicians were setting up.

Surprisingly, Balanchine didn't stay with the company for the entire trip. I believe he returned to New York to spend time with Tanny, who was convalescing and confined to a wheelchair. Class was often taught by principal dancers, Maria Tallchief or André Eglevsky. Dancers who are still performing tend to give classes that suit their own needs, and for much of the time we were abroad I felt deprived of the usual company class.

Still, in many important ways, the tour was beneficial. I was getting to see more of the world, learning what it was like to perform on unfamiliar stages in faraway places. I learned about makeup, how to line and shadow my face, and how to take stage lighting into consideration when making up. I learned about costumes, and how to make minor tailoring adjustments. Madame Sophie Pourmel, the girls' wardrobe mistress, had to keep after me about keeping my hands clean so I didn't soil a ballerina's tutu when I was partnering her. And I finally got used to wearing tights.

Eventually on the tour, I got to learn and perform many new roles, and because of this I was introduced into the Byzantine world of ballet politics. New York City Ballet politics were unique. Balanchine had eliminated the old-world Ballets Russes star system perpetuated by temperamental ballerinas and haughty premier danseurs in which certain roles were reserved for the few. In his company, Balanchine had the final word about casting.

In Australia I got a glimpse of how things worked and

55

what could happen. At this time, Tallchief left the tour briefly and her role in *Swan Lake* was going to be danced by Diana Adams. But Diana was injured on the day of the performance, and Balanchine had let it be known that, in such a case, Allegra Kent, whom Mr. B was entranced with, was to dance the role. This infuriated Melissa Hayden and several other senior ballerinas. Hayden, one of the company's leading dancers, believed she should have been next in line. But it was out of the question to challenge Balanchine.

Milly was incensed, so angry that she took her rage out on her partner during a performance of *Firebird*. As she whirled around doing a pirouette, she attacked the poor man with her outstretched arms and dug her feet into the floor so that he had a hard time lifting her. What could the poor guy do? He was helpless. Humiliated by Balanchine, Milly would have exploded at anyone unlucky enough to get in her way. What other recourse did she have? She knew she was competing with Allegra Kent, Balanchine's newest muse. And that was not an enviable position.

As a rule, all of us tried to look out for ourselves and work as well as we could within the guidelines Balanchine had set up. Many knew how to play the game and get his attention. I knew that strategic alliances were being formed by various dancers and ballet masters and mistresses, but I wasn't really able to recognize or describe the maneuvers I was witnessing. I just sensed what was going on.

Among the members of the company on this trip were two dancers in their thirties, a man and wife who had joined NYCB mainly to travel to the Far East. Members of a troupe Alexandra Danilova had brought to Asia two years before, they had never been paid by the Japanese promoters for their efforts. They wanted to return to Tokyo to see if they could get the money that they were owed.

My impression was that Balanchine had brought them on the tour because he needed seasoned performers. These were not the kind of dancers he intended to build a repertory on. Nor did they represent the future of the New York City Ballet. They were both charming, delightful, lovely people, and one of our ballet mistresses became very friendly with this couple. In her professional capacity, the ballet mistress had the power

56

to hand out roles, and since Balanchine wasn't always around, she cast the man in several important ballets.

One afternoon during a rehearsal of *Con Amore,* a ballet by Lew Christensen in which Jacques D'Amboise danced the lead, this dancer showed up to understudy him. I happened to pass by, looked in for a moment, and went on my way. As I was leaving, Jacques broke away and called me over.

"Why aren't you in the rehearsal?" he asked.

"What are you talking about?"

"You're supposed to be understudying this. You should be here."

"This is the first I've heard of it," I said.

"Well, I happen to know. You're the understudy."

"How do *you* know?"

"Well," Jacques said, "I've seen the understudy list of leading roles prepared by Balanchine, and you're doing this one."

I had no idea that such a list existed.

At this point in the conversation, Jacques and I noticed the ballet mistress standing nearby glancing at us suspiciously.

"I'll talk to you about it later," Jacques said, and he returned to the rehearsal.

Later, I met him in the dressing room where he told me about the list. Somehow he had seen it and knew what roles were on it. While we were talking, the door flew open, and the ballet mistress rushed in in a state of controlled hysteria. She looked at me, and before Jacques or I could say a word, she said, "You know, Eddie, there's a whole series of roles I'd like you to learn," and she reeled off the names. They were all the ones Jacques had mentioned. In addition to *Con Amore,* they included third movement *Symphony in C,* Robbins's *Interplay,* boys' regiment *Stars and Stripes,* and third movement *Western Symphony.* These were choice roles, excellent pieces that required a great deal of jumping that suited my allegro technique. I assumed the woman knew that Jacques had told me about the list and was cornered into admitting she had disobeyed Balanchine's wishes by promoting her friend. Now she was forced to teach me the parts. By the midpoint of the tour I began to appear in many of them.

There were repercussions. A number of dancers resented me. I learned that before the tour, a mature soloist had had a

57

screaming argument with Balanchine about the number of roles I was getting. He got no satisfaction and quit. Coincidentally, Robert Barnett, another dancer in the company, left and I inherited his parts. I suddenly had a repertory of my own, and a very good one.

I didn't want to gloat. It wasn't pleasant to see other dancers hurt and unhappy. But of course I was pleased by the chances coming my way. I was gaining confidence in myself. Even in the corps de ballet I'd been aware of the audience's interest in me, and I adored the attention. I was ecstatic about the opportunity to learn these roles on tour before having to perform them at City Center.

Back in New York by summer, during preparations for the new season, I felt like a rising young star. I was called to rehearsals for *Interplay, Stars and Stripes, Western Symphony, Symphony in C,* and *Agon.* Balanchine had no choice but to use me in *Agon.* Todd Bolender was taking a temporary leave.

"You're going to do it," Balanchine told me.

I was intimidated, and I tried to pull together what I remembered. When Balanchine first asked me to understudy the role, he was just finishing choreographing it, and I had learned the role in bits and pieces. I had never rehearsed the ballet from beginning to end. I had never rehearsed the opening canon with the three men who would be doing it with me. Performing it was going to be baptism by fire, though Balanchine coached me himself one afternoon in the variation. It was the only section of the ballet on which he personally worked with me.

The first thing he had said was, "You shouldn't do it like Todd. You should dance your way because you are en l'air dancer. Be aware of that."

He told me not to dance it softly. "Dance like a man. Just attack, and dance like a man," he said.

That was comforting to me because Todd's approach was very mellow. His gestures had no edge and he moved softly. His movements had a wonderful, natural, flowing quality. I had another personality, another temperament, another attack, and Balanchine was urging me to do it my way. That gave me the confidence to let go. But I was still afraid.

Lincoln Kirstein came back after one of my first performances, and I asked him what he thought of what I had done.

58

"Not very much," he said.

My heart sank. I repeated what I had been saying over and over to myself. "I don't quite know what I'm doing."

Lincoln faced me squarely standing over me like a giant. As always he wore a black suit, and a white shirt and tie, and he was scowling more than usual. I think he was trying to shake me up a little, trying to get me to think.

"You look like the same old Eddie Villella. You have to make your own comment," he said.

As the fall 1958 season got under way, there was a great buzz about me in the theater. People must have been thinking, "Who is this kid dancing such important roles?" No one had really seen me. I had danced exclusively in the corps during my time with the ballet—except for *Afternoon of a Faun,* in which I had the lead. I was an unknown commodity, a boy who'd left the school and didn't grow up in the company, and here I was —all over the place. I stood out, and I reveled in it. But there was a lot of pressure on me. I had often read about actors and other performers who had trouble handling overnight success; now I understood.

One night, early in the season, I performed *Interplay,* which opened the program, and also danced the principal role in the third movement of *Symphony in C.* I loved ending with this ballet. It was something I knew I could really do—it suited my abilities. I could hear the audience gasp and hear the round of thunderous applause when I made my first exit during the movement. The gasp and the applause rang out again when I did the repeat. It stirred me up, higher than I'd ever been.

Years later, Arlene Croce, *The New Yorker* dance critic, described her initial impression of me onstage that night:

I saw a dark-eyed devil in an orange sweater fly backward through space about seven feet off the ground.

That was for starters. He returned in *Symphony in C*— leaping on in the third movement at the moment when, after the opening fanfares, the music catapults to an A chord from an octave below. Then, with the music rebounding to a persistent keening chord in A, he continued to leap and land, circling the stage on a stream of air while murmurs of amazement ran through the house.

59

EDWARD VILLELLA

Coming to rest beside his partner, he began an amusing little vamp in plié, then launched into sautés downstage and up, looping the sautés together with a jaunty turn or two en l'air, after which he shot out of sight in a jump that touched off pandemonium.

The buzz died down, we settled ourselves expectantly, and then he was back, and the miracle happened again: the unstraining, space-swallowing round of sauté, grand jeté, sauté, saut de basque, the climactic grand jeté off. All just as before, only higher. And grinning like a tiger the whole time.

I had purchased two balcony seats that night, all I could afford, and sent them to my parents. They had reluctantly agreed to come to the performance, under the impression that I'd be dancing small roles, struggling in the corps. I think they were shocked to see me in two leading roles, and were even more taken aback by the audience's enthusiastic response.

After the curtain came down, I was still in costume standing on the darkened stage with Balanchine. My makeup was running and sweat was dripping from my body. Balanchine was telling me what I had done right—and wrong—in the ballets. The curtain was up again. The house was empty, and a stagehand had put on the night-light, one dull bulb.

After Balanchine and I finished talking, we shook hands. He went off in one direction. As I started to move toward my dressing room, I saw my mother and father standing in the wings in tears. The three of us fell into each other's arms and laughed and cried and hugged and kissed. From that time on, my father carried my picture in his jacket and flashed my reviews all over the garment center. My mother made my father buy her an electric juicer for Christmas. Each night she prepared celery shakes, and jars of carrot and spinach juice. She'd leave them out for me to drink when I returned home from the theater.

60

FIVE

Generally speaking, there are two kinds of dancers: those who can't wait to get onstage and those who are scared, who wrap themselves up in nerves. There was never much doubt about the kind of dancer I was. I couldn't wait to get onstage, and I couldn't wait for the curtain to go up. I was always on. I left nothing in the stable, nothing in the rehearsal studio. And I always felt that I was commanding the stage when I stepped out on it. I wasn't always in control of events in my personal life when I was a young man, but onstage it was simple. I gave everything.

I attacked every role I danced with abandon. For me, the real excitement was in beginning to formulate my style of dancing. I was trying to define a concept of what a position is and how it's achieved, how a dancer links gestures and moves on, passing through each balance to get to the next position.

Everybody has his own quality of movement. I was able to dance fast, move with power, jump high, and do intricate beats. People say I brought my athleticism to dance. It was always inside me. It *was* me. The energy and attack that was essential for this kind of dancing was second nature to me, part of my temperament. And it was what Balanchine wanted: attack, speed, angularity, getting from position to position by passing through, not by landing and posing, waiting and pre-

61

EDWARD VILLELLA

paring for the next step. Balanchine wanted linkage, the steps linked to one another, the dancing linked to the music. What was hard for me to do was to extend and elongate, to develop a more lyrical sense of movement. In order to achieve this, I was going to have to work through my physical problems and develop an inner understanding of neoclassicism in my body and my mind.

But it was wonderful for me at first to see my instincts confirmed by the artistic direction Balanchine was taking. He was turning away from the overly adorned, the self-conscious, mannered style of Western European and Soviet ballet. Imperial grandeur and posturing—posing—were passé, no longer a vital part of twentieth-century dancing.

Although my career was beginning to take off, there were great gaping holes in my technique. Inside, I suspected that I was getting away with something—temporarily. I was dancing on raw talent, using devices to cover up my inadequacies. Sooner or later, I was afraid that someone was going to see through me, and I'd be exposed. I had raw talent, potential. But I didn't really know the nature of my potential, or how to develop it. Balanchine kept casting me, but I think he was beginning to categorize me as a bouncing ball of energy without much artistic depth.

As time went by, I began to realize that Balanchine was using me in a very specialized area, in such roles as *Western Symphony* (third movement), Candy Cane in *The Nutcracker,* and the Thunder and Gladiator section of *Stars and Stripes.* I had danced more strictly classical roles, such as third movement *Symphony in C,* and the *Glinka Pas de Trois,* but it was almost as if I were a kind of demi-caractère performer and not a true classical dancer, a danseur noble. A character dancer often performs national folk dances and doesn't have classical technique or have to be classically placed. He enjoys a lot of freedom and can dance on instinct. Demi-caractère dancing is somewhere between character and pure classical ballet dancing.

Dancing all those pyrotechnical, allegro roles could have made someone happy, I suppose. But I wanted to become a complete dancer. My mother, who wanted and needed so much in life, had raised me to play for everything I could. I

62

was determined to break away from being typecast. I wanted to be considered a premier danseur, a classicist.

I also didn't want to limit myself to the repertory that Balanchine had reserved exclusively for short people.

In a way I never really accepted that I was small. But I *was* short for classical ballet, five feet eight, and in Balanchine's company this was a particular liability. He loved *tall,* long-limbed girls, and they towered over me on pointe. But I had good proportions. Offstage, people would stop me, saying, "You can't be Eddie Villella—you look too small." People repeatedly told me I looked like a six-footer onstage. Yet Balanchine didn't seem to recognize that. Offstage, I tried to please him and did everything he asked for in class, but it didn't make a difference in the way he saw me. I decided to fight him. I wasn't going to give in to typecasting, but I wasn't sure what to do. There was no system to help me, and I felt that I didn't have the background or experience to do it on my own. I wasn't exactly sure where to turn or whom in the company I could trust.

Many of the dancers who weren't a part of Balanchine's inner circle tended to emulate Jacques D'Amboise. I thought, "Why not?" Jacques had seemed interested in helping me in Australia. Maybe by modeling myself after him I could figure out a way to overcome the limitations imposed on me by my height.

Jacques was tall and gifted. He was a good partner, knowledgeable about the company style and happy to share what he knew. He was a couple of years older than me and seemed like someone I could be friendly with. We were from similar backgrounds. I'd known him since I was a kid of ten or eleven. We used to roughhouse after class, wrestling and carrying on, which often made me late for my train home. When I had returned to SAB after I'd dropped out of college, Jacques was already a principal. He had joined the company at fifteen, and I looked up to him. He impressed me as El Capitan in *Stars and Stripes* and in the fourth movement of *Western Symphony,* roles choreographed for him by Balanchine. And yet I had reservations. I felt that he was more involved with audience response than with serving the ballets themselves. He seemed superficial.

As I got closer to him, I saw that, behind the easygoing   63

façade, Jacques was ambitious. Company politics were sometimes reflected in his personal relationships. Jacques was shrewd
—he knew how to play the game.

Our friendship soon cooled. Rumor had it he had been
talking about me behind my back to Balanchine and Lincoln,
laughing at me, putting me down, and I heard about it. Jacques
was important to Balanchine. He was a good dancer, an excellent partner, and he was tall. Once the season was announced,
he would decide which roles he wanted to dance and usually
got them for himself and Melissa Hayden, his regular partner.
I didn't understand this. I thought Balanchine made all the
major decisions about casting. Now I understand a lot more
about position and power—and how they are obtained and
used. But as a junior member of the company, I was naive.

Hayden wasn't in the inner circle. She was Canadian and
had begun dancing in her teens, late for a dancer to get started.
She was not a traditional Balanchine ballerina. She lacked the
line and the long legs of Balanchine's ideal; she was fairly small,
with broad shoulders. She survived in the company through
tenacity, passion, and determination. I think her aggressiveness
was really a defense. She was trying to attain the highest level
in the art form, but she wasn't playing with the best hand. But
she was devoted to ballet, and nobody ever worked harder.

Milly had a distinctive speaking voice, nasal, urban, deep
throated—not the soft, wispy feminine voice most people associated with ballerinas. She was tough. She used to give herself vitamin B_{12} shots for energy. One day she said to me,
"Honey, take down your pants." I obliged and she poked me
in the behind with a needle.

We used to call her Old Ironsides, and we meant it with
affection. I had tremendous admiration for her because, like
me, she didn't fit the ideal. I identified with her because I was
also ignored by the tight group of company insiders. Many
times I missed out on invitations. Balanchine always asked several dancers and other company associates to his apartment on
Easter Sunday. He was an excellent cook and invitations were
highly coveted. I was never included on the guest list, and it
hurt.

Still, I tried to cling to the idea that everyone involved in
an artistic organization such as the New York City Ballet was

64

selfless and devoted to a noble cause. I learned that people there were hard-nosed like anywhere else. We all suffer from the same disease—being human. I was disappointed that I couldn't find an ally in the company, saddened that Jacques, because he was so ambitious, was forced to act like an insecure, calculating person, but that was the way it was.

In my experience the only dancers who remained above the fray were Patricia McBride and Kay Mazzo. Kay was always open and honest. Patty was a perfect innocent. She never resorted to underhanded tactics in standing up for herself, yet she persevered, often walking unscathed through terrain littered with minefields.

I was beginning to see that a dancer's world was complicated—and insular. Ballet was an emerging art form in those days in America, a struggle that required commitment. Dancers gravitated toward their colleagues who were fighting the battle with them. Who else could understand the hard work, the discipline, and the sacrifice that goes into such a life? Dancers developed a common bond. Unlike many of my colleagues, however, I had experienced the outside world. I hadn't just danced through my early years. There was no doubt I was an outsider in the New York City Ballet. Just as I had left the gates of Maritime College to reenter the world of ballet, I sometimes left the world of ballet to go my own way.

In 1958, during my second season at NYCB, I made my first television appearance in "Dancing Is a Man's Game," a program conceived by Gene Kelly, which he hosted on NBC-TV's "Omnibus." A number of athletes appeared on the program, including Mickey Mantle, Sugar Ray Robinson, and Bob Cousy. Kelly's point was to draw a parallel between the physicality and grace of dancers and athletes. In the show, which was broadcast live, I danced a ballet solo that was intercut with a routine by Olympic ice skater Dick Button. Balanchine had been very much against my participating in the project.

"The only people you should work for are Picasso, Stravinsky, and Cocteau," he said. Aside from himself, he meant. I saw at once the kind of religious order he was talking about, and I knew who the high priests were. In the 1930s and 40s, Balanchine had had a great deal of experience on Broadway and

65

in Hollywood, and he believed his dancers had to be presented properly in the world of commercial entertainment. But he accepted my decision to participate when I told him I needed the money. He could understand that.

As far as I knew, no one from NYCB watched "Dancing Is a Man's Game"; no one ever mentioned it to me. The show was broadcast live from a vast studio. But it was so filled with lights and technical equipment that there wasn't much room for dancing. Performing for three different cameras presented me with a problem—the front area to which I'd be playing continually shifted, and I had to accommodate myself to these moves as I danced. The show served as an introduction for me to the problems I'd encounter on subsequent television appearances. I found it helpful to have cameramen and directors who were agile and musical and had a sense of movement, even though they were unfamiliar with dance.

I was learning more about my profession every day. I decided to stop worrying about being accepted by people in the company, however, and became even more fanatic about improving my dancing. It was obvious I had to work on partnering, which was a horror for me. Partnering is a crucial aspect of a classical dancer's technique, and I would not achieve the status of a classicist unless I mastered it. It is an art that can't really be taught.

Like the steps themselves, the elements of partnering in a Balanchine ballet are extremely complex. The technique is intrinsically unconventional; it goes far beyond what's taught in the classroom. People can be taught the principles and sense the proper technique, but ultimately a dancer must pick it up for himself.

The natural instinct of a dancer who is an inadequate partner is to tense up, panic, and clutch. But a man must assist a ballerina in a pas de deux. The way she's presented is crucial. He doesn't *hold* anything when he partners, not even a ballerina's hand. He *offers* his hand, and his support, but only the support required. If he grips a ballerina too tightly when she's on pointe, she can't feel her balance; she's trapped, unable to progress in a smooth continuation of movement.

66   At first, I was always a count late. I wouldn't let go of my

partner's hand until I was sure everything was all right. I didn't know my way around a ballerina. An artist has to learn his way around a stage, other dancers, and, especially, his partner. My instinct was to hunker down—big girls were coming at me.

Most of the women in the company, except for a few of my girlfriends, didn't want to work or rehearse with me. Even fewer wanted me as a partner in performance. No one said it to my face as Allegra had, but I was sure they complained to Balanchine. He was very good about it. He'd listen patiently, but continued to cast me. Years later, we discussed it. He didn't rebuke me. He said it took a long time for everyone to learn how to partner. But I believe he left me out of ballets he was creating for Allegra Kent at the time because of my problem.

Of all the New York City Ballet ballerinas, Violette Verdy was probably the most vociferous about not wanting to be cast opposite me. She was French and had danced with Roland Petit's company and with American Ballet Theatre before becoming a member of Balanchine's troupe. She and I were the right size for one another and were often paired. I could sympathize with her reluctance, but I wasn't going to back off. I wanted to take advantage of every opportunity to practice. On one occasion, I had been called to a rehearsal of *Donizetti Variations* to dance the lead opposite her. Waiting onstage for the rehearsal to begin, I looked off into the wings where she and Balanchine were engaged in animated conversation. She was in tears, and I knew at once it was because she had to work with me. Later, after she had dried her eyes, I walked over and asked her if she was ready to begin.

"Oh, no," she said. "My foot . . . I need more warm-up." She began working by herself.

The rehearsal was scheduled for an hour; forty-five minutes later she was still at the barre. She had managed to avoid me for most of the session.

I approached her again.

"Now, I'm ready," she said.

We walked out onto the stage, but before we even began she turned to me and said, "Oh, no. My foot still hurts. Can we do this tomorrow?"

Because she continued to stall, Balanchine intervened and forced her to dance the role with me. Later, she tried the same

67

tactic when we were cast together in *Swan Lake*. She avoided me at every rehearsal. When I spoke to her, she had one excuse after the next: she was injured, hurt, ill, late, busy with another appointment. Rehearsal after rehearsal, there were excuses. She was gambling that I would be too frightened to appear in *Swan Lake* without adequate preparation and would back out of the ballet so that she could dance it with Conrad Ludlow, her regular partner. I had rehearsed with Violette little more than a quarter of an hour for *Swan Lake;* all told, my hands hadn't been on her for more than twenty minutes. And I didn't know the sequence of the pas de deux. But I was not going to bow out. On the day of the performance, Jillana, another dancer in the company, asked if she could help me. Jillana, who used only her first name professionally, was very close to Nelly, as she called Violette (Violette's real name was Nelly Guillerm).

"I'd like to help you out," Jillana said kindly. This wonderful woman knew I was desperate, and she had taken pity on me.

The company was appearing at an outdoor theater in Washington, D.C. Jillana took me downstairs underneath the dressing rooms to a sandpit that was covered with a wooden plank, and there on the afternoon of my debut, she showed me the pas de deux. Up to the last minute, Violette thought that I was going to cancel. She was surprised when I showed up for the performance. We went onstage and did it. It wasn't the smoothest performance the company ever gave of the ballet, but it turned out to be a respectable reading. I think Violette was somewhat surprised that I had the nerve to go through with it. She wasn't totally pleased with the results, but I think she got the idea that I was determined to improve my partnering.

A similar situation occurred when Balanchine cast me opposite Verdy in a production of *Theme and Variations* he was staging for the company in 1960. Originally Erik Bruhn, the great Danish danseur noble, had been cast. He had been appearing with the company as a guest artist. Bruhn was a paragon of classicism, one of the greatest stars in the history of the Royal Danish Ballet. His dancing was based on purity of line, and if any of the positions he hit were even slightly imprecise, he felt it undermined his performance.

68

Bruhn and Balanchine didn't get along. They came from different worlds, and they had a falling out over *Apollo*. Balanchine had taught Bruhn the role and went over it with him in the studio one afternoon before announcing that he expected him to dance the ballet that same evening. Bruhn objected. He hadn't even had a stage rehearsal with the Muses, but Balanchine said, "You know ballet. You can do it."

But Bruhn balked. From his point of view it was unthinkable. He refused and quit on the spot, although he was to return to the company in 1964 for a few performances as Tallchief's partner.

A few days after he left, I was thrown into *Theme and Variations* as a last-minute replacement. *Theme* is a demanding ballet. Of all the roles in the international repertory, it's one of the most challenging for a male dancer. The variations are fiendishly difficult. Of course Violette was terribly upset, and I could understand it. Her opportunity to dance with one of the finest and most celebrated classical stylists in the world had fallen through, and the alternative was—guess who? There was nothing she could do but complain, and she poured her heart out to Milly Hayden. She bemoaned my inability to partner and said that it was awful to work with me.

"He's not mature enough to carry the performance. He's going to ruin the ballet," she said.

"Honey, don't worry," Milly said. "He'll bring down the house with his solo variation and no one will care."

Violette was a consummate professional. Her willful refusal to rehearse with me was an unusual expression of temperament on her part. But from her perspective, she was being realistic, protecting herself. I was a drag on her artistry and she was a perfectionist. She used to wear herself out doing classes and warming up. She was always working. By the time she got onstage, I often wondered if she'd saved enough energy to get through the role. Yet despite my apprehensions, Violette sparkled onstage in everything she danced.

Violette was probably the most musical dancer I have ever met. She could talk knowledgeably about a ballet score, and she'd often inadvertently embarrass a conductor because she knew more about the music than he. Onstage Violette dressed immaculately; offstage she never wore makeup or looked like a

69

star. She seemed dowdy. Her hair was blond and she had large, expressive eyes and a friendly smile. People were naturally attracted to Violette and found her easy to talk to. She was charming. She had a quick, analytical mind and a spiritual, metaphysical side. As time went by we became pals and we danced many symphony dates and guest appearances together, all over the world.

For over three years I worked—struggled—to become a good partner. In the beginning, I thought about it all the time. I tried every tactic possible to improve. And when I began to show progress and felt that I had mastered the basics, I concentrated on the subtleties and began to attend to those. One day I just stopped thinking about it, stopped trying so hard, and because I was thinking about it less often, my fears about it began to diminish. I became comfortable. I was able to place my ballerina on pointe in an arabesque at arm's length with one hand during a performance and feel relaxed. One evening after a performance I said to myself, well, you got through that ballet without thinking about it. You weren't terrified. It just came together. And then I realized, I know how to partner! It was remarkable. I never thought it would happen. This problem that had plagued me for over three years now seemed like my best friend. I suddenly loved it. When Violette found herself the beneficiary of my newfound expertise, she expressed her gratitude in her typically witty way.

We were making a guest appearance dancing *Tchaikovsky Pas de Deux* at Jacob's Pillow in Massachusetts, and as a result of using too much energy or too strong an attack, Violette had suddenly fallen off-balance during a series of turns. But there I was, anticipating her every movement, and I was able to quickly straighten her on her feet. We continued to dance the complicated series of supported turns and positions that close the adagio, which ends when the ballerina, held off the floor with her head down, turns her gaze up to meet her partner's eyes. As Violette's eyes locked with mine, she said, "Thanks!" What amazed me was that she said it in perfect tempo—it was like a tag line to the music. Such quick wit was an example of her humor. Once when we were dancing *Le Corsaire* pas de deux on a concert tour, she came out onstage to dance with me with a carnation between her teeth.

70

Some dancers don't like partnering, don't like performing a service to the ballerina. But I grew to like being a cavalier. Looking after a woman onstage, projecting the sense of caring, of giving something to a woman, is a wonderful, masculine feeling, and it became one of the great sensations of my life.

71

EDWARD VILLELLA

SIX

George Balanchine was stimulated by the energy and vitality of America, by the vast open spaces of the country and the towering cities. He was also fascinated by the people, their daring and abandon, their straightforwardness and enthusiasm. And various elements of American popular culture such as jazz, movies, Broadway musicals, and social dancing appealed to him, too. He once told me, "You know, when I was a young man in Europe, I dreamed of coming to America because I wanted to be in a country that produced gorgeous women like Ginger Rogers."

Balanchine found the materials he needed for his art in America, where speed and syncopation made up the tempo of the streets. He found young people who were athletic, brimming with physical energy and their own complex rhythms. Balanchine drew energy from these young American dancers. He used them to create a pared-down, linear, energetic classicism in an unbroken series of masterworks. I was a part of it.

From my first season with the ballet I had the sense of taking part in something new, exciting, and unprecedented. I was riding a surging tide. At the time, America led the world in the arts, and Balanchine was on the cutting edge. He hadn't always had the money, and he never had the desire to mount the big, old-fashioned, nineteenth-century works everyone had

72

grown up on, so he did something else. He used serious musical scores to create a new look in dance. At first, he couldn't afford costumes, so his dancers appeared in practice clothes, which showed off his choreography even more. Later, it became something of a trademark. He was a visionary.

I was on a permanent high. Early on, there were few conflicts. I didn't have a point of view, firsthand knowledge, or understanding enough to like or dislike what was going on. I was intimidated by Balanchine, and I was always trying to please him. I gave him my life, my blood, my energy, and I went to every class. Anything he requested I did. I was drawn to his confidence and naturalness. He didn't try to impersonate a prince; he was one, more than anyone I ever met.

In all the years of our association, Balanchine and I never had an open, slap-you-on-the-back, let's-go-have-a-drink kind of relationship. I never got closer than arm's length. It wasn't allowed. I was usually tongue-tied around him. I couldn't just let go and get an easy conversation going. He made me uncomfortable because he was so sure of himself and his art. And because I was not yet *me*. I had this drive and passion, but gaps existed in my whole sense of myself. To conceal my insecurities I developed a veneer of brashness.

Maybe Balanchine understood in his way. He was a very unassuming man. He read the *Daily News* and ate in coffee shops. Everyone knew he loved soap operas and Westerns on television, and that he ironed his own shirts. He was friendly with members of the company's production staff, people like Leslie Copeland, our wardrobe master, whom everyone called Duckie. Duckie is a lovely man, English and chatty. Balanchine appreciated his humor. I think Mr. B had the need to relax with some people, to let go and not always have to be "George Balanchine," on top of everything. Duckie once admitted that Balanchine came to him to hear all the company gossip. At some point wardrobe people have direct contact with every dancer, and dancers tend to open up to them because they aren't competitors and don't represent a threat.

But even if he could be unassuming and gossip loving, Balanchine never let any of us forget he was the boss. He enjoyed keeping people in their place. Sometimes he liked intimidating dancers. In conversation, he'd intentionally lead people

73

into areas where they were uninformed. This made him feel powerful and others feel insecure. He also used his ability as a raconteur, his marvelous way of relating an anecdote, to manipulate people, especially the men, and especially me! I think he sensed that I didn't really go out of my way to say what he wanted to hear and that I was beginning to resent his opinion that I wasn't a classical dancer.

I could never score points with Balanchine. Once I tried to ingratiate myself by pretending I didn't know the story, which is apocryphal, about how he came up with the position the women are standing in when the curtain rises on *Serenade*. Each girl is facing the audience, one arm raised up high, palm stretched outward. One of the dancers had inadvertently raised her arm in rehearsal, and Balanchine was inspired to include it in the ballet. Of course he knew I was aware of the story, but I persisted in asking him how he came up with the pose.

"You know," he said sarcastically, "Hitler stole that pose from me and made it into Nazi salute!"

I tried not to listen to all the gossip that sprang up about Balanchine. He was still married to Tanaquil Le Clercq, but I knew he had fallen in love with Allegra Kent. During the two years I had been in the company he had staged *The Seven Deadly Sins* in which Lotte Lenya sang the role of Anna and Allegra danced it. The ballet got a lot of attention from the critics. Mr. B also created a big role for Allegra in *Episodes*. But relations between them were strange. Allegra was very much a free spirit, unconventional, and a bit eccentric. She had been raised in California and dressed with imagination and flair, in flowing skirts and colorful fabrics. Other times she'd string safety pins together, insert them into her pierced ears, and wear them as dangling earrings, and she'd often tie a thread with a single button around her neck and wear it as a choker. She had the look of a hippie, way ahead of the time.

I knew that Balanchine's attentions made Allegra uncomfortable. And he was uneasy with her, which was odd because it was usually men he had difficulty communicating with. He often asked Felia Doubrovska to intervene for him when he wanted to talk to Allegra. But I don't think he pressed his case. He regarded all his ballerinas, not only the famed muses, as members of his own family, and he treated them in a protective

74

manner. He discouraged his female dancers from marrying. He would often say, "Why do you want to get married? Now you're somebody, you're an individual. If you get married, you'll become Mrs. Somebody." But of course, he didn't want to lose control of his dancers, or share them with other men.

Even though Carole Fields and I were still together, I sometimes dated other women in the company. I thought it was ridiculous to avoid asking out the dancers Balanchine seemed particularly interested in. But it was often difficult to form a friendship because many of the women didn't want to become the subject of gossip. Sometimes, women tried to keep other company members from finding out they had accepted dinner dates with a dancer, or with any other man. If one person knew a piece of gossip, invariably everyone in the company did, and it would get back to Balanchine. In a way, he was the worst gossip of all. He loved to dish. He knew everything that concerned his dancers and had an opinion about everything. He knew exactly whom you might have gone to lunch with two times in a row, whom you were fooling around with or planning to get involved with, whom a particular dancer was living with, or might be planning to live with. It was hard to keep anything from him.

I once asked a young woman in the company to have a drink with me, and she accepted. I suggested a local bar.

"No, no. We can't go there," she said. "It's too close to the theater. There might be some dancers around, and if Mr. B finds out . . . ?"

"If Mr B finds out?"

"Well, yeah."

"Now wait a minute. Are you having a relationship . . . ?"

"No, no, but—"

"Well, what do you mean 'If Mr. B finds out'?"

"Well, he won't like it."

That incident replayed itself over and over. Balanchine considered his dancers his own. He wanted to control whether or not a man had a relationship with one of his women. Some years later, after the company had moved to the New York State Theater, an elevator door opened onto the corridor where I was waiting. Inside was Balanchine, surrounded by young   75 dancers, a bevy of healthy, vibrant, corn-fed American beauties. Everyone was beaming, and laughter sounded in the air. I stepped inside with a big smile, only to be greeted by dead silence. Suddenly the energy and life had been drained out of everyone. The elevator went up only a few floors, but it felt like an eternity. I was the first to get off, and it was a relief. I couldn't remember ever feeling like such an intruder.

But in those early years, I persisted in befriending some of his ballerinas, and personal tensions grew between Balanchine and me. I wasn't competing with him, but I didn't want him telling me what to do with my personal life. And no matter how hard I worked, I approached every encounter with him with trepidation, feeling tremendously inferior, like a stepchild trying to please the great father who had no use at all for his inadequacies. Around Balanchine I often felt as if I were not the person I ought to be, and I wasn't sure how to respond. But I knew I had to find a way.

Balanchine was a father figure for all of us. He represented ultimate authority, and much more. During the time when my relations with him were growing ever more complicated, I realized that my need for my father's approval was still very much unsatisfied. I knew that in order to please him I had to be more than a ballet dancer: the most important thing I could do for him was to graduate from college. When I had been in the New York City Ballet for two years, I decided to return to college and get my degree. The company was going to be in town for a long stretch, from February to June, and I enrolled for the spring semester.

My schedule for those months felt like the labors of Hercules. I was taking twenty-eight college credits, a tremendous load of work in addition to my performing career, but I managed my best semester, a 3.7 average. I was still living at home in Bayside, and every morning I rose at five, studied for three hours, and arrived at school in Throgs Neck by eight-thirty A.M. After classes, I departed for Manhattan by midafternoon, in time to take ballet class at SAB and rehearse. In the evenings, I performed, often in more than one ballet, I ate a sandwich, drank a beer, and went home. I'd get to bed by one or two and get up again the next morning by five.

There was no time for anything else. I had every minute

76

of my day organized, and my social life came to a halt. Carole began complaining about our relationship. She wanted our affair to occupy a more central position in my life, but she understood how important it was for me to graduate from college. When my colleagues in the company or at school were going out or relaxing, I was studying or rehearsing. The fifties rock generation passed me by. I was unfamiliar with the music of Elvis Presley and all of the popular rock groups, and even with the new dances people were doing. I never went to bars or dance halls, and there was no time to listen to music. It wasn't until the 1960s that I became aware of rock and roll or discotheques.

During that last semester at Maritime College, I would arrive at SAB or the City Center in my military uniform and spend time in the dressing room between ballets studying my college text or doing semaphore. There were great demands on me at that time in the company because I was appearing in such roles as *Agon,* which continued to be a big challenge. The day I graduated in June 1959 and received a bachelor of science in marine transportation, a review of my performance in *Agon* appeared under a photograph of me in the *New York Times.* It was the first time a head shot of me had ever appeared with a review, and sometime after graduation my professor of astronomy showed me the clipping, which he had cut out of the paper.

Looking back, I'm not sure how I was able to do it. But I was driven. I was energetic. There was a need in me that would do anything to get satisfied.

The major breakthrough in my career came in 1960. I was cast in *Prodigal Son,* and in typical New York City Ballet fashion no one ever talked to me about it officially. I wasn't even aware that *Prodigal* was being revived. I was standing around waiting for a rehearsal to finish when Diana Adams turned to me and said, "Oh, congratulations."

I said, "About what?"

"Don't you know?"

"Know what?"

"You're going to be cast for *Prodigal Son.*"

Though I had never seen the ballet, I could tell from the

77

way she spoke that this was important, and here I was, finding out about it by accident. This is how things were done in the company. Generally, we found out about new roles we were going to do by looking at the rehearsal schedule, which appeared daily. I had already been named a soloist and was about to be elevated to the rank of principal dancer. No one ever informed me of these promotions. I learned about them by reading my contracts.

I had had no indication that something of such magnitude was in the offing, and I hadn't even imagined the possibility. In a sense, the role of the Prodigal wasn't a strictly classical role, and the partnering required strength and dexterity more than finesse. But what a part it was! The opportunity to dance it floored me, but the last thing I was going to do was back away.

Balanchine knew his dancers well. He'd seen us grow up in his school, and after we joined the company, he watched us in class, in rehearsal, and onstage. And he got to know us inside and out, and not only what we could do physically, but what we were made of, who we were. He knew just what we were right for and never exposed us to something we weren't capable of doing. He also had a great sense of the moment. He knew when to give a dancer a special role, and he often cast dancers in a series of new roles all at once. A dancer either accepted the challenge or not. It was up to you. In the New York City Ballet, dancers weren't brought along gradually. A lot of dancers were not able to accept this. But life in the company is not about dancing twice a week, or twice a month, as it is in many European and Soviet companies. It's about dancing eight times a week, dancing more than forty roles a year. A New York City Ballet dancer had to be prepared for this and hold up his end of the bargain.

Balanchine didn't want dancers who needed six months to make a debut in a ballet. Instead we were allowed to develop our interpretations of roles as we danced them. I did this with *Prodigal Son,* and with everything I danced during my career. Balanchine didn't want dancers to analyze and intellectualize about parts. He didn't like discussing a ballet to death. His credo was, "Don't talk. Just do." He'd say it over and over.

The first time I danced *Donizetti Variations,* I didn't even know the exact order of the sequences in the choreography. I

78

wasn't sure of the counts, whether I had to count to eight or sixteen bars of music to get onstage, and I wasn't sure of exactly when I had to make my entrances. There are something like seven of them in *Donizetti,* and I didn't know their proper order. I asked Jonathan Watts, another dancer who knew the role, to sort of function as a traffic cop for me backstage, and he virtually propelled me from one side of the wings to the other, pushing me onstage for each entrance.

In the 1959–1960 winter season, my third in the company, I think Balanchine felt that I was ready to accept a major challenge, to move on to the next step. I don't think he had much enthusiasm about the revival of *Prodigal Son,* or for that matter the ballet itself. The assignment to choreograph it had been imposed on him in 1929 by Diaghilev, who needed a Serge Lifar vehicle. Lifar was a leading Ballets Russes star. Balanchine didn't have much respect for Prokofiev, who had composed the score and who treated him as an upstart. Making the ballet had not been a joyous experience for anyone concerned. Nothing proceeded easily or on schedule, and in order to get the painter Georges Rouault to finish the sets and costumes in time for the premiere, Ballets Russes officials had to lock him in a hotel room, stand guard over him, bring him food. He was literally imprisoned until he finished his task. Sometimes it seemed to me as if Balanchine were reviving a dusty work he didn't care about just for my benefit. Maybe he was staging the ballet because he wanted to see it again, but I hoped that he was searching for a role with which to develop me. Even so, he didn't seem terribly interested in what we were doing.

The dramatic element in *Prodigal Son* was the major challenge for me. I had never seen a Balanchine work like this ballet, and I didn't really understand its tradition. The Prodigal is a demi-caractère role with nothing delicate about it. I was comfortable with that. I hadn't yet achieved classical proficiency. But the ballet tells a story, and I had to create a character. The style puzzled me. I had to figure out a way to perform the gestures without feeling self-conscious.

Although it has a narrative (unusual for Balanchine's work), *Prodigal Son* is still very much a Balanchine ballet. The plot is told economically, the choreography is tied to the music,

79

and there's a great deal of invention in the dancing. Balanchine expanded the opening variation for me making it more bravura. Yet dancing the title role wasn't as simple as *Square Dance* or *Symphony in C*.

It was a question of understanding how to make a dramatic moment "tell." I had to learn to sustain drama onstage without the aid of pyrotechnics. After the big variation at the start of the ballet, the action proceeds. The Prodigal leaves his father's home and travels to a far country. As the story unfolds, the steps become pared down; the ballet ends with the Prodigal crawling on his knees, with no steps whatsoever. I felt in a void. The ballet was layered with meanings, filled with references, and I knew none of them. I understood it was an enormous opportunity in the eyes of the public and the critics. I knew it was a chance to influence Balanchine's idea of me. But I was searching in the dark. It made me grow up real fast.

The critic B. H. Haggin asked Balanchine at the time, "Why Villella? Why are you putting Villella in such a major role? He's just a kid."

"Well, Villella, you know," Balanchine said, "he looks like nice Jewish boy."

This statement encouraged me a little. At least I looked right for the role.

I tried to read as much as I could about the ballet. I had Balanchine's book *Complete Stories of the Great Ballets,* and I read the entry on *Prodigal* over and over. I even read the Bible. I examined the Rouault sets and costumes, I looked at photographs, and I listened to a recording of the score by Leon Barzin. The tempi were slower than the pianist played them at rehearsal, but at least I could listen to the music and get to know it. I wanted at least to absorb the atmosphere of the ballet. At home in Bayside I worked in front of a mirror, trying different expressions.

Balanchine taught me the part, but typically he didn't spend much time doing it. He often relied on ballet mistresses to teach his choreography to the male dancers, and he worked more closely with the women. My feeling was that he wasn't really interested in working with anyone on this role.

I learned the opening and closing scenes in two twenty-minute sessions with Balanchine. He taught me the pas de deux

80

in a half hour, and then I didn't see him again until the final rehearsal on the day of the performance. A former ballet mistress, Vida Brown, was coaxed out of retirement to stage the ballet because nobody in the company remembered it very well. Lifar had created the role, and Jerome Robbins, Hugh Laing, and Francisco Moncion had each performed the part with great distinction. But I didn't really have an example before me when I began to develop it.

Balanchine had first staged the ballet for the company in 1950. Robbins and Tallchief had danced the leads. Moncion, who had most recently danced the role, was still a principal, but in typical NYCB fashion no one asked him to come to the rehearsals to help out. It must have been a painful thing, and I think he suffered terribly. No one said, "Frank, this role is now being passed on to another dancer. We want you to understand." No one had that sensitivity. It was a Balanchinian, old-world, Russian way to deal with a difficult situation.

I could see that Frank was hurt, but there was no way I could help. And Balanchine discouraged it. "No, you don't need Frank," he said. "Frank is big, big man. Big muscle man. You're boy."

Balanchine abhorred anything that might create confrontation, and everyone took the cue from him. We just swallowed hard and put up with what he dished out. We had to carry around our feelings of pain and rejection—and anger. We couldn't express them to his face.

Vida Brown's rehearsals, concerned mainly with reproducing the ballet and setting it on its feet, were useless for my purposes. Recreating a ballet section by section is painstaking work. Scenes or movements are often staged out of sequence. Eventually, usually at the last minute, it all comes together. Most of my time in these rehearsals was spent working with the boys who played my drinking companions. Balanchine showed up on one occasion to look at what the boys were doing. As I watched what he showed them with his own body, how he related gesture to music, I began to sense the basics of the style.

Balanchine never spent a great deal of time talking about his choreography or telling us, for example, about the biblical story of the Prodigal, how he had researched the story for the 81 scenario, or arrived at particular moments in the action. But his offhand conversations contained key phrases. I had to be on the lookout for them and recognize them. They were gone fast. I sometimes felt he was not only testing our ability to understand but our commitment.

At one point during the rehearsal, he said to the boys, "You're protoplasm." The word suggested an image of primordial slime, and this was very helpful. Later, working on the section in which the drinking companions run their fingers up and down the Prodigal's exhausted, nearly naked body as if to strip it further of worldly goods, Balanchine said to them, "Like mice." It spoke volumes. It was as if they were going to eat my flesh, and it made me cringe.

At the dress rehearsal, Balanchine's comments were eye-opening. In the ballet's central pas de deux, a difficult moment occurs when the Siren sits on the Prodigal's neck, without holding on to anything for support.

Balanchine said to the dancer, Diana Adams, "Well, it's like you're sitting and smoking a cigarette," and that remark recalled to me images of models in old cigarette advertisements. I could see the way she would be sitting, the way she'd pose, and the way I would have to balance her. It was an image of female dominance at the expense of male immaturity and intimidation.

At still another moment in the pas de deux, the Siren rests on the Prodigal's head as he sits with his knees raised. She puts her feet on his shins, just below his knees, and he holds her ankles. She then rises up from his head into a standing position as he lowers his knees to the floor. Now she's in an upright position, and she steps off the Prodigal's legs onto the stage. Balanchine said, "Good. You lower her like elevator." I was to feel like her servant, like the elevator operator, if you will.

These simple statements conjured up images of what Balanchine wanted the ballet to look like. He made more brief comments that helped me. At the start of the pas de deux the Siren and the Prodigal stand on opposite sides of the stage. They put their hands on their hips and lean toward each other. "You really have to lean into hips and put hands like they're growing out there," Balanchine said. He was trying physically and mechanically to explain the gesture. Then he stopped,

82

looked us in the eye, and said, "Icons. You know, dear. Byzantine icons."

I said to myself, "Oh my God, icons."

The image made me understand the movement and I looked at as many reproductions of Byzantine icons as I could find.

Diana Adams was also a help because she intimidated me personally, and I could inject this element of fear into my onstage relationship with the Siren. Diana was an experienced ballerina of great technical accomplishment and considerable distinction. She had a perfect neoclassical body, and Balanchine admired and respected her. By contrast, I was just a kid. Onstage, one look from her menacing, steely eyes would send a shudder through my body. She embodied the mythic qualities of Woman, Mother, Religious Goddess, Sexual Goddess. It was just a pretense, of course, but onstage it seemed real to me. And she towered over me. On pointe she was over six feet tall.

Offstage, she wasn't easy for me to talk to. Her façade was impenetrable. Looking back, I would characterize her as highstrung. She was withdrawn and tense. Her glance shifted all the time, and her hands were always moving. She didn't easily bare her thoughts or reveal herself; she was someone with whom it was difficult to be intimate. Of course my state of mind made her seem that much more remote.

During the technical rehearsal, I tried to get a sense of the lighting and what the set looked like. Sometimes dancers are sort of detached from these sorts of things. In performance, we're enclosed in the proscenium arch, inside the ballet. Because of the side lighting, the footlights, and the spotlights, we're often in a ring of light. We look out into this black tunnel, which is the audience. A dancer gets a different sense of a production when he looks at the set from the audience's point of view. I could see that the slashes of black on the backdrop corresponded to the slashes of black on the costumes and bore some relation to gestures and the bold colors of the music. It all began to come into a kind of focus I still couldn't articulate.

The early performances of *Prodigal Son* were quite successful and received good reviews. John Martin wrote in the *New York Times* that I danced the role like "a house on fire . . . *Prodigal Son* dates back thirty years . . . but it may very well

83

be that it has never been presented so beautifully as this. Edward Villella in the title role and Diana Adams as the Siren have evolved characterizations of extraordinary authority and richness of color, and they play together with an unbroken line of tension. It is a pleasure to see Mr. Villella the master of such a close stage relationship. . . . He's high-tempered, callow, passionate . . . what is notable is that he communicates this so convincingly in terms of his actual dancing, technical though it remains. His final return and repentance are profoundly moving."

Balanchine said little about the performance. He didn't rush backstage and congratulate me or anything like that. But he continued to cast me in it, and as time went by, every now and then he offered a few words of illumination about my performance.

This was the beginning of my relationship with the role that I was perhaps more closely associated with than any other. *Prodigal Son* was the first ballet that made me think and start to expose my real self. I continued to investigate this role until the day I stopped dancing, and in fact, the process of investigation continues today, when I stage it with my own company, the Miami City Ballet, or when dancers call and ask me to coach them in the role. I gladly give whatever advice I can. As I worked over and over on *Prodigal Son,* through every phase of my career, it occurred to me that no one had the same interest in this ballet as I did. People began to think it was created for me. In the second season of the revival, Balanchine himself said to me, "This is your ballet. I stage it this time. Next time you stage. I'm never going to stage it again."

PRODIGAL SON

SEVEN

Crucial to my development as a dancer, and my approach to classical ballet, is the fact that I was separated from the art form during my four college years. But these four years, frustrating as they were, paid off. They gave me another perspective on dancing and kept me from becoming too ascetic or pretentious. One problem with ballet and the discipline it requires is its distance from the world. Very young dancers are forced into a cloistered existence. My experiences as an athlete, a college student, and a naval cadet got me out into other kinds of life and helped me recognize the closed nature of the ballet world. I developed a disdain for the artifice and posturing that prevail in some parts of the community.

But physically, my enforced hiatus from dancing was a catastrophe. Sports had nearly destroyed my finesse and flexibility. The bruises and crippling spasms I suffered after I returned were signs of problems to come. I didn't realize then that if I had returned to dancing more slowly and patiently, the results I was working for would have come sooner. But I was in such a hurry to catch up I did everything wrong, trying to cram into a matter of weeks what it should have taken four years to accomplish. During the early years of my career, I felt as if I were racing against time. I concentrated on big spectacular steps. I could jump, but my landings weren't light and

85

soft. I landed like an athlete, directly on my heels. I didn't have the strength or the knowledge to cushion my landings by allowing my knees to bend over my toes. This would have softened the jarring impact to my heels. I did hundreds of entrechats-six a day, that is, jumping in the air beating my feet, but I didn't have the technical understanding to do them properly.

I was thrashing around. I needed to build myself up, so I pushed my body mercilessly. I was working from all areas through my shoulders, using tension and hunching up, rather than working from the inside out and developing turnout, which is essential for a ballet dancer. Turnout isn't a position. It's the constant rotation of the body outward from the center. Investigating the concept of turnout has been a lifelong process, and it continues to occupy me today. Turnout initiates movement; turnout extends movement. But tension shortens gesture. Tension affects muscle tone and produces spasms that shorten a dancer's line.

These problems, which plagued me during my first two years in the City Ballet, came to a head around the time of my first performances in *Prodigal Son*. Before this, my body had been giving me warnings, telling me things to heed. Now, every time I danced, I suffered cramps so intense that my movement became limited. And my body took on a misshapen form, rather than a long, lean classical line. I had abnormally large thighs, and thick, tight muscles that obstructed my ability to develop the look of a classical dancer. Pain was constant. I was traumatized physically, and I didn't have a way of relaxing the tension in my muscles. I found myself trying to do less, concentrating on class and walking through rehearsals without doing steps full out, because the more I danced the more I hurt. "Marking" rehearsals in this manner was earning me the reputation as the Bad Boy of ballet. But class had to come first, and I hurt too much to do both. Furthermore, I never wanted to be overrehearsed. I wanted to be spontaneous in performance.

In my pain and confusion, the glimmer of a heretical—and somewhat horrifying—idea began to form in my mind: Balanchine's class was hurting me and was contributing to my difficulties. Once this idea took hold of me, I couldn't shake it.

86   Balanchine's classes were famous, legendary—and para-

doxical. Dame Ninette de Valois, founder of England's Royal Ballet, once described them to me as choreographic rather than pedagogical. She was right in a way; they existed as a lab for his choreographic experiments. They were meant to replenish the body, but they didn't do that for me. Once I started to question them, my misgivings multiplied. They were simply chaotic, formless exercises, and I never knew what to expect. Everything Balanchine said was intellectually illuminating, but the class itself didn't unfold in a logical progression. Structure was predicated on Balanchine's mood or his whim, or by what he was interested in at a given time.

His approach to warm-up was frenetic, haphazard, a tensing of already taut, inflamed muscles. The speed he required was no problem. I could dance as quickly as I had to. But working frantically during warm-up diminished my natural speed in the actual class. In order to produce speed, a dancer has to be able to articulate the entire range of a step to get that push-off. But Balanchine's class didn't allow for that. In effect, Balanchine wanted instant speed. This translated into tension for me, which resulted in muscle spasms. It was a terrible bind.

In a session, Balanchine would sometimes eliminate pliés almost entirely, but then he'd get stalled on battement tendu, and he'd have us do this for twenty minutes. Or he'd get focused on a fondu and give variations on this exercise for a quarter of an hour. Some days, he wasn't interested in the barre and wanted only to get to center work on the floor, so he'd work us at the barre for less than a quarter of an hour. Everybody was aching, sore, barely able to move, but they'd be saying, "Oh, yes, Mr. B. Of course, Mr. B." I didn't say anything. I was trying to figure out what I was getting out of what was going on. Everything was just thrust at me. Nothing was explained, and I developed no inner understanding.

Once, when the company was on tour in Los Angeles, Balanchine gave one of his fifteen-minute barres, and the first exercise we did in the center was sous-sous, entrechats-six to a grand plié. First of all, no teacher should have dancers jump before they warm up, and we'd barely worked for a quarter of an hour. And not only did we jump—we jumped to a full plié. Muscles and tendons, knees, ankle joints, and backs were put at risk. The combination was the most illogical exercise I'd ever

87

been asked to do. Balanchine also just forced turnout. He'd grab a leg and twist it in the socket. The result would be that the dancer's raised leg, the working leg, would turn out while the hip, the knee, and the ankle of the supporting leg just twisted up. Achieving turnout by straining the joints on the supporting leg made no sense to me.

Balanchine's focus in these classes was mainly on the women. Because his ballerinas were long-legged and coltish, they were kind of splayed, in dancer's jargon, "all over the place," arms and legs waving. He was trying to get a better articulation of position, to facilitate moving from position to position without sacrificing speed. He wanted speed, so he just had everyone do everything fast. But a driver can't start a car at one hundred miles an hour. He must go through first, second, and third gears. An engine must be warmed up slowly, the oil flowing and all the mechanics working properly before a car hits the highway. Balanchine had no regard for that. He led us out onto that highway at high speed without warming up the engine. And for me, in particular, it was terrible because my muscles were so sensitive, raw, and hardened; they had nothing to build on.

I got to a point where I could barely move, and I couldn't even tell if my feet were pointing or not. My legs were numb between my lower calves and ankles, and because my metatarsals had sustained contusions and some of the bones were broken, I lost the ability to grip the floor with my feet. Every fiber of every muscle was taut, and it became more and more difficult to warm up and make my muscles flexible and easy. They retained their tension permanently, it seemed, and they'd begin to spasm at any time of the day or night. At first in class, I had been able to do a barre (which was usually easy and warming), get to the center, and perform the small jumps. But by the time I got to the big jumps, the spasms occurred. After a while, in Balanchine's class, they started earlier and earlier; eventually, they'd begin as soon as I left the barre. Then they started at the end of the barre, until—I couldn't believe it!—one day my muscles spasmed doing my first demi-plié, the first exercise in class. These weren't tiny twinges, they were massive contractions. To my further horror, my legs no longer shaped themselves into smooth lines. Before my eyes, my muscles clumped,

88

tightened, and protruded in knots at the tops of my thighs. Enormous, well-defined, solid lumps with ridges and valleys rose up out of my legs, the size of golf balls.

I was desperate to be a dancer, but I was destroying my own body. And yet I couldn't afford to stop working, to take time off to heal myself. I had already lost four crucial years and couldn't afford to lose any more time. It was a frightening dilemma, and I felt trapped. I looked everywhere for help, but it was before the days of sports medicine, and not much was available. I experimented with massage, but Balanchine was against massage and wouldn't allow a masseur in the theater. I went from doctor to doctor, to chiropractors and to osteopaths, and I did Pilates exercises with Carola Trier. Pilates, named for the person who developed them, are a series of exercises in which a person works for the most part with the weight off his feet to strengthen, stretch, and elongate muscles. But nothing I did worked for me.

It was the dancer's responsibility to arrive at Balanchine's class warmed up, so I took another class beforehand. But it didn't help at all. Then I tried to supplement company class by studying with other teachers. I worked with all my former SAB instructors. Muriel Stuart was sensitive to my needs, but I felt that Felia Doubrovska came the closest to helping me. Pierre Vladimiroff gave a brief barre in his class, and Anatole Oboukoff's didn't address the problems I needed to work on, so I started looking elsewhere. I began a major search to find a teacher and went through every one on the scene at that time: Bill Griffin; Igor Schwezoff, a man who carried a riding crop; Valentina Pereyaslavec, who was another Russian émigré; and Vladimir Dukadovsky. One day in Pereyaslavec's studio I paid close attention to Erik Bruhn, who was also taking class. He represented perfect placement to me, and I couldn't understand why I couldn't achieve it. Analyzing it, it was obvious that the muscles in my upper thighs were hampering my ability even to sense and feel my placement.

I was searching for someone to explain the mystery. The teachers around me didn't really *teach* as much as *give* class. It seemed to me that everybody else was dancing better than I was with superior placement, but I'm not sure they understood what they were doing either. No one seemed to have made a

89

real investigation into what classical ballet was all about. And Balanchine, demanding highly advanced technical ability from his dancers, expected them to have a secure foundation from which to work. But it just didn't exist for me.

I toyed with dropping Balanchine's class, but that didn't seem right to me. I wanted to participate in what he was doing, be part of it. Balanchine's classes were the heart and soul of the company. Everyone gathered in his class; it was where Balanchine let you know what he wanted. The classes had a communal, family atmosphere. By not attending them, I'd be missing out on what he had to say, and more, separating myself from him and the company. That was something I couldn't afford to do. But I could no longer function. If I had had any sense, I would have stopped performing, taken time off, gone back to school, and rejoined the City Ballet a year or two later. As a matter of fact, one day in class Erik Bruhn suggested that very thing. As the days went on, I became more and more desperate.

How could I approach Balanchine and discuss the situation with him, especially when I was actually saying that *he* was my problem? After all, I was just a young dancer starting out, and in no position to argue with him about the principles of teaching. I felt that it was an unresolvable dilemma. Here I had this great genius before me, yet another Mozart who was going to be the dispenser of knowledge.

In the winter of 1960, Balanchine approached me one morning, and speaking casually said, "You know, dear, I'm going to bring in a new teacher in a few weeks, this guy from Denmark, because he knows how to work with dancers, how to make people move."

My interest was piqued by this, although I didn't hold out any great hope. I had expected an older man, someone in his sixties, but the man who showed up was in his midthirties, trim and dancerlike. His name was Stanley Williams, and he looked even younger than he was. Stanley had severed an Achilles tendon and had been forced to retire early from dancing. He had studied in his native Denmark at the Royal Danish Ballet School where, of course, he was taught the Bournonville style. Like neoclassical ballet, Bournonville dancing required

90

clean, fast footwork, beats, ballon, and good placement. *Scotch Symphony* and *Donizetti Variations* were examples of ballets in which Balanchine had incorporated the Bournonville style.

Stanley had been a pupil in Denmark of Vera Volkova, a disciple of the great Soviet teacher Agrippina Vaganova. He was also conversant with all the principles of Russian academic classical dance.

Balanchine first met Stanley in Denmark when Tanaquil Le Clercq became ill. Later, they met again when Mr. B returned to stage a ballet for the Royal Danes. During this trip, Balanchine watched Stanley teach a class and, according to Stanley, left without saying a word. Five years later, Stanley received a letter from Balanchine inviting him to teach the New York City Ballet for three months.

The day of Stanley's debut as a teacher with the New York City Ballet began inauspiciously. The pianist hadn't shown up, and a replacement couldn't be found. Occasionally, this happened. As Stanley later told me, "You can imagine how I felt. Out of the blue I get a letter from George Balanchine, whom I haven't seen for four or five years, and who had barely spoken to me when we did meet, inviting me to teach his company. Not the school. His company! Can you imagine my anxiety, the insecurity I felt? I walk in, and all these strangers are staring at me. Balanchine introduces me, and I look around and say, 'Where's the pianist?'

"And he says, 'Oh, no, we don't have today. But it's all right. You can count.'

"Here I was at the famous New York City Ballet," Stanley said, "a fountain of creativity and development, teaching in the most primitive conditions imaginable. I came from a staid, formal state theater. I couldn't understand the casualness. I was a total nervous wreck."

"You know, dear," Balanchine said to the new arrival, "it's okay. There's no music. It's okay, it's okay. Just teach."

I liked Stanley immediately. He was slight and had dark hair, and a wiry, dancer's frame. He didn't have leading-man looks, but was handsome in his own way. He was very polite. I could sense that he was nervous. But when he started to teach, it was a revelation. Halfway through the barre, I said to myself, I know this is it. This is what I've been searching for! My throat

91

tightened, and my pulse began to race. I felt exhilarated, but I was also worried. I couldn't get it all in one day, but I knew it was what I needed. Here were all the ideas scattered throughout Balanchine's class pulled together in a harmonious, sensible, coherent whole. And there was time to go slower, and yet not waste time.

After the class, Stanley and I chatted in the dressing room. He wanted to know where to catch the M104, the Broadway bus to take him back to his hotel. I walked with him to the bus stop, and an hour later we were still talking. We were comfortable with each other immediately, and we became friends. Stanley was in New York for three months, and from that time on I started going to every one of his classes. There was a quiet logic in what he taught. We always got to the place where Balanchine wanted us to be, but Stanley and I arrived twenty minutes later, thoroughly prepared for what came next. There was a simplicity about the teaching that approached genius. It resembled Balanchine's choreography; everything was spare and simple. Nothing was overly adorned or explained to death. This simple style of instruction helped me execute steps and combinations of the highest complexity.

Stanley also gave classes at SAB, teaching the B level. I stopped going to Stuart and Doubrovska and went to Stanley's SAB classes instead. That breached protocol and Balanchine was upset. He told the school administration that I was not to be allowed to take anything but classes for professionals. In effect, he barred me from taking Stanley's B-level class. I wasn't to be deterred, however. I felt as if I had only three months in which to pick up everything Stanley had to offer. So I waited in the corridor until the last minute before Stanley's class and then slipped into the studio. I stood at the farthest end of the room where they couldn't force me out until break. This way, I could at least do the barre. After the barre, they unceremoniously threw me out. It seemed as if I were offending everyone in the school administration by what I was doing; and also offending Balanchine himself. Eventually, Mr. B came to throw me out. He told me I was distracting all the young girls, diverting their attention from their exercises by my big jumps. I replied, "Well, I won't do the jumps." This was only the beginning.

92

As time went by, Stanley and I grew closer, and I began to take class with him privately. He was an emerging teacher, and I was an emerging, mindless talent, a wounded physicality. He was finding his way through me, and I was finding mine through him. It was a fascinating, intense situation in which two neophytes were motivated by the same passion and desire for knowledge, one for teaching and one for dancing. But the presence of Balanchine always hovered over us: icon, father, God. I felt as if I were defying the master in order to understand him better and interpret his work more successfully. Stanley was fascinated by Balanchine and what he taught, and he would watch his classes and then incorporate his principles into what he was doing. Their methods were complementary; their classes supplemented one another.

Stanley was easy to talk to and we'd go to the Carnegie Tavern and talk for hours over dinner and drinks until three or four o'clock in the morning. We'd discuss the most elementary and sometimes abstract questions of dance: what turnout is, or how to execute a plié, and what exactly constitutes battement tendu. According to Balanchine, battement tendu, a simple basic exercise, is the most essential step in classical ballet.

"How do you initiate movement?" I'd ask Stanley. "Do people just move or do they take a position?" Or I'd ask, "How do you move classically? Is it the rotation, one side against the other, which is the continuity in the gesture?"

Many people are just natural talents, and they just move, they don't think of all the ramifications. I wanted to uncover the essence of the movement, the mechanics of every step.

Stanley and I fed off each other. I'd ask him a question. He'd stop and say, "I hadn't thought of that." We'd grapple.

"The Russians have taught us holding balance," I'd say. "They showed us how to do a big double cabriole and hold the landing. But you've stopped the movement, stopped the ges- ture. It's the linkage that makes the dance. Doing a big double cabriole, and landing and stopping, is an acrobatic feat, the trick of a gymnast. But if you tie it to a line of continuing gesture, and a line of continuing musical gesture, and within your body you project a style and a theatrical point of view, now you're dancing, aren't you?"

Anyone who knew even just a little bit about Balanchine   93 could well imagine how little pleased he would be at the idea of two arrogant novices doing something behind his back. We weren't alone, however. Many other dancers were eager to work with Stanley, but they were all afraid. A certain group of dancers began to resent me because I was getting private attention, and some people started rumors about Stanley and me. I didn't care.

One night during one of our marathon talks at Carnegie Tavern, a storm that had started earlier in the evening turned into a blizzard, and by the time we paid the bill there were snowdrifts in the street three feet high. I couldn't even find my Corvette—it was buried in the snow. It was impossible to return to Bayside, so I went to Stanley's hotel and slept on the extra bed in the room. We were seen leaving the hotel together the next morning by a dancer in the company. She had developed a crush on Stanley and was quick to spread the word that Stanley and I had spent the night together. She probably called half the people we knew, including my girlfriend, Carole, who knew better and was quite amused by the insinuation. I understood that some people resented me. The opportunity to study with Stanley was available to everyone, but others were afraid to take advantage of it.

Eventually, several dancers got up the courage and also began to work with Stanley during our private sessions. First one or two people showed up, then, gradually, still more appeared. It was amusing to watch them slip surreptitiously into the classroom. We all tried to be discreet. But you can't keep anything quiet in ballet companies. Ballet companies are run on rumor. Balanchine knew exactly who was there, and who was taking class, and he used to make fun of us. Of course, he was also aware of the quality of Stanley's teaching. He used to talk about getting him to stay in New York on a permanent basis. "We're going to seduce him so he'll stay in America," he said. "We are going to poison him. We're going to poison his mind, infect his mind with our poison and he will be seduced."

Before I knew it, Stanley's three-month period was up. I didn't know what I was going to do. By now, I was dependent on his class and our sessions. I felt as if we had barely touched on what I needed to know. The company was about to have a two-month layoff between seasons, and it seemed like a natural

94

progression of events for me to continue my studies during the break.

"Do you think it would be all right if I go to Denmark and continue to work with you?" I asked Stanley.

"It would be fine as far as I'm concerned, but you must do this officially," he said.

I must have looked crestfallen.

Stanley continued, "I work in a state theater run by a bureaucracy, and everything must be done properly. And you're a Balanchine dancer. It could be very complicated." I felt dismayed. "What you should do is have Balanchine write a letter to the Royal Theatre and ask for permission for you to study there."

"Oh, Stanley, no!" I cried. Actually to confront Balanchine with such a request, a request that would perpetuate a situation that had become more than just bothersome to him! How could I do it?

Asking Balanchine's permission to study in Denmark with Stanley took all my courage. I had already stopped going to Balanchine's class, and he knew I was studying only with Stanley. But he had never said a word about it. Now I was going to ask him in essence to approve my defection. It took a lot of gall. Which I had. But I also had a great deal of fear. I wasn't comfortable asking him for anything, but I would have been far more uncomfortable not having done it. I told myself, this is very important, and then did it.

I went to see Balanchine in his office. I started talking as soon as I entered the room. I took him by surprise. He was stunned.

"Why do you want to go to Denmark?" he said. "We have wonderful teachers here, wonderful."

"I know."

"No . . . no. Why, why do you want to go?"

"Well," I said, "I've benefited from Williams, gotten to understand so much. I would like to continue because I've just begun and I'd like to grab ahold of it . . ."

"But there are wonderful teachers at SAB."

"Yes, yes," I said.

"Then why go to Denmark?"

"Yes, the teachers are wonderful at SAB," I said, "but I

95

have this special rapport with this man. I feel very comfortable, and when you make that kind of connection, you don't want to sever it."

"No," he said. "You don't want to go to Denmark. Stay right here." His brow furrowed over, and he fell silent. Suddenly he looked up at me and said, "I . . . I . . ." He held up his finger as if he had hit upon the perfect solution. *"I will teach you."*

This was the worst possible thing he could have said. I didn't want to reject him outright. An inspiration struck me. "That's great, that's great, Mr. B," I said. "But you have no time."

We went back and forth like this for a while until, finally, with a wave of his hand he stopped the conversation. He looked disturbed for a moment. Then he walked away. Our meeting was over. But he wrote the letter for me, a charming introduction to the head of the theater of the Royal Danish Ballet, saying that I was one of his principal dancers, who was going on holiday in Denmark, and would he please be so kind as to allow me to take company class. It was perfect. How could they say no to Balanchine? Other problems presented themselves. I had no money to make the trip. But I borrowed three thousand dollars from Chris Allen, a friend of mine who was a publicist, to cover the air fare and my living expenses, and I flew to Denmark for two months.

Thus began the most painful phase of my relationship with George Balanchine, my artistic father. I hadn't meant to reject him with my so-called rebellion. I didn't intend to rebel. I was looking for the most effective way to articulate the man's genius. Leaving Balanchine's class was a great embarrassment, a deep humiliation for me. But working with Stanley enabled me to gain greater understanding and dance Balanchine's ballets in a way that would please him. What I did was complicated. It wasn't easy. Soul-searching, discretion, and courage were required. I knew what I was in for, but after I analyzed the choices, I realized I had no choice after all. If I had said to myself, "Stay here and go to Balanchine's class and everything will be fine," that would have been totally untrue. If, on the other hand, I stopped going to his class and started my training all over again so that my body could withstand the physical

96

Watermill—the second time around. Back on stage, June 1990. My chance to say good-bye.

Early activities in Bayside.

My sister and me after First Holy Communion.

OPPOSITE
Local celebrities—Carol and I entertain in Queens . . . my first tarantella.

Balanchine demonstrates what he wants us to do at a George Platt Lynes photo session. My sister is second from left.

GEORGE PLATT LYNES

My first European cruise.

Hanging out with Bayside buddies—pegged pants and gold key chain.

My mother keeping an eye on me.

Dad and me backstage.

Taking out my frustrations on the heavy bag.

My first lead—*Afternoon of a Faun*.

TWO PHOTOS: © MARTHA SWOPE

Proving myself in *Agon* with Milly Hayden (right); Arthur Mitchell, Diana Adams (center); Richard Rapp, Patricia Neary (left).

Distracting Carol Sumner with my flashy jump.

Balanchine (right) brings Anton Dolin, next to me, and other guests backstage after a performance of *Prodigal Son*.

Rehearsing *Faun* with Jerry Robbins and Patty McBride.

© MARTHA SWOPE

Lincoln, Violette,
and me.

ALEX COSTE

The Siren (Karin von Aroldingen) strips the Prodigal.

The Prodigal searches for his homeland.

Prodigal Son curtain call. Suzanne Farrell is the Siren.

The Siren (Karin von Aroldingen) wraps herself around me in the *Prodigal Son* pas de deux.

OPPOSITE
Encircling me like a human doughnut, the Siren (Suzanne Farrell) slides down my legs.

Scene from *Prodigal Son*—the Prodigal with the Drinking Companions. Patricia Neary looks on.

OPPOSITE
Violette and me with Princess Margaret at RAD Gala. Robert Irving looks on.

Janet and I toast our wedding, February 1962.

New York City Ballet—Russia 1962. *Front row seated:* (from left) Allegra Kent, Edward Bigelow, Patty McBride, John Taras, Jillana, Billy Weslow. *Second row seated:* Kay Mazzo (third from left), Karin von Aroldingen (sixth from left). *Middle row:* Arthur Mitchell in striped T-shirt. *First row standing:* Mr. B (fourth from left), Diana Adams (in plaid robe), Sara Leland in sweater (eighth from right), Earle Sieveling, Janet, me, Milly Hayden (seventh, sixth, fifth, fourth from right). *Back row standing:* Jacques D'Amboise (open collar), Robert Irving (in light jacket, shirt and tie).

At the barre.

Jerry Robbins watches Patty and me rehearse *Dances at a Gathering*.

Mr. B helping me with my role in *Pulcinella*. Francisco Moncion follows.

Cutting up with Mr. B.

At SAB: I jump, Stanley Williams watches (Robert Weiss on bench).

OPPOSITE
With Stanley in class.

Top, my nightly liniment rub.

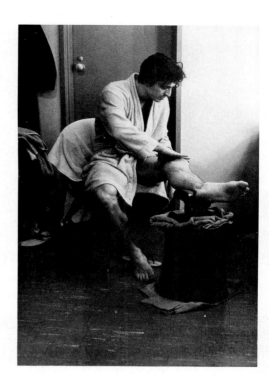

MAX WALDMAN

Discussing a score with Violette.

La Source with Violette.

Tchaikovsky Pas de Deux with Patty.

OPPOSITE
An erotic encounter with Allegra Kent in *Bugaku*.

Playing Oberon to Suzanne Farrell's Titania—the film of *A Midsummer Night's Dream*.

BERT STERN

Apollo and the Muses: (left to right) Suki Schorer, Patty McBride, Carol Sumner.

Pulcinella—in the costume and the mask.

Tarantella.

Patty and Eddie, Columbine and Harlequin.

Developing a long, classical line for *Donizetti Variations*.

Below, Coaching Misha with Patty in *Rubies*.

OPPOSITE
Watermill 1971—as naked as I could be.

Le Corsaire, with Violette Verdy, at the White House, 1975, under the chandelier.

TWO PHOTOS: © MARTHA SWOPE

Exchanging vows, May 24, 1980:
(left to right) my dad, me, Linda,
Lauren, Linda's mom and dad.

Linda, Crista (three months), and
me.

Crista Francesca, age 3, and her dad.

The proudest day: Linda, Roddy, Crista, the old man, and Lauren at Roddy's graduation.

With my dad.

GEORGE SCHIAVONE

Working with dancers at Miami City Ballet.

Lecturing at West Point.

STAN GOLDBLATT

Showing battement tendu.

Passing on the legacy.

DAVID WALTERS

Demonstrating *Prodigal Son* to Miami City Ballet dancer Yanis Pikieris.

demands of the art, I had life. The other way I was facing death. There was no choice. But by studying exclusively with Stanley I seriously offended Mr. B.

On many occasions I tried to talk to him about it, but he'd say, "I don't worry about you, you know how to do battement tendu, is fine, is okay." He meant that I knew the basics. But until his dying day I don't think he ever forgave me for not praying at his altar. And that's a very painful thing. All I wanted to do was please him. But I was not willing to destroy myself in order to do so. I was dealing with survival. The end result was critical. I was not willing to be a device for a couple of years. In a way, one can look at it like that. We were all devices for his choreographic genius, all of us in the company pressed into his service. I wanted to serve, but not to the point of destroying myself. I would be a very angry son of a bitch right now if I had made any other choice. I would have been finished with bravura dancing in three to five years and would have functioned in a limited capacity with an abbreviated repertory. I would have been very, very bitter.

Stanley gave me an extra fifteen years of dancing.

What I was going to do with Stanley was to change my entire approach to dancing. I was a principal dancer who was going to start over in midstream while I was dancing eight times a week, carrying a full repertory. I was going to learn how to become an artist. I knew I was gambling, but I felt the hand I held was strong enough for me to bet the bank. And that's what I did. I bet that the company would see the wisdom of what I was doing and not label me an arrogant troublemaker. But I was beginning to be known as someone who was a bad influence, someone engaged in a conspiracy to undermine Balanchine.

Despite the cost, I think I succeeded in what I set out to do. I now have deep insight into the Balanchine style mainly because Stanley was able to articulate and communicate the basics of the technique and the musicality in a way that freed my body to absorb all of Balanchine's principles. My body is my mind in terms of the Balanchine style. Of course, a dancer must consciously analyze what he's doing when he dances Balanchine. But if he doesn't have brains in his body, if his musculature doesn't have an intelligence of its own to express and

97

EDWARD VILLELLA

articulate movement and gesture the way Balanchine wanted, then it doesn't matter how much he understands. So I needed both: I needed my mind, and I needed brains in my body.

I took up residence in Copenhagen in a small pension across the street from the Kings Theater. All day I spent in class. I worked at the barre for an hour to an hour and a half. I resolved to take my time. Despite what Balanchine had told me, it took me two years to learn how to do battement tendu properly. I learned to stand with my legs crossed, bringing both heels and the inside of the thigh forward as one foot extends to a full point. In order to do this correctly, I had to work on turning out, and because the muscles in my outside thigh continually spasmed, this was hard.

Stanley and I discussed every possible facet of this exercise and what it actually *means* to point a foot. We not only continued our classroom work in Copenhagen, we resumed our lengthy discussions about ballet into the early hours of the morning over late-night beers. I attended performances of the Royal Danish Ballet, a company rich in tradition, and formed a good impression of the male dancers.

Sometimes I had the feeling that many of the people I met thought Stanley and I were lovers. It didn't faze me. The Danes are hospitable, and I was always being invited to dinner. Aquavit and beer play an important role in Danish sociability. During a meal, a guest never takes a drink by himself. He makes a toast. He raises his glass of aquavit, which is potent alcohol, looks down the table, calls out someone's name, and says, "Skoal." The person he names looks back and lifts his glass. Both diners now look each other in the eye, nod, and take a drink. Then, looking back at each other, they nod again, put the drink down, and chase it with a beer. The Japanese have their tea ceremony and the Danes have a drinking ceremony. In the course of an evening in Denmark, everyone will toast a guest. And the larger the party . . . Well, you can imagine how much I had to drink some evenings.

Eventually, it was time for me to go back to New York. I was asked to return for rehearsals of *Creation of the World,* a new ballet Todd Bolender was creating for the company. As I was getting ready to leave, an idea struck me. I asked Stanley to write out classroom exercises so that I could compile them in

98

various formats. I then bought a tape recorder and hired a Royal Danish Ballet pianist to play music, which I recorded to accompany Stanley's notes. When I returned to New York, I'd be able to give myself class on tape. It was necessary to do this in secrecy, and I found a space on the fifth floor in the upper reaches of the City Center in an area the company never used. Here I would hide away and give myself a class in nearly total darkness. It wasn't easy. Reel-to-reel tape recorders were cumbersome, and mine weighed over thirty-five pounds. I'd shut it off at the sound of any unfamiliar noise or intrusion. Using these tapes in the theater made me feel as if I were bringing a copy of *Playboy* magazine into church. But now that I could work this way on my own, I made what turned out to be an irrevocable decision: I never again attended Balanchine's class.

Although he didn't comment on my absence, Balanchine somehow found out about my giving myself class on my own, and he made snide comments about it, but never directly to me. It seemed that one of the dancers in the company was going to go away for a brief period and was concerned about missing company class.

"Don't worry, dear, I'll make tape," Balanchine said to the dancer during a rehearsal. I was standing nearby and couldn't help but overhear.

I got the point. He was obviously angry. I don't think he respected my decision or trusted my motives for no longer studying with him. I think he believed I'd been swayed by the fact that Stanley had paid attention to me. Balanchine's attention in 1960 was still primarily directed toward Allegra. His main aesthetic concerns revolved around her. I hovered on the edge of his consciousness. I think if he could have afforded to do so, if there had been other dancers like me on his roster, he would have dismissed me on the spot. Rumors that I was going to be fired were already flying throughout the company. But I was arrogant enough to believe that there weren't any students of my potential at SAB, either. Balanchine needed me. I hoped.

99

EIGHT

arly 1961 brought some excitement. I was going to dance *Stars and Stripes* in a ceremony at President Kennedy's inauguration in the ballroom of a large Washington hotel. A hastily erected platform in a large arena was going to serve as the stage, but adequate rehearsal and warm-up space with mirrors and a barre were not provided. We had to improvise. The security was so tight that it was difficult moving from one area to the other without a pass or badge of some kind. As the time of the performance approached, I was standing alongside the platform upon which we were going to dance holding on to a stanchion, trying a few exercises. One of our stagehands, Bob Bostwick, came up to me and told me that I had to move. I assume the Secret Service had told him to clear the area.

"I can't move," I said. "I've nowhere to go. I'm going to go onstage in about fifteen minutes, and I have to finish my warm-up."

"You've still got to move." Bostwick stood over me. He was at least six foot four or five inches tall.

I tried to explain patiently that in order to perform I had to be warmed up, but he continued to hassle me. Finally I looked directly into his eyes and said to him, "If you don't get away from me, I'm going to break your fucking nose." It worked. He stepped back and allowed me to finish my barre and go onstage.

100

I liked being part of the presidential inaugural celebration. It made me feel I was making good and gave me a sense of myself as someone people respected. And despite my conflict with Balanchine over class, it was clear I was making good in the company, too. He kept casting me.

In March of that year Violette and I starred in *Electronics,* a ballet Balanchine choreographed to a taped score he was unhappy with. The decor of the ballet was futuristic. I wore a unitard as Apollo, and Violette had silver tinsel hair. When we did the ballet on tour in Los Angeles at the outdoor Greek Theater, Balanchine had the volume of the tape turned up and created a minor disturbance. People who lived in the vicinity called the police because of the noise. Local cats and dogs began to howl. Minor landslides occurred near the bowl-shaped theater. I think Balanchine was tickled by the fuss. I saw the glee in his eye and a mischievous grin on his face. The people in the audience bellowed out, "Turn down the music!" during the middle of the ballet. By the following season, the ballet had disappeared.

On that same trip, Balanchine took especial pleasure in criticizing the men in the company. One morning he suddenly turned on us during rehearsal.

"Men," he sneered. "You're nothing! Nothing! *Porteurs.* Servants. You carry girl. That's all."

It seemed most of us were having difficulty picking up what he wanted. Some people were upset by the outburst, but I was amused. It wasn't that I didn't take him seriously, just that I perceived myself as special.

During this engagement at the Greek Theater I made my debut in the fourth movement of *Western Symphony* opposite Allegra Kent. The night of my second performance I was waiting in the wings when I noticed Allegra's costume in the hand of a dresser frantically running around, searching for a body to put into it. Allegra was nowhere to be found, and it became clear she wasn't in the theater. She had obviously misread the schedule. We were all frantic until someone cried out, "Jillana's here! She's in the audience."

Jillana, who had helped me with *Swan Lake,* had recently returned to the company after an absence of a few years. She had danced this movement of *Western,* but obviously not for a long time. Yet what did it matter? A staff member charged   101 out into the audience, located Jillana, brought her backstage, and Allegra's costume was thrown onto her. The last two hooks were being fastened just as the music for the movement began. Without having her hair done, without makeup or time to warm up, Jillana joined me, and the two of us sallied forth. We sashayed out onto the stage. It was only my second performance in the role, I barely knew it—and I can only imagine what Jillana must have been feeling. But we managed to get through the ballet.

After the West Coast tour, Balanchine announced that he was choreographing Shakespeare's play *A Midsummer Night's Dream*. My assumption was that I was going to be cast as Puck. I still thought of myself as more of a demi-caractère dancer than anything else and was convinced that this was how Balanchine still saw me. I was in for a surprise. When the casting was announced, I was listed for the role of Oberon, King of the Fairies. I thought there must be some mistake, and I wondered, what could be going through Balanchine's mind? But I took it as a great compliment and hoped he was trying to stretch my range. I was eager to begin working, but found myself waiting around at rehearsals, doing nothing. Oberon is a presence in *A Midsummer Night's Dream,* but except for his big set piece, the scherzo, he's incidental to a lot of the dance action. Balanchine basically choreographed around me. The full company was called to rehearsals on a daily basis, and a great deal of activity was going on in the studio as Balanchine created the first act. But there was nothing for me to do. Once in a while he'd come up to me and say, "Oh, you have an entrance here, but we'll do that later."

I'd shrug and sit down. I never got used. After a while, I would lie down under the piano and doze. I'd fall into a deep sleep and snore away peacefully while all the creativity buzzed around me. Waking up, I'd begin to worry. Was I being treated fairly? But I believed that Balanchine was confident enough in me to postpone our work. He knew I'd pick up the part fast. Still, I felt I was being overlooked. I got more worried when I realized that the pas de deux and the solos were set and everyone had steps but me.

Less than a week before the premiere, Balanchine started choreographing the scherzo in which I had a bravura variation,

102

but most of what he came up with was for the children, young SAB girls. What he gave to me seemed thrown away, even though I could see that the steps themselves were phenomenal —and phenomenally difficult.

"You'll do this and you'll do that," he said as he showed me the steps, "and then you'll make your entrance here and go off and then come back again."

Then he went back to work with the students. The next day, the same. "You know, you'll do couple of steps here," he said. "Don't worry, we'll fix. We'll do later."

I was perplexed. But Stanley Williams had returned from Denmark and was teaching now at SAB.

"How's it going?" Stanley inquired. "What's it like?"

"I don't know," I answered. "Frankly, it's a real pain in the ass. You know, he's choreographing all this great stuff on the kids. They've got the best music. He's hardly doing anything for me."

"But what kind of role is it? Oberon, King of the Fairies . . ." Stanley smiled.

"Please don't make that joke about 'King of the Fairies.' I've heard it too many times."

He was serious now. "Okay. But tell me what it's like."

"Well, I have entrances and exits, but I don't do much."

"What about the scherzo?"

"I start something, and then I run offstage, and the kids come on. And then I come back on and do something and go off again."

Truly, I was in the dark. At no time during rehearsal did I dance the variation from beginning to end. We did it in sections, and the concept of the role was obscure to me. I never sensed the impact of the choreography.

A few days before the premiere, Balanchine pulled the variation together, finalized my exits and entrances, and told me where to mime the action. I had never done mime before in my life.

"Well, now you call Puck," he said.

I did what he asked.

"No, dear. Is this way." He demonstrated in a perfunctory manner and then walked off. I tried to copy what he had shown me. But the manner of the role was completely foreign to me: 103

it was a style I'd never seen, no less ever had to perform. It was not in the New York City Ballet tradition; no one in the company had any previous experience with it at all. I had no idea how to call someone onstage by miming, or how to speak and emote with my face and my eyes, my arms and my hands.

The following day was a full technical run-through of the ballet, the biggest production the company had done since *The Nutcracker*: scenery and lights, orchestra and children, and costumes. It was pandemonium. Nearly everyone was wearing a wig, and nearly all the wigs were coming loose and falling off. The children were getting caught up in the scenery, everyone was bumping into one another, and there wasn't enough space in the wings for so many people to move around freely.

Dressed in a bejeweled tunic with close-fitting sleeves, wearing a flowing, fifteen-foot-long cape and a headpiece, I felt completely out of my depth. The material for the cape was exquisite and delicate. It had a windblown quality and cost two thousand dollars. In today's market, it would cost closer to ten thousand. I had never worked with a cape before and found myself choreographing its movements so that it flowed after me as a continuation of my gesture. I had to devise a way of moving so that I didn't get caught up in the material, or trip over it. The entrance with the butterflies, the young SAB students who carried my train behind me, also had to be coordinated. If they didn't keep up with me as I entered, the cape would jerk my neck and pull me backward off-balance. And the top I wore also presented problems. Made of heavy brocade, and further weighed down by the jewels sewn into it, it fit tightly, with little give or elasticity.

The rehearsal finally started, and I managed to get through the ballet. But I felt as if I were sleepwalking. Every so often during the first act Balanchine would cry out to me, "Now, you enter now! You come on *now!* Oberon! Now!" I came on and danced or looked around.

"What happened, what happened?" I asked when the rehearsal was over. "What did it look like?" I hadn't a clue as to what went on.

A day or so later, Lincoln Kirstein approached Stanley. "Stanley, Villella's going to ruin the ballet," he said. "He doesn't know what he's doing. Too much sleeping under the

104

piano. Balanchine thinks he's going to ruin the ballet. Can you talk to him?"

"Isn't anyone else talking to him?"

"No."

"Why?" Stanley asked.

"Because he's so difficult."

Stanley said, "He's not difficult. Just talk to him."

Lincoln shook his head. "No. He's very difficult, and no one can talk to him except you. Will you do it?"

"Of course," Stanley said. "Sure."

Stanley searched me out. When he found me, he came up to me and asked, "What do you think of the role?"

"I don't have a clue, Stanley," I said. "I hardly know what I'm doing. They taught me all this stuff as of yesterday."

"Well, Lincoln asked me to work with you."

"Great."

"He said Balanchine thinks you're going to ruin the ballet."

"He—!"

Stanley cut me off. "Let's go up to the studio and work."

The first thing he said to me in the room was, "Show me what Mr. B told you to do."

I said, "Well, I come in here. Oberon is looking for Puck. I stop and turn around and call him."

"When?"

"On this count."

"Well, what did Balanchine say? How would you call him?"

"He said, 'Look this way and turn this way.' " I showed him. " 'And then you call Puck.' "

"Okay. Show me how you call him."

My words accompanied my gestures. "I walk out, and I look around, and no one's there so I call him."

Stanley shook his head. "No one is going to be able to see that. You have to do it deliberately so that it's visible to the audience. Onstage you have to make the statement and let it rest for a moment so the eye can absorb it." He demonstrated the proper way to do it. I was fascinated. I could see that I had to slow down the movement, give it weight.

Stanley walked me through the ballet start to finish, ana-   105 lyzing the character with me, working out gestures that would be appropriate. Oberon is a monarch. He has to have a regal presence. He's willful, mischievous, not sinister, but spoiled, petulant, used to having his own way. I also got insights from Misha Arshansky's makeup, which he created after talking to Balanchine. The makeup was elaborate but not beautiful. There's an otherworldly, alien-being, elfin quality to Oberon, but he has innate grandeur. He's as much creature as he is a character. At rehearsals I watched Balanchine carefully. He just naturally expressed the character in his carriage, the tilt of the head and the bend of the torso. Finally, the character formed itself in my consciousness.

In further sessions, Stanley and I then went through the steps of the scherzo. Careful analysis of the variation brought the character into focus even more. The variation, I realized, tells you everything: the lightness and speed, the darting quality of the attack, reveal it all. It was full of bubbling little delicacies. Oberon's explosive, but not destructive. Balanchine saw the character in terms of his duality: "scherzo" and "power." This is the big challenge of the variation, to have the power of the jump as well as the requisite speed, and it's probably why people have had so much difficulty with the role. They can summon up the power, but not at the high speed required by the music.

The very first pose Oberon strikes is in fourth position, and the choreography that follows makes a vivid impact. It's majestic in its way. Oberon executes the steps and flies off. In the second sequence of the variation, he does a series of brisées ouvertes, behind. What I tried to do is not move any part of my upper body, just let my legs do all the work, as if I were floating, buzzing over the tops of the trees or above the ground fog.

The final segment of the variation is a sustained line of steps, after which Oberon moves backward, skimming the stage. He's flying over the forest.

Stanley and I went over the variation again and again, and we refined it so that we really understood it. He said to me, "Do you realize what an incredible role you have?"

I did now. It was simply a wonderful variation and I was flattered. I felt that it did three things: it assured me that I could jump and beat and turn; that I could do these things with power

106

and speed; and that I could be purely classical. The fun part was making Oberon a little bit devilish while retaining the classical conception. I had to achieve and project a long, extended line. Dancing at such a level of intensity—and at such velocity—I had to be careful not to tense my muscles, not to hunch my neck and shoulders. Nothing in this role can be done abruptly. No shortcuts can be taken. The steps must be elongated; in preparation for the jump, the plié must be articulated in its entirety. I was beginning to understand the concept of slower being faster: in order to dance quickly, I had to take the time to articulate everything to acquire the speed.

I wouldn't have been able to do this without Stanley. It was he who first began to work with me on this refined approach to technique and phrasing. In those days, dancers didn't really phrase. Phrasing is the way a dancer relates the dynamics of the step to the music: How will he hit the note? Is the attack a hair before or a hair after? Does he play with the note? Split it? What about the hand? If he hits the note with his right hand, what about his left arm? Is it in position a little before or a little after the note? The leg? Is it in place on the note or slightly after? What does he do with his head and his eyes? And so on.

During the preparations for the premiere of *A Midsummer Night's Dream,* my father would occasionally come to the studio to watch me work on Oberon. He was growing more comfortable with the fact that I was a dancer, and during those rehearsals I found that I was dancing for him. In the past he used to show up to watch me play baseball and box and would wind up reading a newspaper most of the time. But now he was paying attention to what I was doing.

By the opening night of *A Midsummer Night's Dream* I felt fairly confident. When the curtain went up, I went out and gave everything I could. In a way I felt inspired. In the performance, I tried to sum up everything I had learned about the part in my first entrance with Oberon's first grand gesture. My mother told me that on opening night she didn't recognize me when I came out onstage. She thought Oberon looked six foot two. The scherzo stopped the performance, and I received a prolonged ovation. Madame Karinska, a Russian who designed most of the costumes for Balanchine, announced at the party after the premiere that I had scored the biggest success of the evening. Everyone was all over me with compliments. They

107

all seemed as surprised as I was at what I had pulled off. Nobody had imagined that I could do it. Balanchine hadn't *really* explained the role to me. As with *Prodigal,* he had showed me in the most understated way what he wanted. I had to find a way to grasp what he was saying and then develop it myself.

I don't know why Balanchine wouldn't approach me directly with his concerns, why he left it to Stanley to lead me into the heart of the role. Perhaps it was the growing tension between us that stemmed from my refusal to attend his class. But I don't think Balanchine was capable of any kind of direct communication with people, and certainly not with a man. He might have spoken more openly with women. But I'm not sure that he did, not even with his most beloved ballerinas.

Reviewers praised my performance in *A Midsummer Night's Dream.* P. W. Manchester in *Dance News* wrote, "Great leaps with landings soft as snowflakes, and brilliant turns superbly controlled to each immaculate completion. He is challenging the Russian male dancers on their own terms and he does not come off second best."

I stayed very late at the party the night of the premiere. I was in a state, reeling around, relieved from the demands of the previous days. Oberon was one of several roles I created that Baryshnikov danced during his year with the company, and others who have performed the part have called it one of the most difficult in the repertory. That night I was already sore, and the morning after I could barely move. I got up early and went straight to the theater just to get my body going. I knew it was going to take some effort.

No one had shown up yet. The theater was completely empty. Deserted theaters can be cold and empty places, especially in the early hours of the day. All that was lit up this morning was one bare bulb way up in the flies. I walked to the back of the stage near the big loading door, which opened onto Fifty-sixth Street. Steam pipes protruded from the wall, which was covered with crumbling concrete. I held on to one of the pipes and tried to do a few battements tendus. My attention was diverted by a noise, and I turned around and saw Balanchine, who had almost bumped into me.

He had just arrived, wearing his worn and wrinkled trench coat, and carrying a newspaper under his arm. He saw me and nodded and kept walking on his way. Then he stopped,

108

he turned around and looked at me. He walked up to me slowly.

"You know, last night you danced excellent," he said. "Excellent." He stepped closer to me and put his arm around my shoulder. "Excellent." Emotions turned over in my chest. He was certainly not given to such expressions, and not to a man. I was terribly grateful. I felt that he was trying to shorten the distance that had sprung up between us. He nodded, removed his arm, and walked away. Those words were the greatest compliment that Mr. B ever gave me.

Dancers work a fourteen-hour day, six days a week, and occasionally I had to blow off steam. My metabolism raced for two hours after the curtain came down; "cooling down" after a performance was difficult for me. Often I needed to socialize, go out, meet friends, have a drink, laugh, and party. In the early days of my friendship with Stanley, we had spent a lot of time with a public relations executive named Chris Allen. Chris used to throw parties that lasted until three or four in the morning. Actors, writers, producers, directors, dancers, and singers made up the guest list—it was a cross section of the New York arts and entertainment community, and really fun. There was always music after the so-called squares left at about one A.M. Opera singers partnered ballet dancers, people sang and acted out scenes, and everyone had a ball.

Chris Allen was a great Ballet Theater fan, close to the dancers in that company and to the ABT directors, Lucia Chase and Oliver Smith. He was often openly critical of the New York City Ballet, and of George Balanchine. I was uncomfortable about that; it put me in an awkward position. Chris was not looked upon favorably by the powers that be at the City Ballet. Balanchine became uneasy about my association with him and his friends. I enjoyed the company of these people. I didn't really care what Balanchine and Lincoln Kirstein thought about them. I wasn't committed to Allen and his crowd, but enjoyed their vitality and irreverence. Our relations were superficial. I knew where my allegiance was, but a principle was involved. I wasn't going to be judged by the company I kept.

By the end of 1960, my relationship with Carole Fields had become stormy, but I couldn't bring myself to end our affair. 109

The emotional ties between us were strong. She was the first woman I had ever really cared about. I thought of her as my Siren, but it was not an easy union. After three years we weren't able to resolve some basic conflicts. She wanted our relationship to be my top priority; she wanted us to marry. I still believed that dance had to come first for me.

It was inevitable that we would go our separate ways, a process I found painful. I initiated the split, and Carole was not happy about it. There was tension, and I felt vulnerable. At this time, I became reacquainted with Janet Greschsler, an NYCB dancer I had known before she joined the company, and whom I had occasionally dated.

Janet had qualities I was attracted to. Dark, vivacious, and alluring in her own way, she had an irreverent sense of humor. Being with her offered me a release from my obsession with my career. And there was no pressure—at least at first. She was full of life and had a great sense of style. She loved dressing up and knew all about rock and popular music. She brought me out of my shell. Although I thought I needed a monastic existence, a spartan life centered around ballet, my instincts cried out for something to temper my single-mindedness. Deep down, I knew I'd lost my sense of humor. I'd become square. I was also too self-absorbed.

I think Janet set her sights on me. I was a popular guy, a principal dancer at the start of what could be an important career. Janet had her own dreams of glory and was talented, but she wasn't focused on her dancing, and it seemed unlikely that she would have a major career.

She was willful, unafraid of expressing what she felt. I remembered when we had both been cast in *Creation of the World*. I was the lead and she was in the ensemble. Todd Bolender was choreographing the piece very slowly and the dancers got bored. Sometimes the chatter got out of hand. Finally, Todd lost his temper and cried out for quiet.

"If anybody doesn't want to be in this ballet, he or she can just leave," he said.

Janet picked up her dance bag and her purse and walked out of the studio, the only one to go.

I was interested in her, and after my long-term relationship had broken up, we started to date again. But no matter how I tried to set up boundaries, our relationship quickly became more serious than I had intended. I tried to back off.

"Wait a minute," I told her. "I've just come out of one rocky relationship, and I'm not in a position now to become serious about anything but my dancing."

In spite of everything, Janet and I started sleeping together. Morality was so different thirty years ago that this had a profound effect on our lives.

"You're using me," Janet said. She accused me of treating her like a prostitute, a whore, and she made me feel guilty, as if I were exploiting her.

Janet and I were together for the wrong reasons, but we didn't understand that. If we had had the patience to investigate our feelings, and our situation, we might not have stayed together. Emotionally, I was immature and so was Janet. My real commitment was to ballet, Balanchine and Stanley Williams, to solving my physical problems and becoming an artist. My personal life was secondary. But as time passed, pressures on us to marry mounted, and Janet continued to make me feel guilty about the sex. I told her that if I was making her so unhappy, then we should stop seeing each other, and I broke off the relationship.

Janet immediately became engaged to a wealthy man who gave her a five-carat diamond ring. After I found out about this, she phoned me and asked me to meet her. She told me then that her life was being ruined, that getting married to another man was not what she wanted. Would I please help her out, and could we try again? I relented. She broke off her engagement. We started seeing each other again, but problems set in almost immediately. When I said I didn't want to see her anymore, she began to cry. She was in great despair. So I gave in. We were going to try out the relationship for six months, and I thought if it didn't work then, I'd back out for good. But I was naive. If all this had happened a year or two later, Janet and I might not have gotten married. It was 1962. Janet and I were married in February of that year, on the day John Glenn was launched in space. The ceremony was held at City Hall. A dancer in the company, Marlene Mesavage, and Paul Di Sorvino, a stagehand, stood up for us. (Today Di Sorvino is head of Madison Square Garden.)

111

My parents didn't approve of my relationship with Janet and were dead set against our union. But I convinced myself I knew better—it was my life—and I rejected their advice. I was too young and proud to acknowledge their wisdom. I had to prove my independence. But it didn't take long for me to see that, as far as my marriage was concerned, my parents had been right. Getting married to Janet was a mistake—for both of us.

Not long after my wedding, I was approached by Jean Dalrymple, who was in charge of musical revivals at the City Center between ballet seasons. She had decided to revive *Brigadoon,* the musical about a mythical Scottish village that comes to life every hundred years. Sally Ann Howes and Farley Granger were set to star in the production, and Agnes de Mille was going to restage her original choreography. Dalrymple wanted me to play Harry Beaton. It was basically a dancing role.

I had been convinced that playing in a Broadway show would widen my range as a performer and had already appeared in *Brigadoon* in summer stock and in a production at the Dallas World's Fair. Dalrymple had heard about my success there. When we talked about it, I was frank.

"The reason why I had a success in this role is that for the opening scene in Act Two, I created my own dances. I did all the rest of the choreography in the piece, but I rechoreographed the dances in that scene."

The dancing that opens the second act is essentially nothing but dramatic running. It was obviously choreographed in the original production for an authentic Scottish dancer. Scottish dancing is essentially a par terre form of folk dancing. I was an en l'air dancer and thought it would be dramatically appropriate for me to jump in that scene. I imagined that if De Mille had originally had someone in the part who was good in the air, she might have choreographed it differently. I had performed a number of pyrotechnical jumps in this scene, and I was convinced that this accounted for the impact I had in the role. I told Jean, "You have to decide what you want, whether you want me to come and dance what I did in Dallas, or if you want the original De Mille choreography."

"Well, of course, we want you to dance what you did in Dallas," she said. Naturally, she was interested in having a success.

112

I said, "Fine. But will you please speak to Miss De Mille about it. This is her production, and I certainly do not want to offend her. She might have reservations about changing the steps. So if you want me, I'll do it. But I'll only do it if I can do what made it successful for me in Dallas."

"Of course, of course," she said.

"So you'll speak to Agnes."

"Yes. Of course I will."

Rehearsals began and went smoothly. But when one of De Mille's assistants came in to stage the opening of the second act, it was obvious that De Mille's original choreography was being retained.

I approached the director. "Didn't Jean speak to you?" I asked.

"Oh, yes, yes," he said. "Jean talked to me. But let them stage the scene the way they usually stage it, and then we'll change it."

Time passed, but every time we worked on the scene it contained the original De Mille dances. A week before opening, the choreography still hadn't been restaged. I knew then they weren't going to. No one is going to do anything, I thought. I tried to reach Jean Dalrymple, but every time I called her she was unavailable, and she never called me back. She was out of town. I decided to call Agnes de Mille myself.

"You know, Miss De Mille," I said politely, "this is the most embarrassing telephone call I've ever made in my life. But I've got to tell you something. Actually, I have to ask you something. Have you ever had a conversation with anybody about the choreography in the chase scene?"

"What are you talking about?" she said.

I explained the situation, told her about my conversation with Jean Dalrymple.

"*Well!* I have never, *never* been spoken to like this in my life! *And certainly not by a dancer!*"

"Well, I'm a dancer and I've just spoken to you like that," I answered. "I'm telling you what my understanding is. I had an agreement, a contractual understanding. The reason I'm doing this production is because I was told we would restage the dances in this scene, and if that's not the case, then we don't have an agreement."

"We'll see about that," she said. And she hung up.   113

The next day, both De Mille and Dalrymple showed up at the rehearsal. A look passed between them when I entered, and the atmosphere was tense. De Mille was intelligent and articulate and had a graceful air about her. She was rather petite, but self-confident, used to having people defer to her.

She locked eyes with me. "All right," she said. "Show me what you want to do. But remember"—she pointed a finger—*"there'll be no white tights in the glen!"*

After I performed the variation for her, she saw the value of what I wanted to do and agreed to let me perform it my way. But she didn't say a word to me throughout the engagement. I appeared in five more City Center revivals of *Brigadoon* in which De Mille restaged the choreography. She refused to speak until the third one, when, on opening night, she sent me a bottle of Scotch.

My reception in the revival at the City Center was enthusiastic. The audience greeted me warmly, and the production set box office records. Houses were packed. How did that happen? I believe a substantial group of people who regularly attended the New York City Ballet in that theater were coming to see me there in another vehicle. Although it was never publicly acknowledged, and was something I never referred to, despite the no-star City Ballet policy, and the predominance of the repertory over personalities, the house seemed to be jammed whenever I danced.

The role of Harry Beaton was fourth or fifth in importance in *Brigadoon,* and one of the procedures in a Broadway show is that people take their bows in order of the importance of their roles. But usually stars are catered to in this respect; they often take the last bow. My bow was the third from the last in this revival, just before the leading man and woman. When I came on, I received more applause than the two stars. Sally Ann Howes, the leading lady, didn't like it. It seemed to me that she let me know how she felt about it during the performance.

One of the first lines I spoke in the play was to Howes. She would respond in order. But when I answered, she'd jump on my line. I found out what people mean when they talk about being upstaged. They mean it literally: someone steps in front of an actor onstage and distracts the audience during one of his important moments. I realized that I needed to watch out for

114

my own interests. I came from a velvet world, where I had been cosseted by such people as Balanchine and Kirstein, the best costume and scenic designers, technicians and stagehands, and the finest conductors, all of them involved in an artistic enterprise of the highest level. Moving into the harsher world of Broadway was both enlightening and disillusioning.

115

EDWARD VILLELLA

NINE

Sometime during 1962 a rumor spread through the company that New York City Ballet would be leaving in the autumn for an extended tour of Europe and the Soviet Union. None of us, of course, were officially informed until much later. But that didn't stop the anticipation.

I was ambivalent, happy to have the opportunity to dance in Russia but a little reluctant. The tour of the Pacific four years before had been hard for a lot of reasons, and I couldn't quite get the experience out of my head. I got more excited as people tried to reassure me. Appearing in Europe and the Soviet Union, the very places in which the art of ballet had been born and developed, would be different, they said. This was a much more significant event, with far-reaching implications for Balanchine. He hadn't been back to the Soviet Union since he had left in 1924. Everyone assumed it had to be difficult for him, returning to his homeland, but he covered up any uneasiness or anxiety he felt.

The tour repertory was eventually posted, and I was disappointed. The only roles I would be dancing were third movement *Symphony in C, Agon,* and *Afternoon of a Faun. Prodigal Son* had been listed, then canceled. I took the cancellation personally. I mustered up my courage and protested to Balanchine.

"Why am I going, Mr. B?" I asked. "Why don't I just stay here and work on all the things I need to improve?"

116

He wouldn't hear of it.

"Well, then, why aren't we taking *Prodigal Son?*" I asked.

"The reason is because they won't let us do in Soviet Union. Because of Prokofiev. Because he went to Paris. They hated him," he said. "And they killed him. They hit him on the head and killed him."

I had no doubt that the Soviet government might have had Prokofiev assassinated, but I didn't believe for an instant that this was the reason for *Prodigal*'s cancellation. I continued my protest.

"I'll find something else for you," he said. "I know. We'll do third movement *Western Symphony*. I'll restage it."

Western was currently being performed without the third movement. For a while no woman in the company seemed to possess a sufficiently strong jump for the role, and Balanchine had removed the section from the ballet. Now he said he would rechoreograph it.

"Okay, fine. Thank you," I said.

But as soon as he began to work, I could see his heart wasn't in it. He didn't really want to do it. He demonstrated a few steps, and I followed what he did, but nothing exciting was happening. Steps and movements were not pouring out of him. After an hour, nothing had been accomplished. He finally shook his head and said, "No, we won't do. No, no, no." He left the studio. The next day *Prodigal Son* was back on the schedule.

As it turned out, I found myself dancing far more on the tour than I had ever imagined. Jacques D'Amboise, crossing the street in Hamburg, was hit by a trolley car. He suffered broken ribs and various bruises. He was laid up, unable to dance because of these injuries, for most of the tour. Many of Jacques's ballets were quickly added to my repertory, including *Raymonda Variations* and *Tchaikovsky Pas de Deux*, ballets I had never danced before.

Our first night at the Bolshoi Theatre we performed for an audience of party and union officials who were fairly unenthusiastic. This happened in every city. But audiences on subsequent nights were extremely responsive. Our second evening performance at the Bolshoi Theatre began calmly enough. I was going to dance *Donizetti Variations* opposite Violette, a role I had performed in New York. We went out on the stage and

117

danced the entrée and adagio section of the pas de deux to a round of applause, and I went off, waiting in the wings to do my variation. When I walked back out onto the stage, I was motivated to do well. As soon as I started, I could tell, despite the raked stage, which was unfamiliar to me, that I was "on": I was going to do the best I could do.

In a way, I have always felt that my best performances were too easy. When everything in a performance falls into place, it seems as if I'm not working hard enough. Nights that I felt I was really working were the times I tended to overdance. That night I finished the variation, which included double air turns, landing flat in position, not moving a muscle or a hair or blinking an eye, to a moment of dead silence. But in the next instant, the audience exploded, applauding in unison and screaming their approval, stomping their feet and crying out, "Bis! Bis! Encore! Encore!" The ovation lasted—it seemed to go on and on. Goose bumps rose up all over my body. The sweat kept pouring off me. The audience now started shouting out my name. I kept bowing.

The place was pandemonium. Instead of dying down, the applause and the shouting grew louder and louder. Every dancer who had been down at the canteen or in the studio or dressing rooms rushed to the stage: the wings had filled up with every member of the company. Cries for "Encore" increased in number and volume. The entire theater was going crazy. An encore had never been danced before in the history of the New York City Ballet, there was no precedent for it, and I didn't know what to do. I kept going back and forth into the wing, and then back onstage, bowing and bowing. The stomping and applause refused to die down. In all, I had gone out for something like twenty-two curtain calls.

Next, Hugo Fiorato, the conductor, made a gesture to the musicians in the pit, and they all turned back their sheet music. He signaled for me to start dancing. The audience was still in a frenzy. I figured that if I didn't dance, I'd be bowing all night. There didn't seem to be anything else to do, so I repeated the variation. After the performance I was somewhat stunned, and incredibly elated, but deep down I was worried about Balanchine's reaction. I was afraid he wasn't going to like it, but he didn't say a word. After a while, however, I knew something

118

was wrong. Days went by, and it became clear. Balanchine was ignoring me. It was obviously because of the encore, but I wasn't sure of what to do about it. I did nothing; I tried to cope with the conditions we were faced with in Russia: we were performing during the height of the Cuban missile crisis.

Russia in 1962 was a very, very dark prison where it felt as if everyone were under surveillance. Life seemed grim, and people looked exhausted. They showed little enthusiasm for being alive. Our hotel in Moscow, the Ukraine, was five years old but looked more like forty. It was falling apart. Doorknobs came off in our hands, water was shut off at odd hours, and we couldn't turn off the radio in our rooms. State Department professionals assured us that 85 percent of the rooms in the country were bugged. Most inconvenient of all, elevators stopped only at certain floors. At every landing sat a buxom Russian woman behind a desk who'd check IDs before letting us proceed to our rooms.

We were in a police state, and we felt oppressed by it. Emotionally, it was difficult to live from day to day. It seemed as if we were surrounded by spies, as if every interpreter were a KGB agent. The Russians guided us every step of the way; they hovered over us at each turn, discouraging any contact or fraternization with Soviet citizens. Often I would turn around to find the same familiar face tailing me. If I dined in a restaurant and happened to strike up a conversation with some of the local citizens, four hulking men would materialize, and the person I was talking to would vanish. One or two people drunk on vodka might try to approach me for a chat, and within seconds these people would also be gone. During the day on the streets we encountered people begging for jeans, nylons, shirts, and ballpoint pens. Someone offered me one hundred dollars if I would give him a rock album, and artists would sometimes bestow their work on us as offerings.

One night, a young man came backstage hiding something under his coat. Whatever it was, he seemed desperate for me to see it. At first, I refused to look at it because I wasn't sure what it was and didn't want to create any scandal. No matter how many times I said, "No, thank you," he kept insisting, pressing

119

EDWARD VILLELLA

this gift on me until I looked down and saw that it was an abstract painting.

"I want you to know that this is what *we* do also. Keep it. Don't show it to anybody until you leave the country."

Another evening someone came backstage carrying a photograph of Rudolf Nureyev. Nureyev had defected the year before from the Kirov Ballet, and the Soviet government was then in the process of relegating him to the status of a nonperson. By showing us the photo, Nureyev's fan was telling us he wouldn't forget him.

One official I remember very clearly from those days in Russia was Felix Rosenthal, the interpreter assigned to the company. Felix was Jewish, and considering the Soviet attitude toward Jews, it was unusual that he held such a high-level job. Before this assignment, he used to shepherd parties of tourists around the country, so interpreting for a major visiting cultural organization was a step up for him. We were convinced that Felix worked for the KGB, but we all grew terribly fond of him. He was a sweetheart of a man, very easy to get along with, and he didn't seem like a bureaucrat. We used to secretly give copies of American magazines to Felix and to the players in the Soviet orchestra. They were just amazed at the photographs and the products being advertised: they had trouble believing that these things actually existed.

Many years later, I saw Felix again by chance on the promenade of the New York State Theater, of all places. He was part of a Soviet cultural delegation to New York City and had come to the ballet by himself. He remarked that few of the names he knew remained part of the organization. It was wonderful running into him, to see how he had prospered, and to talk about old times. I was amazed that Felix was actually traveling on his own outside the Soviet Union. That would have been an impossibility in 1962.

Felix was the only Soviet citizen in Russia who befriended us. We didn't really get close to anyone else though we were often surounded by party officials. Most of the Russians were standoffish. It's hard today in the face of glasnost and the changes that have occurred in the Soviet Union and Eastern Europe to imagine how tense relations were between the United States and the Soviet government in 1962. We were

120

mortal enemies. Khrushchev banging on the desk with his shoe at the U.N. and predicting, "We will bury you!" is a stark image I still carry. Although we were on an artistic mission, it was difficult to separate the artistic from the political because politics drove every aspect of that society. Politics touched everything, especially ballet, which was a source of pride to the Soviets. (At a press conference on the tour, Balanchine was asked what it felt like coming back to the home of classical ballet. He shook his head and said, "The United States is now the home of classical ballet. The Soviet Union is the home of romantic ballet.") On that trip I had the distinct sense dancing for my country, and it felt good. Each country was poised to annihilate the other at any moment, and there we were speaking directly to the people with our art. It was a remarkable experience.

Being in Moscow during the international crisis heightened every experience for me—for all of us. Everyone in the world at that time was feeling the heat and pressure of the confrontation between the two superpowers; we felt it more intensely, and we experienced it differently. In the enemy camp, we were cut off from major sources of information. We couldn't watch television even if we could have found one, and it was impossible to buy *Time* or *Newsweek* or a copy of the *New York Times* or the *International Herald Tribune*. Everything we learned came from daily American embassy bulletins. After reading Adlài Stevenson's United Nations address, the enormity of the situation became clear to us.

But we kept our cool. Some days my pulse accelerated, but I didn't allow myself to give in to any fears. Over and over, I noticed the contradiction between the actions of the government and the Russian citizens' loud cheers for the New York City Ballet night after night. Once in a while, though, we did feel threatened. On one occasion, the company was invited to a special luncheon at the American embassy where, unexpectedly, an announcement was made that the dancers should vacate the premises no later than two-thirty.

I asked a State Department attaché what the problem was.

At first, he evaded my eye. Then he answered, "The schools are letting out early, and there's going to be a demon-

EDWARD VILLELLA

stration in front of the embassy. The students are going to stone it."

As we were being ushered out of the building in a state of semi-emergency, crowds of youthful students were gathering. But the strange thing was that the atmosphere didn't seem particularly hostile. The young people, mostly in their teens, stood around in bunches, chatting among themselves. It was obvious that the protest wasn't spontaneous, that it was being staged by the authorities, and that students had been told to report to the embassy after school. But precautions still had to be taken. The embassy staff promptly evacuated everyone, closing windows and drawing shutters so that the building looked abandoned.

As we were walking away from the site, student agitators went into action, and the crowd hurled large rocks, stones, and other missiles at the embassy, shattering glass and scarring the shutters. Giant ink bottles were also tossed, splattering and staining the embassy walls.

The crashing objects and the shouts of the students alarmed me; I thought we were going to be stoned and crushed underfoot by a crazed mob. But I quickly realized that the students were just going through the motions. There was no real emotion on their part. The slogans they chanted sounded empty, hollow. The protest was not at all threatening. Rather than run for our lives, we all proceeded calmly at a normal pace to the local bus stop. Our bus hadn't returned to pick us up, so we were going to have to take public transportation. As I recall it, the bus ride took only a few minutes and left us off at our hotel, which wasn't really very far away at all.

None of these extraordinary events seemed as real to me as my sense that Balanchine was angry with me. The night of my first performance of *Prodigal Son,* which received a great response, I was sitting next to my wife, Janet, on the company bus that was to take us back to our hotel. Allegra was in front of me, and Balanchine got on and sat down alongside her. He had avoided my eye, but I could sense the anger and fury emanating from his body: I could swear that the hairs on the back of his neck were standing up. Finally, he couldn't take it any longer. He turned around and looked me in the eye. On his face was an expression of withering contempt.

122

"You wanted to dance dramatic ballet," he said. "Now *you're* hero."

I felt as if he had slapped me hard across the face. I flushed, my eyes were stinging, and my cheeks burned. The audience's enthusiasm for my dancing in *Prodigal Son* seemed like an affront to him. He couldn't stand it. It was as if he had to punish me. I thought I understood now why he hadn't wanted to bring the ballet on the tour. He had expected the positive reaction, and it was a work he didn't highly regard. He also knew that my performance would be well received. I was probably well down in line of those he wanted to show off. I think he thought of returning to Russia as a chance to present Allegra Kent to this audience and bowl them over. He had no plans for anyone else to have a major success. Allegra certainly did have a triumph, but suddenly night after night I was getting more applause than anyone else. He didn't like it.

He was also uncharitable about Arthur Mitchell, who is black, whom audiences adored in *Agon.* At first, the Russians were mystified by the ballet, and by watching a pas de deux danced by a black man and a white ballerina. But after a while they began to really appreciate the intricacies of the ballet; they also loved *Episodes,* another purely neoclassical work. Their appreciation of *Agon,* however, was most clearly expressed in their approval of Arthur's performance. Balanchine was furious.

"Look, look at the People's premier danseur," he sneered.

Except for his outburst on the bus, Balanchine hadn't spoken to me for about two weeks when I saw him approach one afternoon as I was walking along a corridor in the theater. He barely acknowledged my presence and tried to move out of my way. Awkwardly we tried to get around each other, each of us gesturing, You go, No, you. I decided to take action, and I stood face-to-face with him, stopping him in his tracks.

"You know, Mr. B," I said, "I don't put much credence in rumor, but quite frankly I've been hearing one I have to get to the bottom of. And that is, you're displeased with me because I danced an encore."

I had never seen Balanchine lose his composure before. He became agitated and started breathing rapidly. He could barely speak.

"No. No. Encore for you no problem. Here, here, won-

123

derful. But if it's London, that's something else because there, all the men there, they want your body. There they ask for encore because they don't know. But not here. No, no. Here they know. I . . . I danced encore here. I did it. No problem."

"Great, great," I said. "Thank you." Then I took another chance. "I also thought maybe you were upset because I no longer come to your class."

He shook his head. "No, no. For you that's okay. You know how to do battement tendu, you know how. No it's fine, dear."

I was relieved, but I wasn't convinced of the sincerity of his responses. Then, a few days after our conversation, Balanchine came up to me. He wanted to talk about the costume I wore in *Donizetti Variations*.

"Your costume's awful, dear, lousy, rotten. You look like a red devil, you look awful," he said.

I completely disagreed with him. The costume I wore in *Donizetti* was very handsome: maroon tights and a maroon velvet tunic with silk sleeves. It suited my complexion and highlighted my dark skin and hair, making me look Latin. It also made me appear taller than I was, creating the illusion of an extended line. I loved this costume. But Balanchine shook his head.

"Rotten red devil. We're going to change."

He signaled for me to follow him. We picked up my costume and walked down a few flights of stairs into the depths of the Bolshoi Theatre into a musty, dingy room. Balanchine plunged his hand into a big wicker basket in the center of the room, pulling out tights and tops and pieces of fabric. He retrieved a pair of particularly loud canary yellow–green tights, the color of baby vomit, and held them up in front of me.

"Beautiful," he said. "Wonderful, great, great. Here. Put on tights."

I thought, oh, no. But what could I do? The man's a genius, he's your boss! I thought. I told myself, put on the tights.

I got into them and looked into a mirror.

"Now, dear," Balanchine said. "Put on maroon jacket."

I did what he said and looked at my image again. The clash of colors was painful. I looked abominable, horrible, outrageous. My heart was sinking. What could I say? Something

124

told me to just go along with it, though I thought I'd never have the courage to go out onstage in such an outfit.

"Now, dear. Maroon shoes."

The effect was completed. Not only did the tights look awful and clash with the jacket, with the slippers on I looked as if I'd been sawed into three different sections. This arrogant, snot-nosed, son-of-a-bitch dancer might have been five foot eight, but standing before the mirror, he could see he looked about four foot two.

"Aw, for God's sake, Mr. Balanchine," I moaned. "I'm not tall enough to wear this outfit."

Balanchine stared at me, beaming. He smiled like the devil. "No, dear," he said. "You're right. If you wore, you'd look like you were dancing on your knees."

Then he walked out of the room, pleased with himself. He seemed satisfied that he had taught me a lesson. He may have said it was all right to have danced an encore and to be in the spotlight for a moment. But he let me know he had the power to humiliate me anytime he pleased. Now he was happy, even though circumstance had given me the victory. I was livid.

A few days later, Balanchine escorted Violette and me to the Palace of Congresses inside the Kremlin one morning after class. He was in a jovial mood. The company was also performing in the huge Kremlin meeting hall, which sat more than six thousand people and had a vast eighty-foot stage. Balanchine was going to redo the variations in *Tchaikovsky Pas de Deux*.

Violette was her voluble self while we were working on the ballet, going on and on about the steps, and Balanchine became impatient with her.

"You know, dear," he said to her, "it's nice simple step, grand jeté, you see. Just watch him. It's wonderful to just watch him jump. Just simple. He just jumps. Wonderful."

In fact, he had given me this big, sweeping variation. He created it quickly and in bits and pieces as was usually the case, and I never had a chance to do it from beginning to end until the night of the performance. The first time I danced it, I became so winded that I could barely see straight. I kept gasping backstage and had to be helped up to my feet, dragged over to the wing, and pushed back out onstage.

125

EDWARD VILLELLA

Overall, I hated Russia, which was gray and boring. It was an uncomfortable place to live and work. We continued our regular schedule of eight performances a week. Travel days were squeezed in between each engagement. I danced every performance. I thought I was going to explode.

My relations with Janet added to my frustration. Anything served as an excuse for either one of us to start an argument. Things were pretty much as they'd been at home. In the States, on the first day of our honeymoon, I'd had a phone call from my sister, Carol. Afterward, I accidentally called Janet by my sister's name. Since Carole was also the name of my old girl-friend, Janet went nuts. I shot back and a fierce quarrel fol-lowed. We hadn't even been married a year, but there rarely was any peace between us anymore. Janet and I could laugh together at times, but more and more we rubbed each other the wrong way. We didn't share the same opinions, and one phrase would mean different things to us.

Things got worse on the tour. One evening after a perfor-mance Janet picked a fight that lasted until four in the morning. I had to be up early the next day, ready to perform *Donizetti Variations* at an eleven A.M. matinee. I barely got through my warm-up and all the other preparations I had to make. Anger and frustration drove me. But once the curtain went up, I en-tered another world. Nothing could touch me onstage.

No one had expected that the tour was going to be easy, but the problems with Janet added to my misery. Before our departure, everyone in the company had been briefed by the State Department on what life would be like in the Soviet Union. They wanted us to be aware of potential problems and restrictions that would be placed on us. But quickly, trouble sprang up. In Moscow one of our dancers was arrested for taking what he thought were innocuous snapshots in a park. It turned out that armed Soviet soldiers sitting in a military vehi-cle were inside the frame of his photo. His film was confiscated. Later, the same dancer was detained in Baku for taking photo-graphs of litter-strewn streets.

We had also been warned that the Soviet Union was not a place for gourmets, and each of us was allowed to bring canned goods and powdered food and drinks with us in footlockers. Items like razor blades and Band-Aids were also packed in ad-

126

vance. Some dancers were really creative, bringing along big jars of Coca-Cola syrup to mix with mineral water for a passable Coke. I felt especially deprived because I was afraid to bring in American or European beer. I don't know what it's like now, but in 1962 Russian beer was nearly undrinkable. We called it Great Bear piss, Great Bear being the Soviet Union. I had managed, however, to smuggle a few bottles of American beer past customs, but they went quickly. I had one left; however, I was saving for a special occasion. But one night when I was ranting at Janet during an argument, she got back at me. She opened my last bottle and poured it over my head.

I had also brought in the country a huge chunk of delicious cheese I had purchased in Vienna. I kept it wrapped in a towel on my windowsill at our hotel in Tbilisi, Georgia, until one of the hotel employees accused me of theft. She demanded that I pay four rubles for the towel, which was worn and tattered and full of holes. Americans were always stealing her towels, she said.

Group outings to restaurants were encouraged by government officials as a way of keeping the company together and under control. Selections were limited, and half the dishes on the menu were unavailable. These dining experiences were never pleasant. Breakfast was a slice of sweating cheese on a plate next to a congealed egg. At other meals, we ate an awful lot of cabbage. The service was execrable. Waiters or waitresses ignored us and mostly stood around talking to each other. Tipping was not allowed, so they had no incentive at all to please us.

We traveled almost everywhere by train. The tour was made even drearier by the fact that there was nothing to do on evenings off, no clubs or movies or new people to meet. We were cordoned off like zoo animals from the real life of the place. Occasionally we'd find a circus or a symphony orchestra or a local ballet company. But these were rare occasions.

Moscow was the most oppressive of all the cities we visited. All the political pressures were palpable there. Everyone seemed suspicious, weighed down by dark clothes and sober thoughts. We couldn't talk to people or buy trinkets from street vendors. We were also discouraged from giving anything to anyone. Kids surrounded our buses everywhere, and we'd pull

127

out chewing gum and various little items like that, but our interpreters frowned on this and I felt as if I were back in grade school—under strict supervision. It was suffocating.

Medicine in the Soviet Union seemed hopelessly primitive. One night Arthur Mitchell gashed his foot in a sauna, and an ambulance had to be called. Into the bathhouse came this forbidding woman, carrying what looked like a wooden crate, a homemade strongbox painted white. Inside were corked bottles containing liquid medications of various colors. Some bottles had rags stuffed inside instead of corks. The woman removed a rag from one bottle, poured out a green substance, and dressed Arthur's wound with it. Then she wrapped his foot in a piece of heavy fabric like muslin; she didn't even have gauze. After that sight, I think we all tried to stay healthy and avoid accidents. I lived in fear of getting a cold!

The most comfortable city we visited was Tbilisi in Georgia, the home of Balanchine's ancestors. The Georgians' sense of their land and their people is fierce. They reminded me of my parents.

Our theater in Georgia was a beautiful old relic, but the plumbing was outmoded and harsh. The bathrooms were like indoor outhouses, and we were uncomfortable using them. I was tired of everything being so rough and primitive. The food in Tbilisi was better than anywhere else; at least there was a wider variety to the fare. We saw fruit and bread for the first time on our trip. The loaves of bread were giant size. I remember grabbing one from the center of a table and breaking off a big chunk. My mouth was watering, but these dark little items were in it. Looking at it, I thought, raisin bread. But on closer inspection they turned out not to be raisins, but cockroaches. It happened all the time. Turning over vegetables on our plates, we'd find the carcass of some insect or other lying there. It was awful. I wanted out—fast.

During our stay in Tbilisi, we came across the once-renowned Russian dancer Vakhtang Chabukiani, who directed the local ballet company. A contemporary of Balanchine's, he still performed, although he was obviously past his prime. A production of his we saw told the story of a group of peasants who storm the walls of their city and triumph over the aristocrats. It was trite propaganda.

128

Violette, despite her usual aesthetic standards, took a great liking to Chabukiani and asked him to teach us the *Le Corsaire* pas de deux, which still hadn't been seen in the U.S. at that time. He demonstrated some brief excerpts but said there wasn't enough time to teach it to us correctly. It took some concentrated attention to pick up the specific style. Instead he offered to teach us a pas de deux of his own. A long, flowing veil was used as part of the stage business. Russian artists had been cut off from outside influences for some time, and this reflected the stifling artistic circumstances. It didn't require bravura technique, and to my Balanchine-trained eyes it was naive, almost funny in its datedness and lack of musicality. Still, Chabukiani took it seriously. He was absorbed in his work and I admired his real devotion to his art.

While he showed us this ballet, we chatted about dance, and he offered his candid opinion about Balanchine's work. He said he couldn't understand the fuss. All Balanchine did was to put classroom steps together. He called *Symphony in C* a classroom ballet and couldn't see why this man was regarded as a revolutionary artist. Violette and I totally disagreed and argued back.

Baku, in the southwest republic of Azerbaijan, had the most agreeable climate of all the cities we visited. Originally, it had been a Persian city, and the old town, a former fortress, was a maze of crooked streets, narrow lanes, and the atmosphere of the Middle East. It felt remote and exotic. Most of the people in Baku were Azerbaijanis, but there were Russians and Armenians also.

Before long, however, we were back on the train. We saw nothing from the window for days at a time but barren terrain, utter desolation as far as the eye could see. There was no vegetation at all, not a tree, not a bush; the countryside couldn't even be described as a desert. I had never seen such a landscape. But the journey gave us the sense of the enormity of Mother Russia.

Occasionally we'd arrive early for rehearsal at the theaters we were performing in, and we'd watch a Soviet opera or ballet being rehearsed on the stage. Usually these pieces shocked us. We'd see singers in blackface being whipped by plantation owners dressed up to look like Uncle Sam in wide-brimmed top hats in operas set in the United States. It was their brand of propaganda.

129

By the time we got to Leningrad, I was feeling less than charming. But the city is beautiful and I liked the people there. The Leningraders had an old-world, European dignity and charm, and their city was elegant and noble. Balanchine spoke often of the St. Petersburg style, which a work such as *The Sleeping Beauty* epitomized. He used to refer to himself, and to Tchaikovsky and Stravinsky, as St. Petersburgers. Russians talk about Leningrad in the same way Italians talk about Florence.

After the Russian tour, Janet and I decided to spend a few weeks in Denmark. Stanley was back in Copenhagen. As soon as he laid eyes on me, he said, "You look terrible."

It was true. We were all exhausted, but having seen each other every day for thirteen weeks, we couldn't tell just how bad we looked. Stanley had a top doctor from a Danish hospital examine me. He was the physician for the company, and he prescribed vitamin B shots three times a week.

Copenhagen was a respite after the horrors of Russia. It was a joyous, friendly, high-spirited city. I loved the look of the place and the food, the smorgasbord and Danish open sandwiches and beer. It was a great place to recuperate in, and best of all, I was able to take class again with Stanley. I also studied with Vera Volkova and with Toni Lander. I felt a little like an intruder. My dancing seemed so bold in contrast to the Danes', it was as if I were tearing up the place.

Almost immediately, Janet and I started arguing in Copenhagen. She was jealous of the time I spent with Stanley and picked a fight one night over my eating out with him. I didn't like it. I felt as if I couldn't pick and choose my friends, as if I weren't supposed to have any friends. Janet wanted me with her always, telling her that I loved her, reassuring her. She wanted to isolate me behind an iron curtain of her affections.

I wasn't sure what to do about my wife. Onstage I had turned into a good partner because I worked hard at it. But offstage I wasn't making much of an effort to improve my partnering at all. I was growing as a dancer but I wasn't growing emotionally. It made me unhappy.

After spending only a few days in Copenhagen, I took a break to fly with Janet to London. I was going to dance with

Violette at a gala performance Margot Fonteyn was putting together at the Drury Lane Theatre for the Royal Academy of Dancing. Fonteyn had contacted us in Russia, and Violette had flown to London directly from the Soviet Union.

I was excited about dancing in England, delighted to meet Fonteyn. She was the prima ballerina of the Royal Ballet, and a great star all over the world. She epitomized the British classical style with her beautiful placement, exquisite line, and innate musicality. She was also a lovely human being, intelligent and dignified, and she really knew how to charm. She could please people by just standing onstage, and she seemed to breathe with the music when she danced. Her dancing was an extension of her human core.

I felt an affinity for English dancers. In the 1950s and 60s, the Royal Ballet and the New York City Ballet were like sister companies and we often socialized. David Blair and Stanley Holden, two Royal dancers I was friendly with, used to go bowling with me when they visited New York, and of course we went out together drinking beer and ale whenever we had the chance.

Violette and I rehearsed on the day of the gala, and all went well. We were scheduled to close the program, which was very gracious of Dame Margot; she was going to dance an excerpt from *Swan Lake* on the first half of the bill in which the violin solo was going to be played by Yehudi Menuhin. In the second half she was set to dance a pas de deux from *Gayané* with Hungarian dancer Viktor Rona as her partner.

As the performance progressed, Violette and I waited in opposite wings, warming up while Fonteyn and Rona danced. When they finished the *Gayané* pas de deux, the response was thunderous. They were called back repeatedly and then danced an encore. I said to myself, how do we follow this, and in Margot Fonteyn's hometown? But then I thought, we have Balanchine's *Tchaikovsky Pas de Deux*. The English audience is in for a treat. It gave us confidence. Violette and I were excited about dancing in London. We were really prepared—we were "on." The audience gave us a stunning reception, even greater than Fonteyn and her partner had received. I like to think I'm not competitive as an artist, but I have to admit that I was sensitive to these things.

131

EDWARD VILLELLA

Everyone came over to us as we went into the wings. They were all saying, "Do an encore. An encore!"

I thought about it for a moment, remembering Balanchine's reaction in Moscow. I looked over at Violette.

"No," I said. "I think that might not be in good taste. I think we should leave it where it is."

The reviews for the performance were great. Mary Clarke wrote in *Dance News* that "[Villella] conquered London with his first jump." Clive Barnes said, "This morning London can hail a new male dancing star, twenty-five-year-old New Yorker Edward Villella." And the *Daily Express* critic wrote, "Last year Margot Fonteyn introduced the Russian Rudolf Nureyev to the British public. And here this year is America's jet-propelled answer. [He] has a distinctively casual elegance all his own. And he can go up in the air like a bird, seem to poise there, and flash a friendly grin at the gaping audience."

I returned to Copenhagen right after the gala and Janet flew home to New York. I was eager to keep working with Stanley. Soon after I got back, an official with the Royal Danish Ballet who had heard about my success in Russia and England invited me to dance with the company in a ballet of my choice. I agreed and contacted Balanchine to see if I might dance *Tchaikovsky Pas de Deux*. He quickly gave me the okay. When I started to rehearse the ballet, the Danes were impressed. Niels Kehlet paid me a compliment I still remember. "You know," he said, "these are movements we have never seen before." I was really pleased.

But as the time of the performance approached, I became entangled in company politics. As a guest, I naturally reserved the right to perform the ballet with the partner of my choice, but Volkova, who had great clout in Denmark, wanted me to dance with a former student of hers who was now a principal dancer in the company. I felt the woman was completely unsuited to the ballet. It seemed obvious to me, and I was surprised that Volkova couldn't see it herself. I couldn't believe that she would willingly subject the woman to the embarrassment of appearing in something unflattering. But the great teacher obviously felt getting her protégé onstage opposite me in a Balanchine ballet took precedence over other considerations.

132

In addition to the matter of a partner, the officials and directors of the company were insisting I dance in the company's smaller theater. The Royal Danish Ballet performs in two theaters, one much grander than the other. The request made Stanley uneasy, and he went with me to look over the smaller house. Performing there was out of the question. The stage was minuscule. There was no way I could propel myself around that constricted area. The variation on *Tchaikovsky Pas de Deux* is about jumping, propulsion, covering space. With Stanley's help we soon worked things out with both the theater and the ballerina.

The five hundredth performance of August Bournonville's *Napoli* was being celebrated by the Royal Danes while I was in Denmark. Stanley said, "The obvious place for you to dance is on that program. You're a Balanchine dancer, just returning from a successful tour of the Soviet Union, and you represent the School of American Ballet and the New York City Ballet. You must be treated accordingly."

Stanley spoke to the company officials. *Tchaikovsky Pas de Deux* was added to the program, and we danced in the main theater. My new partner was the ballerina Solveig Ostergaard. She was the right size for me. She had the necessary speed, attack, and line and learned quickly. She was also easy to partner. And I was delighted with the audience response. Danish audiences have an unusual custom. I had noticed at the performances I attended that applause ends as soon as the curtain falls on a ballet. Once the curtain's down, the audience gets up and leaves. There are no repeated curtain calls. After a few weeks, I'd gotten used to the custom and prepared myself for this kind of reception. I also had to be instructed in the proper manner in which to bow to royalty, because the Danish royal family was going to be in attendance. My first bow had to be directed to them. But at the end of *Tchaikovsky Pas de Deux,* Solveig and I received seven curtain calls. It was quite extraordinary, and I was excited by it. The following day, a front-page story about the performance appeared in one of the city's leading papers.

A review also appeared in the *Berlinske Tidende,* which said, "The audience went wild. It should have resulted in an encore. Villella charmed the audience with his unusual combi-

133

nation of superior dancing and masculine charm . . . King Frederick IX led the applauding."

As it came time to leave Denmark, a curt letter from Betty Cage, the NYCB general manager, arrived. Betty is a kind and sympathetic woman; her tone was surprising. She demanded that I return at once to New York City. In my sensitive state the letter seemed insulting. I felt like a child called back to the schoolyard. Of course, Balanchine was behind it—Balanchine and his resentment of my relationship with Stanley.

I sent back an indignant reply, outlining the terms under which I would return to the company; I asked for a new contract, and a raise. In fact, I felt that the NYCB had not been paying me adequately. After what seemed like a long silence, I received a conciliatory letter that met my terms. I think this latest Balanchine control measure was particularly difficult because of what I was going through at the time with Janet. All around me people wanted to fence me in and circumscribe my emotions and reactions.

The rebel in me was beginning to kick.

134

TEN

When I returned to New York, Allegra and I were immediately cast in a new ballet called *Bugaku*. It was based on Far Eastern dances, but was pure Balanchine. He could adapt the classical vocabulary to almost any style; classical steps allowed him to make whatever statement he wanted to make. In this case, he was incorporating the spirit of a culture that was still, in 1963, unfamiliar and exotic.

Like the work itself, the making of *Bugaku* was quiet, simple. Mr. B choreographed it quickly; it only took about a week and a half. Most of the effort was in moving people around, putting them into position. He worked like a master craftsman, tossing things together deftly and elegantly without fuss or the kind of overconsideration that leads to self-consciousness.

His aesthetic and method were identical. Maybe I admired this so much because I had to work so hard—not just to master the steps but to bring myself to the point where I could forget myself and give a great performance. Sweat was my ethic and aesthetic. By the time we worked together on *Bugaku*, I had learned that if I started to work on a piece by emulating what Balanchine did, absorbing his movements and trying to articulate them, I would be on my way. I had to start out by imitating his style and sense of the musicality of a piece. Then I could work from that.

135

EDWARD VILLELLA

Balanchine usually let dancers go along on their own as long as they respected the basic kernel and feeling of what he was doing, as long as they didn't distort the choreography beyond the boundaries he controlled. If he felt a dancer understood the style of a role, he'd let him build it and shape it. He worked like this now with me. By now, my performing instincts had become sharp and alert, and I could see during the creation of *Bugaku* that Balanchine was comfortable with what I was doing. He looked pleased. "Smaller, smaller. Japanese. Fifth position too big. Just small. Move the head just a little bit." That was the only criticism.

I thought a great deal about the weight of my body and how to carry it in this role. Most dancers, including me, always move upward, outward, and forward. We become weightless, buoyant, pulling the weight of the body up off our feet trying to put space between us and the stage. We never rest flat on our heels but always try to keep them off the floor. The balance of the weight goes over our toes, as with prizefighters. The effect is a lifting, countergravitational sensation. In *Bugaku,* however, the connection to the stage is stressed. I was not trying to levitate.

The use of the floor in this work is totally different from all other ballets. The men's opening entrance walk is rooted to the floor. It's more of a strut than a walk, almost like stomping. Becoming comfortable with this new sense of balance, and different dispersal of body weight, became very, very important. Posture, the carriage of the head, the way I held my neck and wore the headpiece, were crucial in revealing the primitive, innate elegance of the movement. Often, all I had to do was put on the headpiece to feel as if I were an ancient Japanese aristocrat.

The men's steps require just the slightest tilt of the body. We started in a wide second position and lunged forward in attitude, then lunged back. To get this rocking motion right, we had to find the bottom of the step and push off to the next one. This made a powerful effect—we looked forceful and aggressive.

I tried to incorporate the exotic atmosphere and the style of the Gagaku movements that Balanchine captured in his choreography. David Hays's scenery reflected it beautifully. I

136

relied on my memories of the performances I'd seen. Gagaku dancers weren't delicate, they had weight. The basic elements in the ballet that reflected Gagaku movement were the flexed foot with the heel dragged, and the leaning-into-the-plié and the pulling-of-the-arm across the body in opposition to the leg. I thought of samurai warriors. I didn't purposely try to imitate them, but used my weight and stance to present a sense of their masculinity.

The pas de deux in *Bugaku* depicted an intimate, ritualistic marriage ceremony that was highly stylized, erotic, and explicit. Dancing it with Allegra was like having an intimate encounter with a beautiful woman. She was pliant and vulnerable, and a bit aloof. But it wasn't really a sensuous experience. Sexy as the ballet is, sex was the last thing on my mind. Allegra and I were just working—hard. The partnering required was extremely complicated, but I was confident. I was feeling better about partnering.

My performance in *Donizetti Variations* had proven to me what a proficient partner I'd become. In the opening section of the *Donizetti* pas de deux, the ballerina does two supported pirouettes and then executes a flip-jump also supported by the man. The sequence of "double pirouette, flip-jump" is repeated three more times. At first when I danced it, each sequence would be different because I was overcompensating, using too much strength, impeding the smoothness of my partner's turns. But as time went by, I let go of the extra energy somehow. I learned to support the turns and the flip-jump, and put my partner down, by hardly touching her. I could even manage to readjust her skirt. The skirt would twist around the ballerina on the first turn, and if you didn't adjust it, it would wrap around her more and more tightly as she continued to pirouette. I easily took care of this now with a flick of my fingers.

Partnering, I had learned, is a physical conversation, a delicate discussion. I gave the woman freedom and support and allowed the audience to see her without being aware of my labors. The partnering in *Bugaku* was easier because Balanchine created it for me and I could work out problems with him as we went along. It involved my whole body, like the partnering in *Prodigal Son*. I didn't just stand stiff on my feet behind Allegra as she danced in front of me, didn't just put my hands on

137

EDWARD VILLELLA

her waist while she stood on one leg. This was a totally different encounter. I had to get under her, literally, get her over my back and shoulders, and between my legs, cradle her in my arms, and wrap her around my torso.

The lifts in *Bugaku* were difficult. Bringing Allegra down to the floor was even harder than lifting her off her feet, but the problem was my bad back and not the choreography. As with anything that Balanchine created, there was an inner logic to the movement. In this pas de deux there was a dynamic of counterbalance. If I could balance the ballerina against myself when her leg was straight up and she was facing me, using her weight but anchoring her with my body, it would all work.

The pas de deux in *Bugaku* was highly original and, I think, gripping and theatrical. On the whole, the ballet had a startling effect on the audience. They were moved by the beauty of the steps and the erotic tension between the characters. I experienced the pas de deux as an affirmation of my masculinity, both in character as a Japanese warrior and as a ballet dancer. Standing majestically at the conclusion of the pas de deux, allowing the courtiers to dress the ballerina and myself in ceremonial garb, was a way of showing a kind of supremacy, and I felt that I had earned at least a measure of pride.

Bugaku was rewarding and I was feeling confident about myself because of my success in Europe and Russia. Now I very much wanted to dance *Tchaikovsky Pas de Deux* in New York. I was disappointed when I went over the schedule and saw that *Tchaikovsky* was always being done on programs on which I was going to dance either *Prodigal Son* or *Bugaku*. I went to Balanchine to talk about it.

"Mr. B," I said casually, "I notice that there are always performances of *Prodigal* on the schedule with *Tchaikovsky Pas de Deux,* but there's also one on the program with *Bugaku*. I wonder if Arthur could dance the *Bugaku* and—"

The words froze in the air. Just the tilt of Balanchine's head made everything clear to me. This man, I realized, does not want me to dance *Tchaikovsky Pas de Deux*. I flushed, first with embarrassment, and then with anger. I could tell he never wanted me to dance *Tchaikovsky Pas de Deux* again.

"Oh, no," he said, *"Bugaku* is a wonderful ballet."

138 "Yes, Mr. B, but—"

"Wonderful ballet."

"I know."

"Wonderful. You shouldn't step away to dance *Tchaikovsky*."

"Yes. But I think it's very important for me to dance *Tchaikovsky Pas de Deux* because it's very classical, and those are the areas that I still need to explore." The words started tumbling out of my mouth. "This ballet is a major challenge for me, I know *Bugaku* is a wonderful ballet, but for me to be a complete dancer I need to do classical things."

"Oh, you mean, dear, you want to dance *Giselle* and *Sleeping Beauty?*" His voice dripped with sarcasm. He was close to being openly scornful.

"No, Mr. B," I answered, hurt now. "I hope once before I retire I get a chance to do *Tchaikovsky Pas de Deux* again."

I was fuming. He seemed to have reverted to his original idea of me, the Bouncing Ball of Energy to typecast in demi-caractère roles. Was I too ethnic? Less graceful than the others? No way. Was it that deep down he still believed I didn't fit the classic mold? Or was it even deeper: resentment of the acclaim I received abroad when I danced the role? I was going to fight it. Hard. I told him on the spot that if he wasn't pleased with the way that I had danced *Tchaikovsky Pas de Deux* and no longer wanted me to do it, I would take a year off from the company and learn how to dance classically and then come back and show him. And I turned around and walked away.

The next afternoon I received a telephone call from Betty Cage.

"Eddie, Mr. Balanchine asked me to talk to you," she said. "He doesn't want you to think that he doesn't want you to dance certain ballets. Of course he wants you to dance what you want. And he's going to schedule a special performance of *Tchaikovsky Pas de Deux* on the Sunday matinee for you."

"Tell him, thank you, thank you very much. I really, really appreciate it."

And I meant it. But a part of me was skeptical. I imagined Balanchine thinking, give him enough rope and he'll hang himself. I danced that matinee performance with Violette, and I felt it went very well. I thought I had "nailed" it. Balanchine never said a word to me, we never discussed the performance. But he

139

scheduled four more *Tchaikovsky Pas de Deuxs* that season, and I danced every one. The role soon became part of my repertory, and one particular week I danced the ballet five times with five partners: Violette, Allegra, Melissa, Patty McBride, and Anna Aragno. Anna was with the Metropolitan Opera Ballet, and I often made guest appearances with her outside the City Ballet. She was small, compatible with me, and a good technician. She was able to dance all the roles in my concert repertory.

Now I requested *Scotch Symphony*. At first Balanchine scratched his head and looked off into space pensively.

"What's the matter, Mr. B?"

"Well, you know, dear, we have to find a partner." He looked me in the eye. "Somebody *short*. Not Allegra, you know, dear. Not Allegra because she's just a little bit too tall. Too tall for this ballet. So we'll get you somebody short."

It was as if I were being stripped naked. He was saying: Okay, you have the nerve to ask me if you can do *Scotch*. You can do it, but here are one or two raps to the head so you'll know who's boss here. This was his way of getting back at me, by making cutting remarks. I just let them all go by. I could put up with a lot to get what I wanted.

Balanchine certainly wasn't used to anyone like me, and I continued to defy him when the stakes were high. From time to time I wondered if he wasn't just a bit envious of me. After all, he had never had a successful dancing career. Onstage I was a success, and offstage I was young and attractive to women. Now that seems much too simple to explain Balanchine's attitude. Nothing about him could be analyzed too easily.

Balanchine had mentioned in the fall of 1963 that he had an idea for a ballet he was going to choreograph for Violette and me and a small corps de ballet. It would be set to the *Grand Tarantelle* by the composer Louis Moreau Gottschalk. He envisioned nearly nonstop, bravura dancing for the leads in the ballet and thought a small corps would give Violette and myself some support, brief periods of rest in the wings. Violette's foot had been acting up because of an old injury, however, and as soon as Balanchine began working with us, it was clear that she wasn't up to the choreography.

140   Balanchine abandoned the project: when he picked it up

again a few months later, he decided to do it strictly as a pas de deux for me and Patty McBride. He retained his original conception of nonstop dancing, and if anything, the activity in the ballet was now more compressed and intense than before, but Balanchine never called in any other dancers. From the first step he choreographed for *Tarantella,* he just ran ahead of us—he was choreographing it speedily, and we had to run to catch up. Everything he wanted was vigorous and fast, musically challenging, and totally exhausting.

I was especially happy to be dancing with Patty. She was the easiest dancer I have ever worked with. Rarely did anything faze her—she could dance anything, in any style. And I liked her a lot. She was feminine in a way that appealed to me, and we laughed all the time. People were getting used to seeing us dance together. Balanchine often cast her opposite me in the repertory, and we had made several television appearances together. Dancing with McBride, I could practically anticipate by just a look what her next move was going to be. Steady partnerships were frowned upon in the City Ballet, but this was the start of a long, satisfying artistic association.

At the time when most of the ballerinas in the company had been reluctant to dance with me, Patty had acted as if she were totally unaware of the situation. I had been intimidated by many of these ballerinas, but she and I had joined the company at the same time and we were on the same level. When I was insecure and concerned about my inadequacies, Patty and I had worked out any problem in rehearsal. She never made an issue of it, and I'm grateful to her. She helped me and shortened the time it took for me to learn how to partner.

It was a lucky thing we had a good rapport. The rapid-fire pace at which Balanchine was choreographing *Tarantella* didn't leave any time for discussion. As usual, he created the ballet in bits and pieces, and in different sections. At one session, he might work on what Patty and I did together. Another time he'd work with each of us separately. No one except the master himself really knew exactly what the ballet was going to look like. A day or so before the premiere, we were standing on the stage at the City Center, Balanchine was chatting with Maria Tallchief and Erik Bruhn, who had once again joined the company for a season. There was a pianist nearby, and Balanchine

141

suddenly said to Patty and me, as if it were something he had just thought of, "Okay, dear, now let's see. We take a look."

This was our first time performing *Tarantella* from start to finish. We began dancing the ballet full out. We took off. Halfway through, I felt as if I were going to collapse. I didn't think I was going to be able to make it to the end. I had never been so desperately exhausted in all of my career. The driving beat of *Tarantella* didn't allow for inhaling calmly or deeply. The short intervals of music and the repeated landings and takeoffs had the effect of knocking the breath out of me. And a lot of the choreography required bending the body, which restricts the diaphragm and interferes with respiration. During the ballet my sinus passages were constricted.

Long-distance runners and marathon competitors often talk about reaching a certain resistance as they run that makes them feel as if they can't go any farther. It's called the runner's wall, and they must exert themselves even harder in order to produce the energy to break through it. Once they do, they feel as if the extra adrenaline has recharged them and brought them up to an even higher level of speed and performance. This phenomenon happened to me dancing *Tarantella*. I reached a runner's high, and it took me at least two hours to wind down after a performance. I miss that feeling today.

At the end of that first run-through performance, which lasted less than ten minutes, I went crashing into the wings. The tambourine I was carrying went flying into space, and I fell to the floor as if I'd been kicked in the solar plexus. I was flat on my back. But I was happy. I saw *Tarantella* as a great gift to me from Balanchine. It was a ballet that suited my temperament and my background. It set up a series of challenges for me, and full of quick jumps to be performed powerfully, it showed what I could do technically. I hurtled through space and came down at odd angles only to move on again. The ballet was pure dance—absolute dance. *Tarantella* is really about the body smiling—it's just one huge grin. Today everyone worries about doing the tricks in the ballet "correctly," and they approach it too seriously, as if it were a grand pas de deux. Their bodies get tense, and that's not compatible with the wonderful, rhythmic abandon of the piece. The body has to sing the music.

142

The steps for the man require elevation, but because the tempo is so fast and vigorous, I had to get up quickly, sustain the jump to give the impression of the step, and come down so that the landing became the preparation. It requires the intricate ability to phrase and to know how much of the plié you have to use. The man has to shorten the amount of time he spends in the plié as a landing, then take the time he has saved and apply that extra split-second to the push-off for the next propulsion. This is Balanchine dancing.

The dancers in *Tarantella* are also specific characters. Who is this guy? He's a simple, open, sunny kind of person who knows his way around a dance floor. The hero of an Italian village, he's joyful, and he's got his girl, and they're performing the national dance together for an assembled group and for their own pleasure. The style is in his blood, along with his passion for the girl. The relationship between the two dancers in *Tarantella* is all-important—their knowing sidelong glances are part of the ballet. It's as if they're speaking to each other, playing with the music, dancing the steps off the beat. Patty and I had a great deal of fun just looking into each other's eyes throughout. It takes confidence to really look into the eyes of a partner and communicate intimately while being in command enough to direct and control the physicality, the steps and all the other aspects of the choreography. There's a reference in the ballet to the Bournonville style, most specifically to the divertissements in *Napoli,* and this, too, should be incorporated in the performance.

Excitement was in the air the night of the first performance. Here was a Balanchine premiere, and company members who had heard about the extraordinary pas de deux had filled the wings by the time the performance got under way. I was very much aware that it was going to be difficult to get through, and I wanted to pace myself. But as soon as the curtain went up and the music began, I dove right in. Patty and I blasted straight through the steps. I'd go barreling off into the wings for each exit and double over onto the floor on my hands and knees, keeping my rib cage as free as possible to absorb more easily as much oxygen as I could. As the ballet progressed, I knew I was getting fatigued. My legs were beginning to feel heavy, my chest was pounding, veins were bulging in my neck, and my eyes felt as if they were exploding. My shirt was plastered to my chest. There's a moment in the coda when I bend over and tap the tambourine at Patty's feet. I was afraid I'd never be able to straighten up. But somewhere I reached back deep into a reserve of energy and made it through. At the end of the ballet Patty does chaîné turns, I grab her and kiss her. She goes into the wings, and I dive after her. And there I was as the curtain came down, ass over backward in the wings, people scattering everywhere. The next thing I was aware of was tumultuous applause. I was helped back onto my feet, and Patty and I were pushed back onto the stage. It was clear that *Tarantella* was a triumph, and even in my daze I could tell that Balanchine was pleased.

The company physician saw the problems I had breathing during performances of the ballet, and he tried to help me out. He told me that he wanted to set up a stool in the wings with an oxygen tank and a mask so that I might get some relief during a performance. I thought, why not? Great. A few days later, before a performance of *Tarantella,* I noticed the stool and the oxygen equipment, and the doctor, in the wings. I nodded to him. The performance got under way, and halfway through I came barreling offstage. The doctor grabbed me, sat me down on the stool, applied the mask to my face, and told me to breathe. I was gasping and tried to breathe deeply, but nothing was happening, and I felt as if I were suffocating.

"Deeper, deeper!" the doctor cried.

I tried. I was gasping and choking. I felt as I were turning blue, and I didn't want to pass out. Finally, I tore off the mask and rushed back out onstage. After the performance, we both realized that he had neglected to attach the hose from the oxygen tank to the mask. The mask had actually been cutting off my supply of air. We never tried that again.

Balanchine's masterpiece *Apollo* is one of the most coveted roles in the canon for a male dancer, but it wasn't a role I ever thought I'd be considered for, for several reasons: I wasn't tall, I'd had difficulty partnering, and, even by my own standards, still wasn't a finished dancer. My assumption in those days was that Jacques D'Amboise was Apollo and I was the Prodigal. But one afternoon, Balanchine approached me and said, "I'd like you to learn Apollo."

144

I stared at him in disbelief.

He said, "Now go learn it and we'll see."

My reaction was pure terror. I believe that Apollo is the ultimate challenge for a dancer, and I was terrified that I wouldn't be able to get my body in condition so that I could even attempt it. *Prodigal Son* is a different kind of challenge. It's explosive, dynamic, overt. I had the natural ability to be explosive; it wasn't a problem. What was hard was to do a gesture with a minimum of effort and energy. If too little is used, the movement looks limp. If it's overdone, you can look like an acrobat.

Apollo requires a much more subtle physicality than *Prodigal Son*. It combines bravura technique and attack with pure neoclassical lyricism. It's a series of sophisticated dances as opposed to bursts of bravura. A flexible strength is necessary to execute these steps and gestures and link them smoothly. Linkage, a smooth, pure line, is important in ballet. As Balanchine said in a program note to accompany the ballet, *Apollo*'s about eliminating. It's about elongation. It's clear, open. When a body is hunched and bunched, crunched up, there's limited flexibility. The role can't be done working from tension.

Of course I wanted to try it. I learned the part by watching D'Amboise during performance, and by being taught the steps and the counts by Conrad Ludlow, and shortly after, arranged to show Balanchine what I could do. We met in the fifth-floor rehearsal studio in the City Center, just the two of us and a pianist, and I performed the variation.

When I was done, Balanchine looked at me matter-of-factly and said, "No, that's not Apollo."

"What do you mean?" I said. "Those are the steps and the counts."

"Those are the steps and the counts, but it's not Apollo because you don't understand that dancers are poets of gesture."

"I'm sorry," I said.

But Balanchine wasn't dismayed. He simply said, "Dear, I will show you Apollo."

What followed was extraordinary. Sixty years old at the time, Balanchine stood in the studio in a double-breasted gray suit and a green-and-white-stripe cowboy shirt, a string tie, and loafers, and he danced this big variation from *Apollo* for

145

me. It was astonishing. I could see the music emanating from his body.

Balanchine not only "spoke" to me physically; he let me in on his thoughts about the role. He had never done that before, ever.

He began by showing me that the very first gesture of Apollo's variation with the arms up and hands horizontal is really fifth position high. In this one simple gesture of Apollo's, Balanchine just took fifth position and extended it! Neoclassicism is exemplified by that *single* move!

The next gesture in the variation, when Apollo flattens his hands and forearms on his head, is fifth position reduced and flattened. This was followed by a big sweeping gesture, port de bras.

Balanchine turned to me and said, "You know, it's like an eagle on a perch, on a rock, looking down from a crag."

After that, a little Spanish motif arrives in the music. Apollo looks down and raises up his arms and turns around. Balanchine smiled. "It's like the matador watching the bull go by."

He went on, talking about the second-position step in which Apollo kicks left and right with his working leg.

"Soccer step," he said. "Man kicking ball, you know. Soccer." It was even written in the score in 1928, I later discovered. "Soccer step." There's a similar step in the first scene of *Prodigal*. It was Mr. B's soccer period.

Balanchine continued, talking now about the movements from the chariot-race finale, incredible masculine images that evoke Olympic athletes and Greek and Roman heroes and gods.

I decided to ask him a question.

"This gesture, the open and closing of the hands when one of Apollo's arms is behind his back and the other is above his head—where did it come from?" I wanted to know. "It's amazing, really amazing."

He explained, "You know, I was in Soviet Union, awful place, no color, no paint. Lousy. No light. I went first time to London to Piccadilly Circus. Saw for first time flashing lights." In Apollo's vibrant hand gestures Balanchine had recreated his youthful impression of those glittering neon signs. To me they seemed like twinkling stars.

146

So there I was in the middle of eagles and matadors, soccer and London—and Balanchine himself showing me the basics of his style, his connection to the classical tradition of Petipa, and his departure from it. It was overwhelming. And it gave me a point of reference. I got insight into the role itself and into neoclassicism and just what Balanchine was doing to develop it. At that very moment I realized just how much was still left for me to attain, not only in the company and the repertory, but for that man.

I asked him more, about the moment when Apollo rejects one of the Muses after her variation. Apollo jumps up and turns his head away from Calliope after she dances. I said, "What does that mean?"

Balanchine shrugged. He said slyly, "Nothing."

Balanchine was a rascal, and that was the word he used to describe Apollo to me; in fact, he had originally conceived the character as a wild, half-human youth who achieves nobility through art. (A Russian critic at the time of the ballet's premiere complained to Balanchine that Apollo would never have indulged in the actions he had devised for him in the ballet. The critic obviously had in mind the famous statue called Apollo Belvedere, which depicts the god as a more delicate and refined deity. "Young man," he said to Balanchine, "where did you ever see Apollo walking on his knees?" Balanchine replied, "I would ask you, where did you ever see Apollo?")

I'm convinced Balanchine never described Apollo as a rascal to Peter Martins. He was telling me to be myself in the role: a young, lower-middle-class youth from the streets of Queens who played sandlot baseball, brawled, and boxed. But I, too, was learning and growing, developing a new identity, striving for nobility, and a new American elegance, through art. I didn't have to emulate Lew Christensen or anyone else in the role, didn't have to project the lifeless image of a noble god. I could present Apollo as an ideal human being I intimately understood.

I believe there were facets within me that Balanchine saw and respected, an earthiness that appealed to him. The year before, when I had appeared as Prince Siegfried in his one-act version of *Swan Lake,* he had said to me, "Don't pose, don't imitate nineteenth-century European, Soviet style." Certainly I deplored the stilted, old-fashioned manner in which such danc- 147 ers as Rudolf Nureyev portrayed that role, stomping around and posing grandly. Nureyev was a big star and created a lot of excitement, but he seemed to exaggerate elements of academic classicism. On the other hand, Erik Bruhn's approach, which exemplified the true nineteenth-century style and was noble and refined, represented an attempt to get to the heart of the role. I understood finally that Balanchine wanted me to approach *Swan Lake,* and *Apollo,* on my own terms.

At the end of the session in which Balanchine worked on *Apollo* with me, I took away everything I had learned, and shortly after I showed the variation to him again.

"You have a wonderful potential in the role," he said.

I did everything I could to get myself in shape for *Apollo.* In addition to class, I went to a chiropractor and a masseur, I took steam and whirlpool baths, and did stretching and every other kind of exercise. To make it even more daunting, my marriage was becoming increasingly tempestuous. I just wanted to get on with my life. Janet was frustrated. She'd reached that point when she was either going to move up in the ranks and become a soloist or remain a member of the corps de ballet. And she hadn't been promoted.

Janet was a talented dancer. She had been forced into it by her mother but had a facility for it. In a way, it was probably too easy for her. She had ambition but not drive. I don't think she really liked dancing. She would have been happy to have become a ballerina overnight, danced important roles for a couple of years, and then got out of it. As it was, she had made the decision to stay with NYCB through the end of 1965 because she wanted to go on the upcoming European company tour, which was scheduled for that year. She planned to quit at the conclusion of the trip.

Janet and I had moved into a nice apartment on West Fifty-fifth Street near the City Center after we were married, but shortly after I decided to purchase a brownstone on the upper West Side. The company was about to make the move to the New York State Theater at Lincoln Center. I was a principal and Janet was still dancing. We could afford it and were thrilled with the prospect of buying a house. Balanchine hated the idea.

He said, "No. Don't buy. Awful, awful idea. You know, you think you're going to own house, but house will *own* you."

148

I thought about what he said. He might have meant, who was I to have something that grand. He might have been saying, you're an artist. Why bother with material things. The theater is your true home. Actually, I think he thought it would be a lot of bother. He liked to keep things uncomplicated.

Nothing was uncomplicated where Janet and I were concerned. It often seemed that we belonged to different circles altogether. Some nights I had to decide whether or not to go with Janet and her cohorts for a late-night dinner. If I had a matinee the following day, I'd bow out. Janet's crowd belonged to the party-going New York social scene. Janet was a serious opening-nighter, and she believed real New Yorkers were those socialites whose names appeared in *Women's Wear Daily* and who attended galas and media events. I was much more interested in people like Stanley Williams and my agent, Janet Roberts, who were serious about their work.

I had first met Janet Roberts at a cocktail party when she was training to become a theatrical agent. She eventually got a job with MCA and, later, with the William Morris Agency, where she represented me in my commercial ventures in television and on the stage. We were business associates, but we were always friends first.

When we were able to, we used to lunch two or three times a week. I have a great respect for Janet's knowledge and taste in the arts and literature and feel that our lunches were part of my education. As one of my mentors, she is second only to Stanley Williams in my life.

My wife, Janet, knew how much time I spent with Janet Roberts, but she wasn't jealous. It was the time I spent with Stanley, time fanatically devoted to dancing, that seemed to set her off.

In my early NYCB days I also became friendly with William Weslow, a soloist in the company. Billy Weslow was a loose cannon in the City Ballet. He could always make everyone laugh with his outrageous comments, but sometimes he went too far. A lot of people, including me, got angry. But underneath, Billy's a hell of a guy. He had a very troubled early life. His mother committed suicide when he was five or six. His father was a stern disciplinarian, a cripple who suffered from alcoholism related to his physical condition. Taking his   149 background into consideration made it easier to understand him, and we got closer. I needed friends.

My private life with Janet was wearing me out. Many nights I'd go to bed at four A.M., exhausted after a shouting match with her. I'd sleep fitfully for a few hours and then get up to head for the theater. The *Apollo* period was a time of tremendous personal duress. My goal was to eliminate thoughts about my personal conflicts and concentrate only on work. But I felt as if I existed in a state of mental and physical shock.

150

ELEVEN

By the time New York City Ballet took up residence at the New York State Theater in April 1964, I had a reputation as one of the country's leading male dancers. Despite this, I felt that my success was a front, a façade concealing a lack of true accomplishment. I was aware of my natural abilities, and I loved being acclaimed. Everybody does. But a part of me felt undeserving. Insecurity like this can't be acknowledged publicly. Professional decorum must be maintained. But I felt I still had to work diligently on my technique.

The real acclaim for me was when Balanchine praised me after the premiere of *A Midsummer Night's Dream,* or when Stanley came backstage after a performance and paid me a compliment. By 1965, Stanley was in New York for good. He'd given up his job with the Royal Danish Ballet in anticipation of working full-time for the New York City Ballet. But the offer of a permanent job from Balanchine was not immediately forthcoming.

Between them, Balanchine and Stanley kept me honest. I was never allowed to become self-satisfied. My insecurities kept me striving.

Performing on network television was also adding to my reputation. "Dancing Is a Man's Game" was followed by appearances on the "Bell Telephone Hour," "Kraft Music Hall,"

151

and the "Firestone Theater" in the early 1960s. Violette and I danced a version of *The Nutcracker* pas de deux on "Bell Telephone," and Patricia Wilde and Patty McBride performed the *Minkus Pas de Trois* with me on another segment of the show. Patty and I also appeared together on "Bell Telephone" dancing the Bluebird pas de deux from *The Sleeping Beauty*. Later on, we made regular appearances on the "Ed Sullivan Show."

Most of my colleagues in the City Ballet and other companies looked down on me for these appearances. They thought it was demeaning to perform on television, an attitude toward the medium they shared at that time with most Broadway and Hollywood actors. Most artists thought television was beneath them. But I didn't know any better. I didn't know the rules. I made my own rules, and I absolutely didn't care what anybody thought. Of course, I didn't do just anything that came along. When I appeared on TV, I was careful to protect both myself and the art of classical ballet. Over the years I received several requests to appear on television talk shows where I was invited to chat and dance and then, of course, teach the host how to do a few steps that might be good for a few laughs. I didn't think that this would have been in the best interest of the art form and repeatedly turned down these offers. (In the 1970s, however, I appeared on television with Carol Burnett, who satirized some ballet conventions with me on her show. Carol Burnett is an artist with a true comic sense, and she investigated and really understood the art of ballet. Her spoofing was good-natured, intelligent, and a lot of fun. I felt ballet could stand the ribbing.)

Television was hard work. In those days programs were broadcast live, and we danced on cement floors. "Bell Telephone" went on the air at ten in the evening, and we had to be in the studio by eight-thirty A.M., warming up to dance the ballet or excerpt from beginning to end a number of different times. First was a blocking rehearsal for the cameras. We'd walk through the piece so that cameras could be placed and angles chosen. Then we'd do a dance-through based on that blocking. Invariably we'd discover that some of these camera positions weren't working, so we'd make corrections and then have another dance-through. Then a full run-through with all the other acts and individuals who were appearing on the show

152

would follow, and after that we'd have a break. Sometimes the order of the show would then be changed because a director would decide some acts worked better in juxtaposition to one number than another. This would then be followed by a dress and orchestra rehearsal, a full technical run-through. By the time the show went on the air and we were actually performing, we'd been dancing on cement for many hours, our muscles and bones sustaining countless shocks. It took a toll on me; in all, I broke a total of eight toes (not counting the one I broke in Australia) because of landing on cement.

Television directors had never worked with this kind of material before and were inventing a technique before my eyes. As I discovered on "Dancing Is a Man's Game," performing for the television camera was completely unlike dancing within the confines of a proscenium arch. The front of the "house" changed with each new camera angle. It was like another thought process. From time to time, directors asked me which angle I thought they should shoot a particular passage from, and we'd work it out beforehand. But if I thought they were shooting me from a terrible angle, I'd stop and tell them why I thought another one might work better.

We had to teach cameramen to make their cameras dance with us. Cameramen were normally used to shooting singers, comedians, instrumentalists, and actors, and they used mostly stationary shots and cuts from angle to angle as a way of creating action. Zooming in and out, dollying, panning, or the use of the crane were rare. But all these techniques came into play with dance, and most of these camera operators were inexperienced with such maneuvers. No one had any doubt that it was considerably more difficult to shoot a dynamically moving body as opposed to a singer who only moves a few steps.

Soon enough I began to develop various techniques for performing on TV. For instance, I always insisted on a monitor so I could see what each angle looked like, not only during blocking and technical rehearsals, but during the actual broadcast, whether it was live or on tape. Whereas cameramen thought they were blocking out my action and shooting me, I was actually blocking them. I'd have to keep adjusting because a cameraman would miss a shot. He'd either be in too tight or too wide, too far to the right or to the left; sometimes the

153

EDWARD VILLELLA

camera wouldn't be where it had to be at all. They'd wind up shooting the sets or the lights, would be unable to frame me when I did a big jump, and would repeatedly cut off hands and feet. So I used the monitor as a check on the cameraman's inexperience, and to keep an eye on what the director was doing.

One technique dancers devised for TV was to put rubber on the tips of toe shoes that would extend halfway down the length of the sole. The rubber was used only on the front half of the sole on men's shoes, and it created the friction that was necessary for moving on cement stages that were often covered with waxed linoleum tiles. The rubber strips added weight, and an extra dimension of solidity to the ballet slippers and shoes, but this didn't totally do away with the insecurity we felt dancing on slick surfaces.

I also learned how to deal with an orchestra performing on television. At the New York City Ballet, Balanchine worked closely with the music director, Robert Irving, who died in 1991 at age seventy-eight. In twenty years of dancing, I never encountered another conductor with Irving's brilliant musicianship. In television studios, I found I often had to direct the orchestra myself. I had to set the tempi and the timing of entrances, and I became used to consulting a conductor and various instrumentalists.

And I also became knowledgeable about production, lighting, and costuming. I was no longer dealing with costumes designed by Barbara Karinska. I was working with a shop that made costumes for Broadway. I had to guide them in terms of the construction of a ballet costume, the line of its body, how to fit it so that it moved with me. I also had to coordinate the colors. The taste of Broadway designers tended to a broader style; they'd embellish rather than use only what was needed, theatricalize a garment rather than tone down its look. Most of the costumes I wore on television were not right for ballet.

Balanchine didn't have high regard for television or for the experience of the people who worked in it. He thought it was facile. Things were put on and taken off quickly. Quality, development of an idea, the investigation of how a dance could be adapted to the medium, were not given a high priority. There was no time to do anything right. He believed that ballet

154

simply would not be presented properly. But I thought it was important just to present it, to promote a ballet as a popular art form by exposing it on this medium that reached so many people. My point of view was that to improve the presentation of ballet on television you had to engage it. If you ignored it, it would evolve in its own way. I had the sense of being a pioneer, getting out information and knowledge to technicians and directors as well as to the general public.

Conditions have changed greatly. The payoff came when "Dance in America" was created, and funds were used to correct the problems that had previously existed. Today performers dance on wooden floors, and camera angles, lighting, and design have vastly improved. Programs are conceived expressly for television. Balanchine himself choreographed a pas de deux, *Diana and Actaeon,* for Patty and me to perform on the "Ed Sullivan Show," which I recently restaged for my own company in Miami. In the 1970s, Balanchine also staged and taped many of his ballets for presentation on "Dance in America." But in the 1960s he never said anything to me about my various television appearances.

From the start it took some adjusting for us in the New York City Ballet to get used to the New York State Theater, our new Lincoln Center home, which we shared with the New York City Opera. Problems had sprung up even before the company moved in. The theater had been designed and constructed according to the recommendations of consultants from both the City Opera and the City Ballet. In 1962, before we left for Russia, Mr. B had asked me and a few other dancers to test the new floor for the stage to be sure it would work to our satisfaction. It was a webbing of wood in five layers that Balanchine and our stage manager, Ronald Bates, had designed themselves, and it was installed over cement. The cement stage was necessary because the theater had to adhere to building codes. Originally, the Lincoln Center officials were under the impression that dancing on the cement floor as it was would be satisfactory for the company. Balanchine had to set them straight. I remember my first impression of the house that day —the cavernous auditorium that had no seats in it at the time and was dark and empty.

155

Then another problem arose, this one with the orchestra pit. In order to raise extra revenue for the theater, someone had come up with the idea of staging various musicals by Richard Rodgers every summer. It was decided that this summer season could be made even more profitable by reducing the space allotted for the orchestra pit, and adding two more rows of seats on the orchestra level. An orchestra for musicals needs only twenty-two musicians in the pit. Construction moved ahead before Balanchine and Lincoln were informed of it. They were furious when they learned about the plan.

Balanchine shrugged. He told the company, "Well, you know, it's okay, the City Center is a wonderful theater, a good, good theater, excellent. Audience loves us there. It's comfortable. That's where we'll stay. City Center."

He informed Lincoln Center of his intention. His message came through loud and clear. The next day the newly installed rows were removed, and the orchestra pit was returned to its original dimensions, suitable now for a symphony orchestra playing music for ballet and opera companies. So we went to Lincoln Center after all.

The New York State Theater was far more luxurious, commodious, and elegant than the City Center. At City Center we were four to a dressing room that had no amenities but a single sink. At the State Theater the dressing rooms were made to be shared by two principals and were fitted out with double sinks, a shower, a john, and a locker. It was like moving out of an army barracks into a luxury hotel.

The rehearsal studios were large and had sprung floors, and the stage was enormous. It had depth and width, and the height of the proscenium arch accentuated the feeling of great space. As soon as I stepped out onto that stage, I felt taller, more elongated, as if I could fly. And when I danced, I didn't have to hold back as I did, say, when I was dancing *Donizetti Variations* at the City Center. Balanchine opened up many of the ballets the company performed at the State Theater during staging rehearsals in which the pieces were adapted to the new dimensions of the stage. And there was room in the wings for comfortable exits, without calculating when we'd have to stop short, and for grand entrances. It was hard to enter forcefully at the City Center, flying in when only three feet in the wings

156

was available as a runway. I felt that I could stand on the State Theater stage and communicate with every seat in the house even though there were five levels. It felt intimate because it was so beautifully designed by the architect Philip Johnson.

One drawback was that there were no windows in the theater. I'd enter the stage door in the morning, and that was the last I saw of daylight until the following morning.

Shortly after the company moved to the State Theater, Antony Tudor was invited to stage a revival of his ballet *Dim Lustre* for us. Tudor, a distinguished British choreographer, began his career with Dame Marie Rambert in London in the 1930s. In 1940 he came to the U.S. to work with the newly formed American Ballet Theatre. A 1951 NYCB production of Tudor's *Lilac Garden* had been a great success, but by 1964 it had been out of the repertory for over ten years. Rather than revive that work, Balanchine and Lincoln thought it would be desirable to mount a Tudor ballet we had never danced, and it was rumored that Balanchine personally selected *Dim Lustre,* a period piece, choreographed to Richard Strauss's *Burleske for Piano and Orchestra.* It is set in a ballroom. Patty and I were cast as the leads.

Tudor's ballets depict the innermost feelings and emotions of their characters; they're known for their psychological insight and dramatic intensity. Hugh Laing, who danced in the premiere, defined the piece this way: "Two people find they have been caught up with memories, not with each other, and they part." I was familiar with a number of Tudor's ballets and was excited about the challenge of working with such a distinguished choreographer whose style differed so much from Balanchine's. Balanchine was a technical genius. Tudor's talents lay in the dramatic and theatrical, and this was going to be a chance for me to develop in this area. I anticipated that rehearsing with Tudor would be like working with a great director, like working with Jerry Robbins.

Everyone in the company was excited about *Dim Lustre,* and everything possible was done to make Tudor feel welcome. He was given whatever he wanted: unlimited rehearsal time, access to the biggest studio, and the dancers of his choice. Because the ballet was a revival—and one that, I subsequently

157

learned, he had originally choreographed in two weeks—I imagined it would take no time at all to get it on its feet. After that, I thought, we'd be able to delve into the complexities of interpretation. That didn't turn out to be the case.

Rehearsals crept along. Tudor proceeded more slowly than any choreographer I had ever worked with. What amazed me was that he had difficulty remembering the ballet. Then once he recalled a step or a passage to his satisfaction, he would tinker with it and change it slightly rather than set it as it was. The changes were minor, nearly imperceptible—arm movements shifted from right to left and back to right again. It was the same with feet. Counts, too, would go from six to eight for no particular reason. The choreography was vague to begin with, open to various interpretations, and the ballet lacked fluidity and a coherent line of action. Steps were awkward and physically uncomfortable to perform. We rehearsed long hours every day, six days a week, and little progress was made. As the days drifted by, Tudor started losing the attention of the dancers—he certainly lost mine. I felt ready to work, but little actual work was going on, and a lot of time was being wasted. The process was becoming painful for me.

Eventually Nora Kaye and Hugh Laing were brought in to assist. Tudor wanted them to serve as aids to memory for him. Nora Kaye was Tudor's foremost interpreter, and *Dim Lustre* had been choreographed on her and Laing at Ballet Theatre. They were used to Tudor's way of working and were confident they could help, but by the time they arrived it was really too late. I was surprised that Tudor had been so unprepared to remount the ballet and thought that Kaye and Laing should have been brought in at the start. In fact, Tudor should have been working with them before rehearsals began, going over the score and trying to refresh his memory and summon up steps.

Tudor was a tall, balding, dignified English gentleman. At the time, he was in his midfifties. His speech was clipped, and he seemed remote, if not cold. What struck me most about him, however, was that unlike Balanchine, who dressed casually, he wore street shoes and a shirt and tie to work. I sensed a cultural disparity between him and the world of the New York City Ballet and was reminded of several English coaches and

158

teachers I'd worked with, former ballerinas who wore sensible heels, tweed skirts, tailored blouses, and sweaters or shawls to rehearsal.

Tudor's working methods disturbed me. Traditionally dancers defer to ballet masters and don't argue. Tudor took advantage of this convention and bullied the dancers. He treated all of us like children, or worse, idiots, and I saw a pattern emerge. He'd condescend and sneer and single out the more retiring and insecure cast members, ridicule their idiosyncrasies or deficiencies, and criticize them harshly in front of everyone. I believe his nasty and arrogant attitude was a cover for his insecurities. Even so, I loathed his manner. I was sure that he'd be too wary to try these tactics with me, but one day he called me over in a tone of voice I'd learn to recognize.

"Oh, Vil–lel–la?" he said, drawing out the syllables. I looked up. "That's Italian, isn't it?"

"Yes, it is," I snapped. "And I dance the tarantella. What's the matter with that?"

Put off by the edge in my voice, he shrugged and backed away. For the time being, an incident was avoided.

On the day of *Dim Lustre*'s first performance, I still didn't really understand who my character was and what he was feeling. Tudor hadn't been able to offer any help and was still changing the positions of arms and legs to no effect. The ballet was greeted mildly by the audience and the critics at the premiere. It was hardly a success, but as with most new productions, performances were scheduled the following season, and I was still interested in dancing in it. Despite my reservations about the way Tudor worked and treated people, he was still a formidable character, a great talent whose ballets had something to offer me.

At the start of the next season, I approached John Taras, an NYCB ballet master, and asked him to conduct preliminary rehearsals of *Dim Lustre* before Tudor came in to work on it. I hoped that if the ballet was on its feet when the regularly scheduled rehearsals began, Tudor would be more inclined to work on the finer points of the choreography. Taras agreed, and by the time Tudor arrived the ballet had been set up. But as soon as the sessions started, I saw that nothing had changed. He was still involved in making minor changes, positions of arms and

159

legs. Time was being wasted again. I got nothing from those rehearsals, and my mind was somewhere else most of the time.

On the day before the ballet's first performance of the season, Tudor gathered the cast in a group on the stage. I removed myself and sat on the floor at the edge of the stage near the wings. Once everyone was settled, Tudor began. In no time at all what he was up to became clear. He was tearing the New York City Ballet apart, being highly critical of Balanchine and Lincoln. Then he picked on individual dancers and cut them to pieces as well, commenting sarcastically on their looks, their abilities, their intelligence, and the way they worked. One by one, he went down the line. Then he got to me.

"And Villella. Where's Villella?"

"I'm here."

Everyone turned around. The crowd parted on the stage, and Tudor stepped out and walked over to where I was sitting.

"Well," he said, "I had been told that you were going to 'mark' in rehearsals, but I was assured that you would give a performance. Well, I want to tell you that you *marked* your performance!"

I slammed my fist on the floor with a loud crack and jumped up onto my feet. He was accusing me of just going through the motions.

"How *dare* you speak to me like that! How *dare* you say I 'marked' my performance! Don't you *ever* say anything to me like that again!" Tudor looked stunned, and I didn't give him a chance to respond. "My biggest problem is that I *overdance*. I need to learn to hold back. I *never* mark anything onstage. *Ever*."

I lowered my voice and tried to stay calm. "All of us have been waiting for you to give us something to work with, to help us understand the meaning of your ballet," I said. "You've given us nothing and just wasted our time. This is a farce!"

Tudor stood there with his mouth agape, and I glared at him. Everyone was staring at us, and no one said a word. Finally he whispered, "I guess that's all."

I was in a fury, and I stormed up the stairs into Betty Cage's office. Practically shouting, it was all I could do to explain to her what had happened.

"How dare he criticize the company when he's a guest

here! And how dare he speak to the dancers like that! I'm a principal, and I won't put up with it. I'm taking myself out of the ballet, and I will never speak to him again unless he publicly apologizes."

I meant what I said. Frank Ohman, an NYCB soloist, replaced me in *Dim Lustre,* and he did a fine job. I never danced the part again. Tudor never apologized, but I felt I had the unspoken respect of the company because I had the nerve to say what had been on everyone's mind. Years later, Nora Kaye and I discussed the incident. She told me that Tudor had often reduced her to tears during the many years of their association. This was how he worked. Nora was a great dramatic artist, Tudor's foremost interpreter, and yet he treated her in this shabby manner. Having grown up in the New York City Ballet and having worked with George Balanchine, Tudor's behavior was incomprehensible to me.

Balanchine's attitude was nothing like Tudor's. He had his perversities. He tended to control and manipulate his dancers, and God knows I had my difficulties with him, but at least he seemed to have respect for us, for our professionalism. He never consciously created unpleasant working conditions. In all my experience, I'd never seen Balanchine *publicly* humiliate someone. He usually treated us as if we were members of a big family. He set the tone in the company, and I had come to expect the same from all choreographers and ballet masters who had authority over us.

Balanchine's first major project at the New York State Theater was a new two-act ballet called *Harlequinade.* It was my first commedia dell'arte ballet, and I was to dance the lead. The commedia style originated in the rustic farces that were staged in southern Italy in the sixteenth century. Actors improvised routines that consisted of a basic set of characters: elderly parent/guardian types, a pair of lovers, servants and zanies. Audiences loved them. The French commedia characters, Harlequin, Columbine, Pierrot, and Pierrette were based on Italian counterparts. The popular English pantomime character Punch actually comes from the Italian Pulcinella.

Once I had seen an Italian company perform commedia, and I had looked at sketches of these characters in various art   161 journals. Commedia dell'arte impressed me as an Italian version of slapstick comedy and Harlequin as a kind of Groucho Marx character. I was familiar with the story of Harlequin and Columbine, so I had some idea of what the ballet would be like.

Dancers were always thrilled when Balanchine created a new role for them, and I was excited. *Harlequinade* was going to be a big production, a story ballet in two acts. But I was worried about the style. I told myself that Balanchine knew all about this tradition, and as in other ballets, he'd demonstrate what he wanted, and I'd pick it up from his movements.

Balanchine carefully watched what I was doing when we started working on the ballet, but he didn't demonstrate very much. We began with the pas de deux. There were going to be two of them, one in each act, and Balanchine seemed much more concerned with Patty McBride than with me. I thought this was natural enough. After all, Ballet Is Woman, I thought. Of course I wanted him to work with me on the role, to show what he thought it should look like. But it didn't worry me that he paid so much attention to Patty. I was confident. I had fine-tuned my skill and established my own style of phrasing. In a ballet such as *Tarantella,* I was able to phrase in a way that revealed the pulse of the music and demonstrated the relation of the music to the dance.

My boundaries as a dancer were expanding. I owed a lot, as well, to Stanley. He had shown me how to shape a performance into highs and lows, how to build to a climax. He had encouraged me to develop refinement and finish in my dancing. It wasn't that I was unaware of these elements before; it was just that I had been focused more on making an impression onstage.

Harlequinade presented me with a new set of problems. I was playing a particular character; during the dances I had to support the ballerina, as well as maintain the story line and stay within that character. The part called for a broad, farcical approach, and I was shy. I didn't want to make a fool of myself in front of Balanchine and the entire company. I needed a point of view, and because Balanchine seemed intent on letting me flounder about, I developed my own approach. The longer the rehearsals went on, the more uninhibited I became. I performed what I thought was the proper style of mime, even though I

162

felt as if I were distorting my body, shortening my line, exaggerating the character at the expense of the choreography. But Balanchine didn't say anything to me—he let things go.

One day, when he was just about finished choreographing the two pas de deux, Balanchine began to poke gentle fun at what I was doing. Because he hadn't said much to me, I had fallen into a trap and had been accentuating the slapsticky, hunched-over Marx Brothers gestures. I had it all wrong. Now Balanchine stopped me, and his simple words were among the most important he ever uttered to me, not only in relation to *Harlequinade* but in terms of my identity as a dancer.

"You know, dear," he said, "Harlequin is premier danseur."

Everything was illuminated for me all at once. I understood that I had taken the wrong tack. I needed to adopt another approach, not an overly adorned, nineteenth-century manner suitable to a prince; I had to be a charmer, a bit of a devil, but one who was also a classical dancer. Classical bearing denotes nobility and dignity even while the dancer has to perform comically. I knew at once how to create this character (as well as some of the others I was now dancing) because now it seemed that I was finally a classical dancer in Balanchine's eyes. I didn't want to embarrass myself in front of him by spilling over with emotion, but I was very grateful that he had finally acknowledged all my hard work.

He gave me more advice. As he often did, he told me not to imitate anybody. "Be your own Harlequin. You don't have to be a Russian Harlequin or a French Harlequin or an Italian Harlequin. Be your own Harlequin."

I also worked on the role with Stanley. He had danced in Copenhagen in the Tivoli Gardens where commedia ballets were often staged, and he helped me refine what Balanchine had shown me. Harlequin's platform in the ballet is not the full foot but the half-toe. In only a few days, I felt comfortable in this position, pulled up and classical—but with my elbows bent, my palms turned up, and a devilish glint in my eye.

Balanchine's version of *Harlequinade* was based on Petipa's *Les Millions d'Arlequin* to a score by Riccardo Drigo. Mr. B had danced in it as a boy in Russia. The story concerns the efforts of the heroine's father Cassandre to separate his daughter Col-

163

umbine from the penniless scamp Harlequin so he can marry her off to a rich old suitor. Harlequin and Columbine are aided in their efforts to thwart Cassandre by his servants Pierrot and Pierrette.

Harlequinade marked another step in my wonderful relationship with Patty McBride, a deepening of our rapport. There was a wonderful give-and-take between us, a harmony in our work together. Neither of us took anything more from the other than we we gave.

Patty was easy to partner. I just put my hand on her, and she instinctively moved with it. It was as if we spoke as one, as if we were singing a duet in perfect pitch with a single voice. We were really Columbine and Harlequin onstage, but we were also Patty and Eddie. And our offstage relations were just as amicable. Patty never complained, never put up any resistance. She never tried to dominate a rehearsal or a performance.

Harlequinade turned out to require a great deal of stamina; this two-act work was nearly a full evening's entertainment with two pas de deux, two variations, and two codas. Harlequin is onstage throughout, dancing, acting, miming—the works. It was very physical. When I wasn't dancing, I was being chased around the stage or was carrying Columbine in my arms, and all of this tightened the muscles in my calves. Luckily I had a few minutes in the action in which I hid behind Cassandre's house (where some of the stagehands sat playing poker between cues), and I could rest there on a stool and massage my calves.

Balanchine revised and expanded *Harlequinade* a few years after the premiere, adding children to the action, choreographing some music he had originally omitted, and inserting an intermission. He understood the style so well, the subtle differences between French commedia, which this ballet reflected, and the Italian style he would later demonstrate in *Pulcinella,* a ballet he choreographed for me with Jerry Robbins in 1972 as part of the NYCB Stravinsky Festival.

Harlequinade also had a distinctive visual style. The set had been created by Rouben Ter-Arutunian for a New York City Opera production of *La Cenerentola* and was recycled for the ballet. Rouben had designed many NYCB productions. The stage looked as if it had been transformed into a toy theater.

164

The costumes were opulent and colorful. My outfit was patches of wool jersey sewn together. It moved with my body like the skin of a snake. The colors—purple, red, yellow—were especially vivid. A problem occurred after the first few performances; the costume began to shrink because I perspired so much dancing the role. But a way was found to treat the fabric with chemicals. It was then dry-cleaned between performances and retained its proportions. But after a while it started shrinking again.

My performances in *Tarantella* and in *Harlequinade* were linked. In both ballets, the body is smiling. Not a straight up-and-down smile, but one that emanated from deep within and was then released. Everything went upward and outward. It was pure neoclassicism. This smile was the core of my performance. I danced every step and gesture in *Harlequinade* articulating joyousness from the top of my head to the ends of my fingers down to the tips of my toes.

Seven years later, when Balanchine choreographed *Pulcinella* for me, he pointed out the difference between the French and Italian commedia traditions. French commedia was more refined and the Italian more basic and rambunctious. Russian commedia was a mixture of the two. But at that time, when we were working on *Harlequinade* and he had gotten across to me that this Harlequin was a premier danseur, he no longer had to explain what he wanted me to do in the ballet. It was clear. It seemed now that my days of being typecast as a demi-caractère dancer were over.

Balanchine's failure to offer Stanley a permanent job with the New York City Ballet provoked a crisis in Stanley's life. He didn't know how long he could stay in New York without full-time work, and he contemplated taking a job with John Cranko and the Stuttgart Ballet, or working with the Royal Ballet in London. This in turn provoked a conflict in my life. Now that I had found what I had been looking for in a teacher and had developed a close artistic relationship with him, I didn't think I could exist without it. If Stanley was offered jobs with either one of those companies, would I be forced to make a choice between Balanchine and him? Would I defect to Europe? This became a major source of worry to me.

EDWARD VILLELLA

I had at the time become involved in the filming of a production of *The Nutcracker* in Munich by a German named Kurt Jacob. Melissa Hayden and Patty McBride were also appearing in it, and since Stanley was officially unemployed, I paid for him to come to Munich to work with us. He gave class every day for six weeks. In the evenings, we went in a group to dine and relax as a way to recover from the tedium of filming. I also needed an escape from the worry about Stanley's future, and my own. Then, shortly after production was concluded, Balanchine asked Stanley to teach on a permanent basis, not at the New York City Ballet, but at SAB. Stanley was disappointed at first; he took it as an affront. But after mulling it over, he realized that working with young dancers was exactly what he wanted. He still teaches there today, cochairman of the SAB faculty. What relief I felt now that I didn't have to make a choice between my two mentors.

TWELVE

Balanchine's infatuation with Allegra Kent was over by the time the company moved to Lincoln Center. Allegra was an artist of the first order, but she was only intermittently devoted to her career, and Balanchine had already been concentrating on other women in the company who excited him. During the company's last year at the City Center, he became interested in Suzanne Farrell, a young dancer who had been in the company a couple of years. Farrell was a young, tall, lithe, long-legged American beauty. Highly gifted, willing to work, she was eager to let Balanchine mold her. And mold her he did. Almost instantly, Balanchine's interest in Suzanne became an obsession that nearly wrecked their lives and had ramifications for every member of the company.

In 1963, Suzanne had replaced Diana Adams in the premiere of *Movements for Piano and Orchestra,* a new Balanchine work to an extremely difficult score by Stravinsky. Diana had first spotted Suzanne when she was scouting scholarship students for SAB in 1960 and brought her to Balanchine's attention. Not long after *Movements,* Balanchine created a pas de deux, *Meditation,* in which Suzanne appeared as a vision to an older figure who may have been an artist or a lover. She was eighteen and Balanchine was fifty-nine. He was still officially married to Tanaquil Le Clercq and lived with her in their apartment on Broadway not far from Lincoln Center. But by the time of *Meditation*'s premiere, there was little doubt that he was head over heels in love with Suzanne. She'd become the primary source of his inspiration, his most cherished muse. It didn't seem as if he were interested in anything else.

Balanchine in love was a delight to behold. He was a happy man, all aglow. He radiated a warmth and delicacy that was nice to be around. He was like a sixteen-year-old and the depth of his feeling revealed itself in the masterworks he was making. It was a phenomenon. When Balanchine was making a ballet for a dancer he felt ordinary affection for, rehearsals were often formal. There was no tension, but there was definitely the feeling of hard work being engaged in. When Balanchine was in love, however, when he was creating for his muse, the studio —the theater itself—seemed bathed in a glow. Everything was alive, and rehearsals were gatherings in which Balanchine demonstrated the wonder of choreographic possibility. At first, we all basked in the warmth of his infatuation with Suzanne. But as Mr. B's passion steadily intensified, it seemed that Suzanne, and Suzanne alone, had become his reason for being.

Balanchine could hardly contain his delight when he introduced her to Stravinsky for the first time. The composer had been visiting during a rehearsal of *Movements for Piano and Orchestra* and he watched Suzanne dance.

"George, who is this girl?" Stravinsky asked.

"Igor Fyodorovich," Balanchine replied. "This is Suzanne Farrell. Just been born."

In 1965, Mr. B choreographed a three-act ballet based on Cervantes's *Don Quixote* to a commissioned score by Nicolas Nabokov in which Suzanne danced the role of Dulcinea, the hero's ideal. At the premiere, Balanchine appeared in the role of the Don. The ballet generated a great deal of attention in the media, and hopes were high for it.

Nicolas Nabokov, a cousin of the distinguished author Vladimir Nabokov, was a Russian émigré and an old friend of Balanchine's. Mr. B was always comfortable collaborating with his Russian compatriots and often hired many of them to work at SAB. But in selecting a friend to compose the music for this ballet, he created unnecessary difficulties for himself. The consensus was that the score was weak and derivative, that

168

it sounded like movie music. The choreography reflected the score's inadequacies. Consequently *Don Quixote* was flawed and never achieved a major success.

That the ballet was something of a failure did little to ease the feelings of discontent among other dancers in the company. A lot of people resented Balanchine's singular devotion to Suzanne. Melissa and Violette felt rejected and grumbled about it; occasionally they became quite vocal. Milly felt the situation most acutely because she often danced with Jacques D'Amboise, and he had become Suzanne's regular partner. Milly was physically different from Suzanne, but Suzanne's loose limbs and long line represented Balanchine's ideal for ballerinas.

Milly and Violette weren't alone in feeling cast aside. Allegra also expressed her unhappiness. I suppose Patty McBride was upset about the situation, too, but her career was just getting under way, and Balanchine was casting her often and making important new roles for her.

I felt frustrated because I knew I'd rarely get the chance to dance with Suzanne; she was too tall, over six feet on pointe. I partnered her in *Prodigal Son* and in *Bugaku,* and one or two other pieces, but the differences in our height meant that we couldn't appear together in most roles. I thought I was going to be relegated to a secondary position in the company. Jacques was now Suzanne's partner in almost everything she danced. His role in the company became more enhanced, and relations between Jacques and me were not especially cordial. I worried that few new parts would come my way.

I had always prided myself on my serious approach to my career and my commitment to work, but I had to admit that I liked to party. In the 1960s, private clubs had become popular in London, and one of my acquaintances, Sybil Burton Christopher, thought it would be marvelous to open a club in New York where people could go to enjoy themselves. She called the place Arthur.

I invested in the business and was named president of the venture, not because I knew anything about running a discotheque, but because of my association with the New York City Ballet. It lent the club an aura of seriousness. Certain nights the need to go out overpowered the part of me that wanted to go

169

home after a performance, and I sometimes went to Arthur three or four times a week. I often felt guilty about being there, but, in spite of myself, had many good times at the club.

New York City Ballet was flourishing in the State Theater, and Balanchine continued to conceive big-scale ballets with large ensembles to fill the expanse of his new stage. *Brahms-Schoenberg Quartet* was choreographed to a piano quartet by Johannes Brahms that had been orchestrated by Arnold Schoenberg; the music was sometimes called Brahms's Fifth Symphony. The novelty was that it was created as four self-contained sections; each movement had its exclusive cast of principals and corps, none of whom appeared in any other part of the ballet. Melissa and André Prokovsky danced the opening Allegro movement. Patty and Kent Stowell the Intermezzo, and Suzanne and Jacques the finale, Rondo alla Zingarese. Allegra and I led the third movement, Andante, a highly romantic and atmospheric interlude that included some of Brahms's lushest music.

The lyrical section was a change of pace for me. I liked it because the choreography showed off my partnering ability. I saw myself as the protagonist of the piece, and as the only man in the movement, my presence had to balance the ballerina's femininity, the all-female corps, and the highly perfumed aura of nineteenth-century romanticism. The choreography for the corps was especially lovely and involved beautiful patterns and groupings. In a way, I was supporting all the women. I played a forceful figure, aristocratic and refined, a nineteenth-century gentleman whose courtly demeanor hid reserves of power and masculinity that were unleashed during the variation.

This one section of *Brahms-Schoenberg Quartet* was a rare instance in which Balanchine let the choreography for the man rather than for the ballerina dominate. After a brief pas de deux in which the male has to support the ballerina in arabesque while on his knee, the ballerina has a lovely variation to music accented by march rhythms. These rhythms are significant because they set up the man's variation. This is one of my favorite solos; it contains broad, open, confident choreography that covers the breadth of the stage.

Stepping out on half-pointe and waiting a few seconds for the crescendo that marks the start of the dance was like waiting for a countdown: I used to feel as if I were about to be launched into space, propelled into the ozone. The variation called not only for power and the ability to jump, but the ability to do both at high speed. There is a propulsive element to the variation. Each jump requires that the dancer *travel* through the air and then land in the preparation for the next step, which is also a huge jump. The landing links the jumps and provides the choreography with continuity. This continuity is essential to the Balanchine aesthetic—it's why he didn't want dancers to put their heels down onto the floor when they landed: it would slow them down and break the flow of the choreography. But people have made too much of this directive. They've taken him literally and dance on half-toe, and this isn't what he meant.

Balanchine wanted the dancer to place his knees over his toes when he came down to cushion the landing; he wanted the heels to reach the floor but go no farther so that the movement wasn't "down," *"down,"* but rather "down," *"up."* The idea was to pass through "down" in order to go "up." If a dancer doesn't pass through the down movement in this fashion, he will then come to a stop when he lands and lose both his momentum and the music. Soviet-trained dancers have great difficulty with this concept when they approach Balanchine, and I was to witness that when Mikhail Baryshnikov was cast in several of my roles after joining the company in 1979.

The male variation Balanchine choreographed for the Andante in *Brahms-Schoenberg* seems to drive the ballet forward. It injects an element of vigor and energy into the movement and makes the romantic choreography even more lovely and moving by contrast. Balanchine referred to one of my steps, the cabrioles, as the Nijinsky step. I jump in the air with both legs in front of me and do five beats: it's like an entrechat-cinq in front that opens up. It felt natural on me, and Balanchine said I did it better than Nijinsky. Boy, did that make me feel—well, how can I say it? It blew my mind! He praised my performance to Carl Van Vechten, the photographer and critic, telling him I was a better dancer than Nijinsky, and Van Vechten printed what he said. It was a lovely compliment, but I wasn't sure Balanchine had ever even seen Nijinsky dance, and I tried to put his comments in the proper perspective.

The comparison, in any case, was relative. He was really   171

EDWARD VILLELLA

referring to how ballet technique had improved over the years, and this was true. Technique gets better and better with time. In the eighteenth century, the ballerina Marie Camargo raised the length of her skirt from the floor to her ankle so that her audience could see her perform an entrechat-quatre, a royale, and it was a revelation. In our day Merrill Ashley performs entrechats-cinq or -six, brilliant and flashing beats, in a way that would have been unimaginable to that audience. When Roger Bannister ran the four-minute mile in 1954, it was a record, but in our day people run it as a matter of course. Man is a bigger, healthier, stronger animal today than he was at the beginning of the twentieth century when Nijinsky danced.

In my heyday as a dancer, the 1960s, the general level of technique would have made what Nijinsky did look somewhat quaint. I had achieved a certain technical standard and Balanchine was aware of it. But technique isn't an end in itself, and not everyone appreciates that. In ballet today, international competitions are used as a means by which to judge great dancing, but what's really being judged is great technique. Dancers aren't gymnasts or acrobats, however, and something's being lost. This is one of the reasons for the shallow period we're going through now, for what I see as the demise of classicism.

I think of technique mainly as a potential from which artistry can be developed. Artistry can't be taught, and it can't be judged at competitions. It's a combination of a dancer's natural talent, insight, and honesty, his investigation into the essence of a role and a search for the truth. On the other hand, competitions encourage dancers to develop technique at the expense of investigation, and consequently dancers today are mainly interested in pyrotechnics and virtuosity. They want to make their own statements about the art form, but they aren't able— and in many cases don't want—to take the time to steep themselves in its various facets. Most kids of eighteen, nineteen, and twenty don't have the means or experience with which to express themselves significantly. Yet a young dancer of this age will win a competition and be hired as a principal by a company when he's had no time to develop his craft. Young dancers are really shortchanged by these competitions, and because of them, their training is deficient in something vital. Picasso didn't just wake up one morning and begin his career as an abstract painter, the inventor of cubism. His early paintings

172

reflect his formal education and show he was a master of traditional styles. In the same manner, Stravinsky wrote full-bodied, melodic, romantic and classical works before he created his twelve-tone masterworks. Innovation can't occur if the groundwork hasn't been laid.

Patty McBride's beautiful rendition of the Intermezzo of *Brahms-Schoenberg Quartet* is an example of the artistry I am talking about. Her performance wasn't the result of mere virtuoso technique but of technique in the service of artistic vision. Working intensely within the Balanchinian aesthetic, she danced the choreography with the deepest commitment and expression and made a lasting comment on the role.

The *Quartet,* which is still in the repertory, is a sweeping and ambitious ballet, an audience favorite, and a particular favorite of mine. At the time of its premiere, some of the ballerinas resented the way in which curtain calls were arranged: the cast of each section took a bow at the conclusion of its movement. Only the ballerina who danced in the final movement was called with her partner in front of the curtain at the end of the ballet, as if to receive the applause for the entire performance. Since this ballerina was Farrell, it caused general unhappiness backstage. I felt differently . . . happy to bow after the Andante and get home early—the sooner to have a beer.

Every summer since I first became a professional, I had been appearing at the Jacob's Pillow Dance Festival in the Berkshire Mountains. Founded by Ted Shawn and his wife, Ruth St. Denis, the company was a great force in modern dance. They attracted every kind of dancer to their annual summer festival—classical, modern, jazz, and ethnic. Shawn always gave me the freedom to perform anything I liked. He often asked me to choreograph a ballet for him, and the idea appealed to me greatly. In Europe, I had come across *Suites for Ballet* composed by Dmitri Shostakovich, and one summer at the Pillow I decided to try my hand using this music. Shostakovich had written three different suites, and I excerpted eight selections, suitable for two pas de deux, several variations, an introduction, and a finale. Patty McBride was going to dance the lead opposite me, and the small troupe of NYCB dancers I worked with included my wife, Janet.

173

EDWARD VILLELLA

I began to devise some dances. Before this I had together a few pas de deux that I had danced on the "Bell Telephone Hour" and the "Kraft Music Hall," but this was my first formal effort at choreography. The music was straightforward and the orchestrations rather shallow. But I wasn't out to make a work of art, I was just looking for music to set some steps to, and the score suited my purpose. I particularly admired the sections I used for the pas de deux. I felt I was in command of the style. It was basically an *uninformed* attempt at choreography, and everything progressed quite rapidly. The dancers picked up what I wanted them to do, but not unexpectedly, working with Janet was a little awkward. I was her choreographer, but I was also her husband, and she had no compunction about resisting what I asked from her. She was constantly telling me that the movements were uncomfortable. Her variation never got completed. But somehow everything else worked out.

Shostakovich Ballet Suite was meant as a kind of curtain raiser, a novelty. We did it at the Pillow as well as on some of my concert tours, and it always proved a success. But it was a modest effort: it wasn't a ballet I wanted performed at the State Theater. The very idea of presenting a ballet in New York City intimidated me. As part of the New York City Ballet repertory, any ballet I choreographed would have to hold its own against the masterworks of Balanchine, or for that matter, Robbins, and I didn't want to be judged by such standards.

There was never any pressure on me to become an in-house choreographer. Though Lincoln periodically asked me if I was interested in creating a ballet for the company, I was always reluctant. I had no background or training in music and had never approached the art of choreography or examined it from a formal point of view. Yet the idea held some interest for me and certainly held a fascination for my ego. After the Shostakovich success I found myself thinking about other music that might be suitable.

I had read some Dante in college and was intrigued by Tchaikovsky's *Francesca da Rimini,* based on characters from *The Inferno.* I was attracted to a long middle section in the music that I believed would make an attractive pas de deux. But Lincoln shot down the idea.

174

"No, don't do it," he said. "It's already been done as a ballet. Try to find something else."

My friend William Roberts, Janet Roberts's husband, had written a one-act play about a contemporary Narcissus figure. Vague plans were in the works to present the play off-off-Broadway on a double bill with another short play. But when I told Bill I was looking around for an idea or a piece of music to choreograph, he suggested his play, which was called *Narkissos*. Lincoln thought this was a terrific idea, and it was decided that I should adapt it as a ballet for the company. Once we decided to go ahead, Lincoln became more and more excited about the project, and the force of his personality and his position shifted my focus away from Bill Roberts's original conception. Lincoln's enthusiasm was infectious, but he was impetuous. Often his ideas were off the wall, and sometimes it was difficult to stand up to him. We held several discussions about music, and after listening to some work by Robert Prince, who had written the music for Jerry Robbins's *New York Export: Opus Jazz,* Lincoln and I commissioned Prince to compose a score. We felt that his style was appropriate. I discussed my ideas with him at length, and we figured out what was going to be needed for various sections.

The completed score was to be submitted at the end of April of that year, and the plan was to have a major portion of the choreography set by mid-May. We'd hold the premiere in July in Saratoga. The New York City Ballet had now become the resident ballet company at the Performing Arts Center in Saratoga Springs, New York, where it performed for three weeks each summer in an attractive outdoor theater that was modeled after the auditorium at Tanglewood.

The first of April arrived, but Prince's score was not ready. Prince labored over every note he wrote, and it took him longer than he anticipated to create the music. Originally, I had hoped to be able to listen to the score and go over it to see if any adjustments had to be made. But now I had twenty dancers in a rehearsal studio ready to work and no music on hand. Prince did actually deliver some portions of the score in time for the first rehearsal, but it didn't leave me much time to study it in detail. I had to begin choreographing more or less on the spot as I had when I was making pas de deux for television, working

175

on sections in no particular order with bits and pieces of music as they were ready. If I had been a more experienced choreographer, I would have postponed the premiere of *Narkissos* and waited for the entire score before I began working.

Commissioning a score for a new ballet can present difficulties for even the most experienced and sophisticated choreographers. I had just seen Balanchine's difficulties with the music for *Don Quixote,* but of course he was a master and could overcome any problem a score presented him with; I couldn't. I didn't know it at the time, but working with a commissioned score put me at a great disadvantage. Essentially it meant that I could only hear what Prince had written on the piano. Orchestra rehearsals are costly and are scheduled only at the very end of the rehearsal period, so for nearly all of the time we were working I was never able to hear the orchestrated version of the music, never able to get a sense of the colors and the tonal texture of the piece.

As it was, after listening to the material, I felt that Prince's music was incompatible with my ideas. It sounded thin, not nearly dense enough to support the movements of the twenty dancers who made up the cast. Perhaps if I'd been more experienced, I could have provided Prince with the proper guidance to help his work. Still I didn't really feel as if I were in a position to reject his efforts outright. I was youthful and naive and I had my heart set on making a ballet, so I plunged ahead. Gordon Boelzner, who was the rehearsal pianist during those sessions and is now the New York City Ballet music director, is a first-rate musician, and he was able to make some sense of Prince's submissions. With the composer standing at the piano, Gordon reworked his music into a piano version so that I could choreograph some movements to it.

Working with what amounted to approximately a quarter of the score, which was all I had available, I created some dances that seemed to have an impact, and I was relatively pleased. At the time, New York City Ballet held open rehearsals for a group of company supporters called Friends of the City Center, and Lincoln asked me if I would present a section of my ballet at one of these rehearsals. It would be billed as a work-in-progress. He also asked me to talk a little bit about it. The open rehearsal went sensationally. A small section of the

176

ballet was performed, and I spoke to the audience about what I was trying to accomplish. Their reaction was enthusiastic. Lincoln was ecstatic. He rushed up onto the stage, picked me up off my feet, and gave me a bear hug in front of the assembled crowd. It seemed to everyone at that moment as if everything were going to work out, but deep down I knew that it wasn't. These brief excerpts represented the best of *Narkissos*. Nothing else was going to match it.

At the open rehearsal I was able to talk about my ideas for the rest of the ballet, but while I could articulate them quite succinctly, I knew that I wasn't really going to be able to achieve them choreographically. I had the ideas but no real understanding of the choreographic process. I was convinced that the music, my lack of experience, the chaos of the rehearsals, and other difficulties were going to sink the ballet. As I knew they would, things went downhill from that point.

In the first discussions I had had with Lincoln about the ballet, I made it clear that, as an untried choreographer, I wasn't interested in an elaborate production that would cost a lot of money. If it was a failure, I didn't want to be responsible for the company's having made a huge financial expenditure. Ideally, I would have liked to choreograph the ballet and then, if it worked, proceed with scenery and costumes. But from the start, Lincoln felt the work was going to need some production value, and he brought in a designer to create a set. I had no experience working with a designer, and even though we had detailed discussions, I didn't communicate my conception to this man adequately. He went off on a tangent that didn't have much to do with my original intentions, and it was soon clear that the scenery and costumes weren't going to work—they threatened to overwhelm the dancing. But I had become so concerned about the situation with the music, and what I had left to choreograph, that I didn't give the problems with the decor my proper attention.

The remainder of the music that Prince submitted was no more suitable for what I had in mind than the first sections he had handed in, and the problems with the score seemed unresolvable. In a collaboration there has to be an intimate understanding between the participants. As with the decor, I obviously never made clear what I needed. Gordon continued

177

to help me make sense of what we had, but I had to adjust all of my ideas to conform to it. I tended to set the weaker sections on myself, hoping that my dancing could compensate for the inadequacies in the music and the choreography. I knew that the ballet wasn't coming together. I was being pulled in various directions and felt unsure. Instead of imposing a vision on the piece, I was making a series of compromises that didn't lead to anything of significance. By the time we arrived in Saratoga, the ballet seemed like a patch job. The most successful sequence was a pas de deux I created for the character of Narkissos and his alter ego, a somewhat frightening figure. I included this alter ego in another dance, a pas de trois in which he danced with Narkissos and the Echo figure, who was danced by Patty McBride.

In Saratoga it became clear that *Narkissos* wasn't going to be a success. From the start, Balanchine had distanced himself from the ballet. I didn't feel that I could go to him now for assistance, and he certainly didn't offer any help or advice. But what really upset me was that Lincoln also seemed to have abandoned the project. Once he saw the difficulties I was having, he treated me as if I were a leper, saying unkind things about the ballet. This embarrassed me, and I felt chagrined and then very, very angry. It seemed more of an issue than the quality of the ballet. I told myself, "You didn't do a good ballet. So what? This was your first real try."

What hurt was that Lincoln was shunning me, and I was humiliated. This was typical of his behavior. Leo Lerman, the well-known *Vogue* magazine arts editor and a brilliant and flamboyant New York figure, had been a friend of Lincoln's. Once, when we were chatting, Lerman referred to himself as a "Lincoln Kirstein widow." When I asked him what he meant, he said, "For no reason at all Lincoln has stopped talking to me. Damned if I know why." Now in Saratoga I felt like a "Lincoln Kirstein widow," but I *knew* the reason for the silent treatment, and I was very unhappy. I was so hurt that I even contemplated leaving the company. After I calmed down, I told Ronnie Bates, NYCB's production stage manager, how offended I was by Lincoln's behavior.

I was living in a rooming house in Saratoga that didn't have a phone. One afternoon there was a knock on my bed-

178

room door. The landlady told me I had two visitors. I went downstairs to find Ronnie Bates and Lincoln standing in the entrance hall. Lincoln was a particular sight. In the city he always wore a black suit and a white shirt and a tie, but in Saratoga he dressed in the style of a British colonial colonel, khaki shirt and khaki Bermuda shorts. The sight took some getting used to. As soon as we walked back into the living room, he turned to me and shook my hand. He apologized profusely for his behavior and indeed seemed genuinely contrite. I accepted his apology, and I felt a little better about the situation.

I was an audience favorite in Saratoga, and *Narkissos* was received with some enthusiasm. Even so I wasn't happy with it, and if I had been more in control, I would never have premiered it in New York. The choreography needed to be redone, and so did the score. The music had to be entirely reorchestrated. This would have required a lot of time and money—and work—and it would have been an exercise in futility in any case. The music didn't fit the ballet, it never would. The project should have been postponed or canceled, but I was caught up in the momentum. The New York premiere had been advertised and scheduled, and people were looking forward to the ballet, even as a curiosity, so the performances went ahead. Clive Barnes wrote in the *New York Times,* "It remains a first ballet that makes you anxious to see his second rather than discuss this first." I had bitten off more than I could chew, and the experience was painful.

In retrospect I can see how the experience grew out of unspoken NYCB policy, reflecting Lincoln and Balanchine's philosophy. Just as principal dancers without the proper training were hired as soon as they retired to teach at SAB, so were some of the principal men in the company encouraged to choreograph whether or not they were ready or had talent. None of the women, however, were given a chance. In a way, the policy was hard to understand. With Balanchine and Robbins on hand, the company didn't need a farm team. Yet this policy might have been a way of forging a continuity in the company and the school, a way of doing things that harked back to an earlier system, the one Balanchine was familiar with in the Imperial Ballet. I don't think it did the art form a service,

179

EDWARD VILLELLA

however. But for his part, Balanchine was engaged in the heat of battle, choreographing the lion's share of ballets and running both a company and a school. He couldn't really be expected to supervise every aspect of these institutions, choreograph every single new ballet, and also instruct neophyte choreographers in the fine points of the art. So people were given chances, but they had to fend for themselves. For a time, Mr. B instituted choreographic workshops he took part in, but these were soon discontinued.

At that time my natural talent lay in dancing, not choreographing. I should probably never have been encouraged, but I accept full responsibility, and the lessons I learned from *Narkissos* are still vivid to me. I'm sensitive to the needs of young choreographers and the ways they can be developed. People need to understand how a ballet is structured and developed before they attempt to choreograph. They need an environment in which to try out things and experiment. A workshop situation. Even though the process of creating an original work taught me what making a ballet really entailed, it left me gunshy about choreographing for a very long time.

180

PRODIGAL SON

THIRTEEN

In the 1950s, like today, dancers were always scrambling for cash—even those employed by prestigious companies such as NYCB. Ballet seasons didn't last long, and most of us usually worked other jobs to survive. Dancers who were disinclined to dance on Broadway or in Hollywood still considered themselves lucky to find a gig in the commercial theater. It paid; most of the time they had to wait tables or become clerks. Stars weren't guaranteed full-time employment, either. Some dancers scraped by living together in tiny cold-water flats, pooling funds in order to pay the rent and groceries. Some months the rent couldn't be paid, some days people went hungry.

At the start of my career, I was content to scrape by. I accepted things as they were. All that motivated me was dancing and making up for lost time. Before long I rebelled at what seemed the terrible indignity of dancers having to lead the lives we did. The attitude of the business community, and of society at large, toward dancers and even toward the art form itself, seemed insulting. People would often say, "Oh, you're a dancer. But what do you do for a living?" It was as if we were children, marginal figures, second-class citizens, lucky to get paid anything at all. I never really understood it. It made me especially angry when some dance-world managers and administrators adopted this attitude, fostering an unspoken policy of financial discrimination against us.

181

I have never been able to understand why members of the New York City Ballet orchestra earn higher salaries than many of the dancers. It's the dancers that the public is coming to see. I don't begrudge these accomplished musicians or the backstage personnel their salaries. Many of them are my friends. But I believe dancers should have parity, and even today this isn't the case. What makes the situation harder to bear is that dancers' careers are so short-lived; they have fifteen years at best. Most musicians and technicians continue to work to a normal retirement age.

New York City Ballet dancers fare better than most. Ever since I first became a member, the company has always paid above the union minimum. Balanchine, Lincoln, and Betty Cage made sure everyone's salary was above scale. Even so, I never earned more than one hundred dollars a performance with the company. My yearly salary never exceeded $25,000, and most of it was spent on the essentials, and treatments that were necessary for repairing my body. All the extra money I made came from dancing outside the company and from business ventures.

I was a professional, an artist, a top-ranking dancer in America's premier dance company, and I had every intention of living like a member of the middle class. I wanted to see my hard work translated into some comforts. Maybe I felt driven to show my parents that dancing could be a viable—and lucrative—profession. So I didn't always pass when other opportunities to earn money did come my way, though I didn't always accept. I was being considered for a starring role on Broadway in a production of Peter Shaffer's play *The Royal Hunt of the Sun* at a more substantial salary than I was earning. The play had been a big hit in London, and I was tempted. But I thought long and hard about what I really wanted to do, and I turned down the offer because it would have meant spending too much time away from the ballet. If I had accepted, I might have gone on to films and done more dramatic work on the stage and TV. I'm not happy about having missed that opportunity. On the other hand, I might never have forgiven myself for taking the time away, and in the long run, I know I did the right thing.

182   I began to understand that it was crucial for those of us

who could to demand larger salaries from company managers, concert promoters, and arts executives. Dancers were paid a fifth of what show business performers were earning. I wanted to fight not only for my own rewards, but to raise the status of the profession and benefit American dancers in general. I was eager to do this. I felt that as an NYCB principal I was at the highest level artistically, and I was determined to be on the highest level financially. As the saying goes in television, I wanted to be "top of the show."

I heard this expression when I appeared on the "Ed Sullivan Show" in 1966. It referred to the money the biggest star on the program was going to be paid. Bob Hope, George Burns, Peggy Lee, Ella Fitzgerald, were all top of the show, and it was what I demanded for myself. I told television and concert promoters, "You have to pay me half again what you're offering because I'm sure it doesn't begin to match what others are earning." What I was demanding was also known as most favored nations clause: I was to be paid no lower than the sum the highest-paid person was receiving, but no higher.

I wanted to force the commercially minded television executives to acknowledge my contribution. In this way they'd learn to value what I did and understand that it had to be rewarded. It became something of a personal crusade because classical dancers were not normally considered commercial commodities, and *American* classical dancers had no status at all: we were looked on as minor artists, not even the equal of our European counterparts. This was driven home to me the first time I met Sol Hurok, the impresario who brought European and Russian ballet and opera to American audiences. Janet Roberts introduced us one evening at a private screening of a revival of Charlie Chaplin's film *Limelight*. Milly Hayden and André Eglesvksy made appearances in the film.

Janet spoke to Hurok, as she had already, about including me on one of his concert programs.

"Oh, Edward Villella," he said, turning to me. "Yes, I know who you are. You're good."

"So why don't you book him?" Janet asked.

"Oh, you know, I would. But I can't. He's American. It wouldn't go over."

In those days a dancer had to be Russian or at least European to be accepted as a major draw. Singers suffered, too. Many American opera singers had to go to Europe and make a success before they could be accepted at home. But as my career progressed, I think I helped make the idea of a man being a classical dancer acceptable for most Americans. By extension the art of ballet became more accessible to people all across the United States.

I got a little tired of being typecast in the public eye as the macho ballet dancer. It was simplistic to me, and insulting to other male ballet dancers. In interviews, journalists and radio and TV broadcasters always zeroed in on the fact that I had been a welterweight boxing champion in college and that I also won letters playing baseball, an obvious angle for their stories. It was as if they were saying, "Wow, who would believe it? Here's this guy who was a boxer and now he's a ballet dancer!" They didn't mention the fact that there were probably a helluva lot more dancers who could perform respectably on a sports field than there were athletes who could have managed a simple plié. I resented the underlying attitude toward ballet and male dancers that the interviewers' jock talk revealed. I had no apologies to make about my career or my life and neither did my fellow male dancers. I recognized my story as having some public relations value for ballet, but believe me, I know it was a pretty superficial game I was playing. It may have been useful; some men have written to me saying that they wouldn't have become dancers without me as an example for themselves and their parents. But I have to think that they must have been lacking in desire and commitment if they would have been intimidated by the silly prejudices of others. I wasn't.

Another problem I was aware of at this time was the lack of ballet interest outside New York. I wanted to perform all over this country, but except for an occasional tour, New York City Ballet rarely traveled. This drove me mad. I wanted to see the whole United States go ballet crazy. Restricting our performances to New York seemed an elitist concept and ultimately quite damaging.

So I tried to travel—dancing throughout the United States between NYCB seasons got me to places where people had never even heard of Balanchine or the New York City Ballet. Once again, I felt like a pioneer. I had the opportunity of pre-

184

senting a kind of dance most people hadn't seen before, and I became a spokesman for Balanchine's art. Bringing ballet to middle-sized towns and cities gave me the chance to show people that what we were doing was light-years away from anything stodgy or effete.

Traveling around, I learned a lot about the level of ballet instruction in the country at that time. It wasn't very high, and sad to say, the situation hasn't improved much over the years. One reason is that the art of dance is not taught in direct relation to music. The approach is still foursquare, old-fashioned, related to the nineteenth century, not to the innovations in rhythm and syncopation of twentieth-century music. Another deficiency I saw then (that still persists) is that too much emphasis is placed on basic positions. Certainly a dancer needs positions to form gestures, but positions themselves can be picked up from instruction manuals. Attention must be paid to how the positions are connected. Dancers wind up posing when the main idea is *movement* that is directly related to music. In ballet, music *is* movement. They become one.

For the most part, I traveled with Patty or Allegra and a small troupe of NYCB corps dancers. Occasionally Milly Hayden or Anna Aragno was my partner. Billy Weslow usually accompanied us, and that always livened things up. Anna used to travel with her tutu flattened out in a large, round carrying case. She never checked the case with her luggage but brought it on board the airplane. Air hostesses were always intrigued by the sight of this oddly shaped bag that resembled a big pancake. They usually said something like, "How odd. What's in it?" "It's her diaphragm," Billy would yell out.

Milly was also a lot of fun on these trips, and sometimes, when she was also along, Janet could get into the swing of things. She had a dry sense of humor, and God knows, we sometimes needed cheering up. Many of the places we danced in had never seen live ballet before, and some newspapers didn't have dance critics, so music writers generally filled in. Occasionally we were reviewed by sportswriters or someone from the news desk. These writers generally had no background about what they were watching and said things like, "The ballerina danced the entire evening mainly on her toes." And we performed under the most inauspicious conditions. Stages were small, and lighting was nonexistent. I often had to use some kind of extrasensory perception to just feel my way around, but I adapted well enough and began to feel that the worse the conditions were, the more I learned from them.

We always had to be prepared to deal with the unexpected. In Fort Wayne, Indiana, the shoulder strap on Milly's tutu broke during the *Don Quixote* pas de deux. She danced the remaining adagio movement with one hand holding up her bodice, and she was great. Then she rushed into the wings searching for a pin and reattached the strap in time for her solo variation.

On another trip, I arrived for a concert appearance with a symphony orchestra in Bangor, Maine, during a raging blizzard. I was ready to cancel the performance, but the concert promoters assured me that the audience would show up. The local citizens had grit, and the weather was not going to keep them away. They had pride in their symphony orchestra, and the seats would be filled, I was told. I admired their spirit. But the weather still presented problems: the snow and the moisture in the air were making the stage too slick to dance on. Most touring companies transport their floors with them, layers of vinyl called Marleys. These six-foot-wide rolls are laid side by side over the existing stage surface and secured in place with masking tape. Naturally enough, dancers feel more confident dancing on their own floor than on a cement stage or a wooden platform. But I hadn't the money or the means to carry such equipment around the country with me. It was written in my contract, however, that the management had to provide me with rock rosin in which to rub my shoes. The rosin creates friction that helps the shoe grip the stage.

No one in Bangor had remembered the rosin. It was a Sunday, the hardware stores were shut, and nothing could be found in the hall. I insisted that the organizer telephone the owner of the hardware store at home. The man didn't mind being disturbed. He didn't have rock rosin in stock, but he apparently thought linoleum might do the trick. He delivered sheets of kitchen linoleum to the hall during the snowstorm and put them in place, but they didn't work either—the surface was even slicker than the floor. I didn't give up. Dancers often sprinkle an abrasive such as Ajax or Comet onto the stage when

186

there is no rock rosin available. I never liked to use that because the cleanser was unpleasant to breathe in, but it gave me another idea.

We roused the owner of the local soda fountain from his home and asked him to open his shop. We then sent an assistant on a mission through the snow and told him to bring back a quart of Coca-Cola syrup. We mixed the syrup with water and sprinkled it over the linoleum on the stage. Because of the sugar, when the mixture dried, it made the surface sticky and provided the necessary friction to go out and dance.

But we were suddenly faced with another problem. The surface was sticky enough now to support us. But because the linoleum was so thin, it stuck to our feet. When I lifted my leg, I picked up the stage with me. Since there wasn't time enough to get masking tape to secure the floor, the solution was to wet mop the surface so that the syrup spread out more thinly. This worked to a point. I was able to dance, but the sound of my feet lifting up off the stage—like pieces of Velcro being pulled apart—could be heard throughout the concert hall. But at least I didn't slip.

On another occasion, Patty and I were dancing with the Pittsburgh Symphony, performing the balcony scene from *Romeo and Juliet* to Prokofiev's music. We rehearsed with the orchestra in the afternoon and adjusted the tempi with the conductor. Everything seemed fine. The version of the ballet that we were going to dance begins with Romeo entering alone. It ends with Juliet scampering offstage as Romeo picks up his cape, throws it over his shoulder, and also exits. As soon as the performance got under way, however, I could see we were in trouble. The tempo was very slow—it dragged. I wasn't sure what to do, but I thought Patty's arrival would pick it up. When she entered, we started moving, but no matter what we did we went ahead of the music. It was impossible to dance the steps as slowly as the music was being played. There was nothing we could do, so we just danced the pas de deux ahead of the music. By the time we had completed the choreography, three minutes of music remained to be played. For a moment we stared stupidly at each other onstage. Neither of us had the slightest idea what to do. Suddenly a gleam appeared in Patty's eye. She rose up on pointe and started to bourrée off.

187

EDWARD VILLELLA

"Oh, no, you don't," I thought. I ran across the stage to her, grabbed her wrist as gracefully as I could, and bowed, saying under my breath, "Patty, just stay with me. Here we go." I lifted her and put her down. Then I offered my hand and she took it. We improvised two minutes' worth of choreography until, at last, the music was over. Communication between us was so strong that what we came up with was effective. Improvising choreography with a partner who needs to be supported can be risky, but Patty and I were able to pull it off.

I learned how to cope with the unexpected on stages that were never intended for dancing, with conductors who had never led a ballet orchestra, and with audiences who were completely uninitiated in dance. I never knew what might happen. Once during a date with the New York Philharmonic I had to perform *Tchaikovsky Pas de Deux* on twelve feet of stage; the remaining space was taken up by the players in the orchestra. During the rehearsal I noticed that every time I approached the principal cellist, he cringed. He was afraid that I was going to crash into him. I wasn't concerned, however. My built-in radar could navigate a course around a stage within half an inch. This is not an exaggeration. I had developed this talent at Jacob's Pillow, where the stage was so small that I often had to dance on the lip of the apron, the very front edge of the stage; I had learned how to use every inch that was available to me in a limited situation, and I had been dancing with orchestras all over the country, in Chicago, Cleveland, Los Angeles, and Minneapolis.

Admittedly, navigating the male variation from *Tchaikovsky Pas de Deux* in twelve feet of space was a feat of engineering, but I felt that it was manageable. I did the series of coupé jetés, in which I make a wide circle of turns around the stage, by flinging myself off-balance. There were about two inches between me and some of the players, and I thought that was sufficient. But this cellist didn't agree. Every time he saw this whirling dervish coming at him in rehearsal, he went white. Finally, there was a break and he came up to me and said:

M-Mr. Villella, may I h-have a word with you?" He had an old-world accent and a pronounced stutter.

188   "Of course."

"C-c-could you please not come so c-close to me when you dance?" I was about to answer him, but before I could get out another word, he held up the cello before me and cried, "P-please! I beg you! This is priceless. It's a S-S-Stradivarius!"

On another occasion I was booked for a series of performances with the Philharmonic even though I was appearing nightly at the State Theater during a week-long NYCB run of *A Midsummer Night's Dream.* Oberon only appears at the end of the second act of *Midsummer,* so as soon as the curtain fell on Act I, I'd get out of my costume and race downstairs to the stage door. A Lincoln Center policeman would be waiting for me. I'd jump into his security cart, and he'd drive me across the plaza to Philharmonic Hall, where I'd change into another costume. As soon as that intermission was over, I'd dance my number with the orchestra. Then I'd fly out the stage door, my costume still on under my coat, jump into the cart, and be driven back to the State Theater. In the wings I'd reapply my makeup, get back into Oberon's costume and headpiece, and get ready for my entrance for the last scene of the ballet with seconds to spare.

This was not the least of my moonlighting. During one Christmas season, the midweek and weekend schedule of early-evening *Nutcracker* performances during the month of December allowed me to appear in yet another City Center revival of *Brigadoon.* Some days, after the matinee of the musical, a waiting taxi would speed me through midtown traffic to Lincoln Center where I'd dance a performance of *The Nutcracker.* I'd arrive in time for the second act, the only one in which the Cavalier appears, for the pas de deux. Then I'd return to City Center for the evening performance of *Brigadoon.* Once in a while I wondered if this whirlwind of activity was going to finish me off, but instead it energized me. I thrived on it.

The brownstone near Lincoln Center that Janet and I had moved into had brought about a temporary truce between us. Decorating it was the one area in which we were compatible. Working with Arthur Weinstein, an interior designer, we turned the top two floors into self-contained apartments we rented out and used the rest of the house for our living quarters. The five-story house cost $65,000 and we spent another

189

$130,000 renovating it, a lot of money at the time. When we bought it, it was just another unoccupied, run-down, upper West Side rooming house, indistinguishable from the others in the neighborhood. Inside, there were beat-up sinks and refrigerators everywhere, but the plaster moldings, the wood paneling, and the parquet floors were beautiful.

I found I had developed a fondness for collecting beautiful objects. Janet had terrific taste, and we decorated each room in a different style. It took a few years, but when we were finished, we were pleased. The ceiling in the library had mahogany panels and we lined the walls in red fabric. The upstairs drawing room was done in pastel colors, pale yellow, green-beige, and robin's-egg blue. The room had a marvelous delicacy to it—an eighteenth-century feeling.

Still, we lived informally. We ate out a lot, occasionally asking friends to dinner. Once we gave a dinner party for twenty people and hired a cook for the occasion. We also bought a German shepherd we named Ruby for the new ballet Balanchine was beginning to choreograph for Patty and me. Because Janet and I both felt something for the house, I thought we just might be happy there.

In 1967, in a great blaze of publicity, Balanchine choreographed *Jewels,* an evening-length work billed as the "first three-act plotless ballet." The company seemed to be attracting more and more attention in the media since the move to Lincoln Center, and more than ever, Balanchine was a grand celebrity.

In fact, *Jewels* was not a three-act ballet; it was a triptych, three separate ballets set to music by three different composers. The ballets were unified by the decor, which reflected the motif of precious gems, and each represented a different facet of neoclassicism. "Emeralds," the opener, was a dreamy, romantic work set to music by Fauré. Violette Verdy and Mimi Paul were the leads. "Diamonds," the finale, was for Suzanne and Jacques. Set to music of Tchaikovsky, it was an homage to the nineteenth-century Imperial style. "Rubies" came in the middle. Choreographed to music by Stravinsky, it was made for Patty and me, and was, in the words of Clive Barnes, "the most American part of the trilogy."

190   The music for "Rubies," Capriccio for Piano and Orches-

tra, is vintage Stravinsky—dry, witty, and syncopated. The score was a favorite of Balanchine's. He choreographed the ballet in the State Theater's large Main Hall, which was usually crowded when he worked there. One afternoon there must have been fifty people gathered inside: the cast, understudies, dancers who'd dropped in to see what was going on, pianists, Lincoln and Madame Lucia Davidova (a friend of Balanchine's and Stravinsky's), and various relatives, wives, and lovers of company members. Everyone was animated, and during a break the chatter grew louder and louder. Balanchine stood by himself in the center of the room staring intently at the score in his hand, deaf to all the noise. It was as if the only thing that existed for him was that score. All of a sudden he raised his head, put down the score, and loudly clapped his hands together to get everyone's attention.

"Okay," he said. "Let's work."

The room went dead quiet. The visitors retreated to the walls, and the dancers who were needed immediately took their places in the center of the studio.

I have always felt a personal connection to "Rubies." I felt Mr. B used everything he knew about me in the piece, and his intimacy with my technique gave me security. Balanchine's familiarity with my life, who I was, where I came from, how I lived, made me feel valued. The section after the pas de deux in which I dance with the boys chasing me was straight out of my street days in Queens. It was as if he had tapped into my memory. There was always a leader of the pack in those days, always a chain of kids behind him. The movement called for self-assured, cocky gestures. It was aggressive and reminded me of playing roller hockey. Home turf, all the way.

I marveled at Balanchine's ability to use what he had observed. He was fond of horses, adored the Lippizaners of Vienna. And the company had recently been spending time in Saratoga, during the racing season. The track atmosphere was one of the many elements he was integrating into "Rubies"; horse racing seemed to be behind all our prancing. The women were fillies and the men were jockeys. During the pas de deux I felt I was holding the reins, leading the ballerina through her paces, directing her movements around a track.

There were other influences on "Rubies": Degas, Astaire,

EDWARD VILLELLA

the world of jazz and show dancing, the brashness and confidence of Broadway nightclubs. Balanchine choreographed a tango into the pas de deux. He even worked cakewalk movements into some of the steps. This kind of layering is a part of every Balanchine ballet and gives them an extra dimension, a subtext that he rarely took time to point out or discuss. On those rare occasions, he'd open the door a little bit and let in some light. But just a glimpse.

Balanchine choreographed his ballets in no particular order. He liked to start with the finale. He once said, "If you start at the end, at least you know where you're going." It was always a revelation seeing the complete ballet emerge at a run-through, and we never knew exactly what to expect. When the company saw the three ballets that made up *Jewels* for the first time, everyone was surprised. I think Balanchine's intention had been to open with the quiet, lyrical "Emeralds," move on to the neoclassical, vaguely demi-caractère novelty "Rubies," and knock 'em dead with "Diamonds," a glorious evocation of the nineteenth-century classical style. But as it turned out, "Diamonds" was somewhat anticlimactic because Balanchine had outdone himself with "Rubies." I think Mr. B was caught off guard by its success. It seemed like a wonderful irony; he had obviously seen "Diamonds" as a tribute to Suzanne. He wanted to give her a great triumph. But "Rubies" was the tour de force.

In 1967, Balanchine took eighteen dancers to the Edinburgh Festival where the company had appeared in the early 1950s. On that first trip, the Scottish countryside had inspired him to create *Scotch Symphony*. I was included in the small group on this second trip along with Patty, Suzanne, and other principals. Jacques had been scheduled to go to dance with Suzanne in *Tchaikovsky Pas de Deux* and *Apollo,* but he dropped out because of an injury and she was left without a partner.

Balanchine sent John Taras to Europe to see if he could find a replacement, and in Copenhagen Vera Volkova recommended Peter Martins. Peter had danced *Apollo* with the Royal Danish Ballet, and after auditioning for John he traveled to Edinburgh to dance with Suzanne in what would turn out to be a rather historic occasion: his first appearance with the com-

192

pany. I remember the first time we met. I was chatting with Stanley in our hotel in Edinburgh. In walked this tall, handsome Dane. His reserve made him seem slightly arrogant, but I could tell he was really a little unsure of himself. We shook hands. Stanley had been Peter's teacher in Denmark, and like so many of Stanley's students, Peter was devoted to him.

Peter saved the day by dancing *Apollo* with Suzanne, but Balanchine also wanted to show her off in *Tchaikovsky*. Since no one else in the contingent knew the ballet, he decided that I should partner her. I thought I was going to look silly and said so.

"Oh, you know, don't worry, dear," he said. "We fix."

I wasn't convinced. I knew Suzanne was six inches taller than me on pointe, and that it would be impossible to partner her in classical pas de deux. But Balanchine was adamant.

"No, no, no," he said when he saw the look on my face. "We fix."

A rehearsal was called, and Suzanne and I tried to dance the pas de deux. We had a hard time and it was clear to everybody—even Balanchine—that it wasn't going to work. It looked ridiculous. I could dance *Bugaku* with her, and *Prodigal Son,* but not a classical pas de deux. We were physically mismatched. Balanchine was disappointed, but there was nothing to be done. I danced several ballets in Edinburgh, but *Tchaikovsky Pas de Deux* wasn't one of them. The ballet was dropped.

By taking me out of *Tchaikovsky Pas de Deux,* Mr. B saved me from looking like a fool before an audience. But our relationship was still complicated. Once before, when the company had been abroad in 1965, he had played a little joke. We'd been appearing at La Scala in Milan, and Balanchine said he wanted to take me shopping at Gucci's. He wore Gucci loafers and thought I ought to have a pair. He always ridiculed my deplorable taste in footwear.

"Have you heard of Gucci's?" he wanted to know.

"Yes, of course."

He didn't seem entirely convinced. "Well, I'm going to take you there and see what we can do."

One afternoon I met him at the theater after rehearsal and we went off together to the very expensive store. As soon as we entered, the salespeople flocked to his side. Some of the

193

employees had seen the company dance, and they paid him the greatest respect. They showed him around and called him "Maestro." He was having a great time, but he finally got down to business.

"I'd like you to meet Villella," he told the salespeople. "He is a first dancer with our company." He signaled them to come closer, bowing his head and lowering his voice. Pointing to me, he said, "Mafioso!"

Everyone stepped back automatically, looking me over from head to toe. I don't know if they were startled, embarrassed, or frightened, but they all bowed respectfully. No matter how intimidated they were, however, they still let me pay for the shoes. "Balanchine didn't often take dancers shopping, and I don't think he really meant to make fun of me. I think he just wanted to smooth out a few of my rough edges.

As soon as we returned from our successful trip to Edinburgh, preparations for the fall season got under way. I was worn out. My body felt depleted. I had a full repertory to dance, but in addition to that, I was being trailed by an NBC-TV camera crew shooting a profile on me to be broadcast as a special on the "Bell Telephone Hour." It was going to be called "Edward Villella: A Man Who Dances." They'd been working on the program for nearly a year and were about to conclude the project.

One afternoon as I was being filmed in my dressing room, Milly Hayden knocked on my door and came in. She wanted to know if I would dance with her on a matinee performance of *Raymonda Variations* because Jacques was injured. I was already scheduled to dance *Tarantella* in the afternoon and "Rubies" in the evening. Both were going to be filmed by the video crew, and I was exhausted at the thought of it. But I wanted to be a gentleman, and I agreed.

I got through *Tarantella,* cameras shooting me in the wings as well as onstage, and changed quickly into my costume for *Raymonda,* which the crew wasn't to shoot. There hadn't been time to negotiate the film rights. The performance began well enough. Milly and I danced the pas de deux, and I went off into the wings. I sautéed out to perform the first step of my variation, a jeté, and while I was in the air, a cramping pain shot

194

through my thumb and adhered it to my palm. I couldn't move it at all. Almost simultaneously, small muscles in my arms, and the powerful muscles in my thighs, calves, and back, all started to spasm at once. My entire body was rigid. I landed from my jump onto muscles that were completely spasmed, and only the weight of my body broke them so that I was able to do a small plié without shattering any bones. I tried to keep going, but I felt nearly paralyzed, and after four or five steps, I collapsed onstage.

My muscles had stopped functioning, and I crawled off on my hands and knees. Milly Hayden, trouper that she was, dashed onstage and improvised the rest of my variation. I was lying on my back in the wings, and someone threw a blanket over me to keep me warm. Faces I barely recognized hovered above me, and everyone was frantically trying to figure out what to do. A doctor appeared, but he seemed as confused as everyone else. All around me I heard the question, "Should we bring down the curtain? Should we bring down the curtain?"

I told the stage manager to notify the conductor to cut my second variation. Nobody could believe that I would be able to dance the coda and the finale. I had been on the floor for about ten minutes when I struggled onto my feet and took a few tentative steps, shaking out my legs. The spasms had abated somewhat, and I could work my muscles well enough to move. When I heard the music for my entrance in the coda, I simply sautéed out and tried to dance the choreography, big cabrioles and turns. I was not performing but was simply executing the steps to finish the ballet. Clive Barnes wrote in the *Times* the next day that an ashen-faced Villella somehow managed to get back onstage. He said that I looked shaken.

After the performance, I took a hot shower and was examined by the company physician. Billy Weslow massaged my aching muscles and someone sent out for food. I ate a sirloin steak and a baked potato. But the question was: Could I dance "Rubies" that evening? I felt a tremendous responsibility. "Rubies" was in its infancy and I wanted to appear in every performance. Moreover, my understudy, Paul Mejia, had never done the role, and he didn't feel he was ready. And since he danced in the corps of the ballet, he'd also have to be replaced. The television cameras were set up. This performance was the cul-

195

mination of the project the crew had been working on for a year, and I didn't want to let them down.

I would *try* to dance, but I warned everyone that I didn't know if my muscles would hold out. They might seize up and spasm at any moment, and if they did, I didn't know what would happen. It was decided that Mejia's understudy, John Clifford, would stand bare-chested in the wings in tights. If I gave out, the plan was to remove Paul's top and put it on John, then take my top off and put it on Paul, who would then complete my role in the ballet.

Backstage everyone was fraught with anxiety. We all held our breath as the ballet got under way. I felt stimulated, turned on by the excitement. I get off on risks and high stakes. I have a taste for drama. That night I took one of the biggest risks of my life. I could have sustained a serious injury that might have had dire consequences for my career, but luck was with me, and even though I kept crashing breathless into the wings, the performance passed without a hitch. I'd do it again in a minute —just for the rush.

196

FOURTEEN

In 1968, I turned thirty-two. I wondered if my *Raymonda* disaster was the result of my age. Thirty-two isn't old, but a dancer in his thirties has lost the first bloom of youth. I tried not to obsess. Usually I was able to work my body so that my muscles didn't misbehave so flagrantly. But because I had been dancing two or three times a program, eight times a week, for sixteen straight weeks during each NYCB season, physical problems were becoming more and more of a concern. I was never free from the pain of swollen joints and severe backaches. The tendons in my legs were often inflamed, and tendinitis is extremely painful. Complete rest would have helped, but I was never able to slow my pace.

I'd go home as quickly as possible on the nights when a major performance of, say, *Prodigal Son* was on the next day's schedule. I'd work hard to cool down. As my metabolism slowed, my muscles cramped and my body tightened up. Joints —especially my knees—became inflamed, and my back ached. Sitting was torture. Supper would be light. I'd still have a few beers during the meal but forgo the luxury of an after-dinner liqueur. If Billy Weslow was available, he'd give me a massage. Since his habit is to go to sleep as the sun comes up and get up at one in the afternoon, massaging me after performances suited his schedule. Before going to bed I'd rub liniments into my muscles, and I'd sleep with a heating pad strapped to the small

197

of my back. Some nights I wore a back brace to bed. I had three of them. The heaviest I wore in airplanes or when I drove a car. The lightest, the most flexible, I wore under a costume for performances. The midweight brace was for rehearsals and bed.

Most mornings I hurt so much I could barely get out of bed. I worried that I was becoming crippled. Once I got up, I'd lean against the bedroom wall, and supporting myself with my hands, push my way toward the bathroom. I'd soak for twenty minutes in a whirlpool bath before I'd be limber enough to get up and go about my business. There were days that the soreness and stiffness were so bad that I had to crawl on my hands and knees to the tub. After the bath I'd rub liniments into my legs and wrap them in lightweight cloth to retain the warmth as the day progressed. Most of my day was spent getting my body to move. Then I'd gulp down orange juice, yogurt, and coffee for breakfast before rushing off to SAB for Stanley's ten-thirty class.

Dressed in woolen tights, rubber dance pants, and a sweatshirt, I'd take my place at the barre. After working there, dancers are divided into two groups to perform exercises in the center. Normally I worked with both groups. For the most part, I'd do whatever Stanley asked for in the first group; in the second I'd concentrate on the areas I felt I needed to practice, making sure I practiced entrechats-six, cabrioles, and double tours. I needed to fine-tune my muscles, bring them along slowly, flush them thoroughly in class. But if a heavy evening was coming up, I'd cut way back on my classwork. Instead of repetition, the preparation for the jump or the landing became the object of the exercise.

At noon, I'd arrive at the theater for rehearsal. I approached these sessions as I did class, saving myself for the performance. I never rehearsed full out. If I had to practice a pas de deux in which there were lifts, I'd only do one or two, and I'd mark the steps in my variation. Often I'd show up for rehearsal in sweat pants and character shoes so everyone could see I was not prepared to *really* dance. People may have thought I was being arrogant, but I had no choice—I had to reserve my strength. Balanchine was often irritated with me. He didn't see me in class and I didn't rehearse the way he wanted—he was

198

forced to wait until the performance to see what I was going to do.

Between rehearsals I'd always schedule a trip to Dr. Richard Carnival, my chiropractor, and if there was time, have a massage. Being massaged was one of the high points of my day, and very important to my mental health. No one could find me or tell me what to do. The phone wasn't ringing, and I wasn't driving my body. At the theater Billy usually had to work on me in some out-of-the-way corner so that Balanchine didn't see us. Mr. B's attitude toward massage remained unchanged. I'd always doze off during these sessions, and if time permitted after Billy was finished, I'd go for a swim.

At four in the afternoon I'd eat my main meal of the day: steak, a salad, vegetables, and something to drink. I'd also bring a cup of Jell-O or yogurt into the theater with me and put it aside to eat just before the performance. The sugar in this food provided me with a burst of energy. If I was particularly tired and sore, I'd substitute honey for the yogurt. Honey is a predigested food, and it's in the bloodstream in a matter of minutes, and many nights a jar sat on a table in the wings. A belt of it would sometimes give me a boost during a performance.

On most evenings (but *always* when *Prodigal Son* was on the program), the ideal situation was to take another SAB class with Stanley, this one at five-thirty. I always needed to work twice a day. Walking through roles and marking choreography requires warmth and flexibility, and the morning class provided it. The evening class was more of a complete warm-up, after which I'd hurry to the theater. Of course, it wasn't always possible to attend the five-thirty class if it conflicted with rehearsals.

Warming up on my own ordinarily took an hour and a half, but cooling down took minutes. So, for most ballets I liked to warm up as close to curtain as possible. Then I'd go to my dressing room to slap on makeup, work on my hair, and spray-paint my ballet slippers. They had to be dyed to match my tights for most roles.

The company procedure was for dancers to give slippers to Roland Vasquez, one of the assistant stage managers, who'd take them to the spray room where he had a supply of paint in

199

EDWARD VILLELLA

over fifty colors. But I didn't bother with this. I hated breaking in new slippers and used to make one pair last the season. That meant they had to be sprayed for every performance, often twice a night. I had my own spray room under my dressing table and spray cans in five or six colors, depending on the roles I was dancing that week. Sometimes thirty layers of paint accumulated on one pair of shoes. I was constantly spraying, eternally grateful for the invention of paint that dried instantly. I tried to be considerate of my dressing room mates, however (first Conrad Ludlow and later Peter Martins), and did my best not to asphyxiate them.

Once I was done spraying, I'd get into my costume and go downstage. I'd check tempi with the conductor, do a few stretches, and try out a few steps. I was notorious for being late, however, and often a dresser was sent to knock on my door to hurry me along. After the dresser, the stage manager came upstairs to call me. When Ronnie Bates, the production stage manager, was at my door, I knew I was in trouble.

Warming up for *Prodigal Son* was special. The body makeup took a half hour to put on, and if I applied it before warming up, it rubbed off while I worked. Putting it on after warm-up meant that my muscles would cool, so I had to put it on before. (I once tried dancing the ballet without body makeup, but I felt unclean, and under the lights my skin had a sickly, washed-out glow.)

Before applying the makeup, I'd swallow a few muscle relaxants and then examine the chafed or worn-away skin on my knees and feet. Once the body makeup was on, I'd warm up in an empty studio. Then I'd get into my costume and go down to the stage, keeping warm in the wings by doing very gentle tendus in the minutes that remained until curtain. In most ballets I wore tights; in *Prodigal* I was bare-legged and barefoot in my slippers, and that took some getting used to.

No matter how hard I tried to stay warm in the wings, however, my muscles soon cooled down because of the scanty costume I was wearing. But if I put on tights to keep myself warm, the makeup rubbed off on them. The solution I came up with was leg warmers, woolen leggings that cover the dancer from the thigh to the ankle. And I'd also wrap a towel around my neck and shoulders and put a robe on over that,

200

tight enough to keep me warm but loose enough to let me work and not rub away too much makeup. By now the picket fence and the flat that depicted the tent, the basic scenery for *Prodigal Son,* were in position onstage. I'd finish this mini-warm-up and then step out and try out the steps of the variation from the first scene.

I sometimes felt that success of the opening movement—indeed the whole ballet—depended on this variation. It contained the jump that had become the signature pose of *Prodigal Son.* The variation is dramatically important to the narrative. I sauté high in the air with one leg out in front of me, the other tucked in under my torso, my arms up over my head in the air. It's a leap of defiance, the gesture of someone desperately seeking freedom. It should come as a shock, a surprise. But at most performances it seemed as if the audience was anticipating the jump; even those people who'd never seen the ballet had heard about the step or seen a photo, and they were waiting for it. It was always absolutely necessary to be certain that the jump was firmly established in my muscles and bones so that it was like a conditioned reflex. Once the jump occurred, the audience would relax, sit back, and enjoy the rest of the ballet. I would feel better, too.

The Prodigal exits in the first scene by jumping over the fence downstage right, turning, and running off into the wings. I always practiced this jump, too. Billy Weslow would hold his hand higher and higher for each jump, and I'd try to reach the level of his palm. Going over the fence could present a problem. If I was tired, my left leg sometimes went limp. This was my turning and landing leg. I had previously injured it and it worked slower than the right one. A couple of times it came up so late on the jump that it grazed the top of the picket fence.

If the dancer who was playing the Siren was unsure about sitting on my head or my neck, as she had to do during the pas de deux, we would try out the movement. I'd ask the conductor to go over the opening variation for me. The tempo attacks the dancer. I wanted to attack *it,* so I'd set it with the conductor and go through the whole variation.

It was also important for me to check the stage, especially the areas where I had to move on a diagonal or cross from one end to the other. Because there are such abrupt movements in

201

the ballet, I really had to have a very secure sense of the floor. During a performance the stage can become a slick. I didn't want to push off and have my foot slip and slide and twist in the opposite direction.

By now "Places, please" was being called, but a part of me would still resist. There was always one more thing I wanted to do. Making a last-minute check of the stage, I'd remove the towel and the robe, but not my leg warmers. I'd wear them until about twenty seconds to curtain. By then I'd be in my place onstage behind the tent waiting to make my entrance. I tried to get the time I stood behind the tent down to a matter of seconds. But in those remaining seconds I'd eliminate everything but the performance from my mind. I'd be scheming, calculating, preparing all day for this moment, and now I'd narrow my concentration into a simple straight line focused solely on my physicality. I'd feel very alone and revel in the solitude. It wasn't a meditative or spiritual moment; it was just that I could stand there and, no matter who was around me, feel calm. I'd wait for the curtain to rise and the music to start, and I'd burst out onstage. Sometimes I had to go into overdrive and call on an extra reserve of energy to propel the performance because I was fatigued mentally and physically, or because I'd be dancing through a sprained ankle, a bruised toe, an intense backache, a stiff neck, or an inflamed elbow. But usually I had energy to spare now no matter how tired I was.

I love leaping into the air while simultaneously exerting the most precise control possible over my body. Onstage I get an exhilarating sense of abandon and freedom when I move. The sensation of piercing the air, of the air passing my ears as I jump, always thrills me. And I love the fact that the audience is watching me. Stepping out onstage, I would feel more alive than I had during the entire day. This is how it was.

When I hit the stage as the Prodigal, the character is alive inside me. My enthusiasm bursts forth without restraint. But I have to make the character circumspect. The Prodigal is from a noble family. Balanchine adapted the story of *Prodigal Son* from the New Testament. He described the tale in his book *Complete Stories of the Great Ballets*. "A son said to his father, Father, give me my portion of goods that has fallen to me . . .

202

[he] gathered all together, and took his journey into a far country, and there he wasted his substance with riotous living."

The Prodigal has two servants. I must retain a sense of his position, which is revealed in the way I present my body. My gestures are economical, my demeanor calm and reserved until my sisters, who are attempting to stand in the way of my adventure, arrive. Each puts up a little bit of opposition and I become agitated.

The first movement that I do in the variation is to slam my fist into my thigh. In the early years, I'd get bruises the size of half-dollars on my left thigh because I didn't know how to project the moment convincingly. I had to cover these bruises with an extra layer of makeup. Later I learned how to project that moment in a more stylized manner.

After the Prodigal pounds his thigh, he throws up his hands, and the gesture must radiate tension. I never fake this—I know how to produce tension. But I must release it for the next step, the celebrated jump.

The jump is followed by turns, and the most difficult moment of the scene. This is when I come out of the turns, run to the tent, and stop on the very last note of music without moving a muscle. If I lose the beat in this passage, the opening section is ruined, for this is the Father's entrance. The moment is crucial.

In the action, I play off the Father, whose movements are stylized to suggest a sort of Moses or Abraham character. I look to my servants and then over at the gate and perform the act I'd been preparing for—I leave home. I repeat the variation, with great intensity. I leap over the fence, and in a last scream of defiance, I fall into the wings.

As I catch my breath, my chest heaving from the variation, I head for the rosin box, rub my feet in it, and feel the friction that I'm going to need. I cross over to the other wing to make my next entrance. Makeup and costume adjustments are made, and I grab a Kleenex and pat the sweat off because perspiration can cool the muscles as well as make arms and legs slippery for the dancers who have to grab me onstage. I look for the Siren in the wing, and we nod, just to make contact.

I enter downstage left for the second scene. Getting ready, I position myself just outside the edge of the proscenium arch

203

EDWARD VILLELLA

so I can get on quickly. As the time approaches, I politely ask people who are watching from the wings to move aside. Their response makes me uncomfortable. They become intimidated, as if they are actually dealing with the Prodigal Son, and they move away quickly, apologizing, as if they are intruding on a sacred moment. The fact is I just want them to move out of the way so I can get onstage.

As I enter, the drinking companions are clustered downstage right. I look around—it takes a few moments for me to become aware of them. I feel their eyes on my back at first and play off that. I slowly walk over to them, and one by one they offer their hands and I reach out. But almost cruelly, they pull their hands away. Sometimes the boys are off the music and the offering of the hands is rather chaotic, but I work with that and use it in the performance. It's a rare performance when all those hands come out exactly in time to the music. This ballet is not a favorite among young corps de ballet boys. They're covered in ugly headpieces and unflattering costumes, and their gestures are goonlike and grotesque. I understand the lapses in their concentration. When I'm being touched by the goons, I imagine green slime is pouring over me, that eels are slithering across my skin, and the image chills my bones.

I command my servants to offer the goons wine. They swarm around me. I give them wine and some of my other worldly goods to keep them from pawing me. I'm drawn into their activities and I begin to take on their character and form. My body lowers itself, my head goes forward and my shoulders rise up. The sense of nobility I projected is gone: I'm subsumed into the slime. I jump over the table, thinking of myself as the leader of the revelers, when I'm suddenly aware that the Siren has appeared.

The Prodigal is the center of the drinking companions' attention until the Siren arrives. My first reaction is annoyance that the drinking companions are distracted. They're no longer giving me the attention I feel they owe me. But once I take in the sight of the Siren, it's as if a bright light has been shoved in my face, and I flinch. I want to protect my eyes. Then I hold back from the sight, but I'm powerfully drawn to it. I can't resist this overwhelming monument to sensuality. It's my awakening. The Siren's legs are long and voluptuous. Her red

204

cape streams from her, and she is wearing a kind of headdress that seems like an extension of her body. The Siren is a strong, controlling woman, a force. Her movements are cool, frightening. First she spreads her legs. Then she does a backbend and walks on her hands and her pointes. I leer at her legs and am consumed with the thought of touching her limbs, caressing them. Now my glance moves all over her body to her waist, her breasts, her buttocks. It isn't that I want to kiss her, it's strictly sexual, and at that moment when I feel I can touch her, she covers herself with her cape. I inch forward, pull off the cape, and staring at her, think that I must have her.

The pas de deux is critical to the success of any *Prodigal Son* performance. It's a rite of passage from innocence to maturity, but it almost has the force of a rape. I let the Siren dominate me and I feel a sense of release. At the start her arms go around my neck, and she pulls my head to her breast. I'm lost.

I danced the Prodigal opposite many different women, perhaps more than a dozen. Each one had a distinctive style, temperament, and sense of musicality. Each had a different degree of confidence in my ability to partner her. And of course they were all different sizes, and it was up to me to accommodate all of them. Early on I danced the role opposite Gloria Govrin, who has been described as "a magnificently outsized" dancer. Gloria was six foot three inches on pointe, her thighs were bigger than mine, and each of her breasts and my head were roughly the same size. A grand, voluptuous woman, she was well cast as the Siren, but the first time we danced together we had problems. At a crucial point in the pas de deux I hadn't positioned myself correctly with the proper support, and when I put my head through her legs and tried to lift her with my neck during rehearsal, I staggered slightly. Balanchine and half the people watching leapt out of their seats to come to my assistance.

Karin von Aroldingen was stately and sensual. Suzanne Farrell was somewhat girlish, petulant, a bit vulnerable as the Siren. Jillana, on the other hand, was wonderfully feminine. Her line was one of the most exquisite in all of classical ballet and was shown off beautifully in the role. Of all the women, 205

Diana Adams, however, left the strongest impression on me. She was passionate, yet utterly ice-cold: she froze my blood. Diana, of course, had worked extensively on the role with Balanchine. She was a very intelligent dancer and she was especially well suited to the part. I had made my debut in the ballet with her, and I felt that she guided me through the part, teaching me about it from her own experience. In later years, I was often in her position, the experienced performer leading newcomers through the intricacies of this extraordinary pas de deux.

The trickiest moment in the duet comes when the Siren gets into second position on pointe and, straddling the Prodigal, who is sitting on the floor, sits on his head. Once she's there, there isn't much I can do to help. She has to shift her weight from two legs and her buttocks to one leg and her buttocks. Sitting on my head, she's still on pointe, she's totally unsupported. It's a precarious moment, and each ballerina deals with it differently. If the Siren panics or loses her balance, I have to anticipate it and be fast—and flexible enough—to handle it. Somehow I always manage to avert disaster.

The next moment in the pas de deux the Siren, still on the Prodigal's head, cups her feet over his knees or his shins and rises up to a standing position as he lowers his legs to the floor. The moment the shank of her ballet slipper touches my leg, I grasp the foot and hold it fast, and this gives the Siren a sense of control. I repeat the process with the other foot, but the hair-raising moment comes when the ballerina has to rise up to her full height balancing on my legs while I straighten them and bring them down to the floor, supporting her only with two hands. It's here that Balanchine would say in rehearsal, "Like an elevator." The ballerina has to have confidence in my ability to counter her balance: if either one of us moves too far forward, we can both roll over onto the floor in a heap.

There are other parts of the pas de deux that require the utmost dexterity. At one instance the Prodigal approaches the Siren and, ducking, places his head between her legs and lifts her into the air. I always think of this moment as a unique instance of foreplay. Without changing the position of her arms, the Siren crosses her legs and sits calmly on the Prodigal's

206

neck. It's the moment when Balanchine would often tell the ballerina, "Relax, smoke a Kool."

At another point I take hold of the Siren, swing her in the air, wrap her around my waist like a belt, and hold her there. The Siren then slides down to the floor, and I control her descent by bringing my feet and thighs together; I'm partnering her with my legs. Once she's at my feet on the floor, I lift her to her knees, and sliding my feet underneath them, I walk her while her knees are pressing into my feet.

The pas de deux ends with the Siren and the Prodigal sitting on the floor entwined in an embrace. One of the Siren's arms is wrapped around the Prodigal, but the other is raised behind her head, her fingers fanning out above her headpiece and radiating like a halo, another reference in the choreography to images from Russian icons.

The momentum of the ballet slows down somewhat during the pas de deux, and performing it, I often experienced the most uncanny phenomenon: I was able to monitor the performance from a point of view outside myself, from somewhere in the upper reaches of the theater. A dancer works in front of a mirror taking class and rehearsing, seeing his image come back at him for much of his life, and I think this sense of monitoring the performance can be explained as a consequence of my having looked at my image in the mirror so continually during my career. The phenomenon helped me anticipate mishaps that could occur during the performance so I could avoid them or integrate them into the action.

The pas de deux is followed by another intensely physical scene. In this sequence I am set on by the drinking companions, who tear me off the Siren, turn me upside down, and throw me from one end of the stage to the other. I charge at the boys and try to run through them. They have to stop me and then propel me from one side of the stage to the other. Sometimes a few of them panic. There are times they become a little more physical than necessary, times I find myself crashing onto the floor from ten feet in the air.

At the end of this sequence, I jump up on the table and run along its length to escape the Siren. But the drinking companions block my path by lifting the table at one end on a steep incline so that I can't climb any farther, and I slide down it on

207

my back. At one performance, a shooting pain nearly took my breath away as I slid off the table. After the performance, the pain in my back was worse, but I still couldn't tell what was wrong. The pain persisted for days until one night in my dressing room I was bare-chested and someone said to me, "My god, you've got a splinter in your back the size of a nail."

The scene in which the boys attack the Prodigal ends with him stripped of all his worldly goods, nearly naked. Left for dead, the Prodigal slowly regains consciousness and comes out of his stupor. In his nakedness and his abject pose, he resembles the figure of Christ. Drained of all his strength, he's aware of what's happening to him and is filled with the most overwhelming despair. He sinks very, very slowly to the ground.

Balanchine once told me, "You have to move in this scene as if you are not moving. You have to make it seem like you are disappearing."

I think of sinking, drowning. The challenge here is to sustain the level of physical intensity I achieved at the beginning of the ballet, but to do so without the benefit of steps. I desperately turn my face up as if the water level is getting higher and higher around me, and this contributes to a theatrical effect because my eyes catch the overhead key light. Collapsing to the floor, I remain completely inert. But after a few beats of music, I set my fingers twitching. I reach out blindly, holding on with one outstretched hand to the upended table. The table is the pillar against which I have been savagely attacked. It supports me and helps revive me. (The table is a fantastic prop that goes from being a picket fence to being a table, a pillar, a crucifix, and the bow of a sailing vessel. In the final scene it's a picket fence again.)

In my wretched and remorseful state, I plead with God to restore my strength, and the depravity into which I have sunk becomes real to me. The Prodigal Son falls three times in the scene as Christ did on the road to Calvary, but I don't know if Balanchine was making a conscious reference to that or, for that matter, if Prokofiev was. (When I questioned Mr. B, however, he said, "The falls are in the music.") As the scene progresses, I crawl along and mime the gesture of finding water and drinking it with my hands. It's helpful in a way that I'm parched and thirsty, for it adds to the realism of the moment, but I'm always careful not to carry this too far. I get myself into a fetal position

208

and crawl off into the wings. I try to avoid the patches of sweat on the floor as I crawl because the squeaks can make the scene look hokey.

I spend a brief interlude in the wings, standing on a big sheet that is spread out on the floor. The trunks I'm wearing are removed, and I get into another pair. Misha Arshansky works furiously, streaking slashes of grease over my body with water to depict my begrimed and bedraggled state, his fingers and elbows poking me in the eyes and ribs. And Duckie Copeland and his assistant also hover over me, waiting desperately for a moment to tie my leggings and throw a sackcloth on my back. I grab the staff as all these people are still tugging, pulling, and tearing at me, and as the bars of the music for my entrance sound, I lower myself onto my knees and crawl out for the final scene.

The Prodigal, near death, crawls on with the aid of his staff, blindly in search of his homeland. By now I'm really exhausted, and sometimes it's difficult to differentiate between what I'm supposed to be experiencing as the Prodigal and what I'm feeling myself. Balanchine told me not to wear a facial expression in this scene. He wanted everything as simple as possible. But as time went by and I grew more confident in the role, I came up with an idea to make the moment feel more convincing to me. I behaved as if I were really sick, physically wounded, ill. I crawl as if I can hardly hold up my head and slowly allow my eyes to come into focus. I stare out into the audience looking desperately for my home. Balanchine was not at all pleased that I moved my head to look out into the audience. He wanted the Prodigal to show no emotion at all, to cross the stage on his knees, look up to God, express resignation, crawl farther, see the gate, and collapse.

"I don't want you to act," he said once.

"Why?" I asked him.

"Dear, don't be movie actor," he said, and walked away.

Balanchine didn't want dancers to get carried away and overinterpret his ballets, exaggerate their subtle points. But I didn't want to be a slave even to his genius. I couldn't stop thinking for myself. I felt comfortable with the movement, and I continued to look out to the audience. He must have grown resigned to it because he never objected to it again.

•

209

EDWARD VILLELLA

In this scene I'm discovered by my sisters nearly unconscious outside the fence. The girls come out and gently lift me up and drag me through the gate. The scene has a particular beauty and poignancy, with a sister on either side of the Prodigal framing him as in an Italian Renaissance painting.

The most moving moment in the ballet for me comes when the Prodigal touches his home ground for the first time; it's almost as if he's being swallowed by it. The Father enters from the house. I see him and make a supplicating gesture. I strive to communicate the terror of the moment for the Prodigal, for even in his daze he's afraid that his father will reject him.

A sweet, intensely lyrical passage sounds in the score as the Father slowly offers his hand to his repentant son. The Son is on his knees now, unsupported by the staff. Placing his arms behind his back, and bowing his head, he walks on his knees to his father. The crawl is difficult to perform because I am hunched over. I get within the reach of the Father, then collapse with my body going forward and my hands up behind my head, a gesture inspired by a Rodin sculpture. I need to calculate this fall because I don't want to land flat on my face at his feet. But if I land too far away from him, I'm not able to grab his shoes and his legs. And I have to be careful gripping them. If I clutch too hard, I throw him off-balance. On my knees, I reach up to his shoulders and I haul myself up. I put my arm over his shoulder as he covers me with his cloak. He cradles me, and the curtain falls.

Shaun O'Brien (who usually plays the Father) gently lowers me to the ground. I can hear the applause from the other side of the curtain. The performance has taken its toll on my body: my knees are skinned, my insteps are bleeding, my elbows are bruised, there are welts on my arms, and my back hurts like hell. Usually my toes are bleeding, and dirt from the stage clogs my nose and mouth. I'm covered with grime from head to toe. I'm gasping for air. I have just enough energy for the bow.

Onstage there's a commotion, people rushing on and off from the wings as the cast takes places for the curtain call. We organize ourselves in a line for the call, and the Siren and I thank each other. The curtain goes up. It's always a wonderful

210

feeling to be engulfed by the warmth of the audience, and thrilling to come forward for a solo bow. The curtain comes down and I am presented in front of it.

Stepping back inside, I wander around for a minute or two in the midst of the general hubbub. The stage is being swept for the next ballet, and dancers are arriving and warming up. My energy is high but unfocused. I receive a few compliments. The conductor's backstage now and I thank him for the tempi. I have an eye out for Balanchine. He and Stanley are the ones I want to please most. I see Mr. B but wait for him to walk over to me.

I know from experience that Balanchine seldom articulates his feelings about a performance. We all yearn for him to talk to us, and it's a rare occasion when he does. Some dancers linger in the wings trying to catch his eye, but it's futile. It's hard to accept, but this is how Balanchine deals with us. If he says anything at all, it's usually about the music—the tempi were too slow or fast, the orchestra sounded good. He might make a technical comment about a gesture or a step in the pas de deux, and that's all that's necessary. Whatever he says is satisfying. The connection is made, I can return to my dressing room.

Despite the nearly universal regard for the piece, Balanchine remained indifferent to *Prodigal Son*. I think he was tired of it, bored by it. Some years after I had made my debut in the role, the director of the National Ballet in Washington, D.C., was eager to stage a production of *Prodigal* that I would dance, but he was uneasy about getting Balanchine's permission. He asked me if I would approach Mr. B for him, so I did.

"Oh, no, dear," Balanchine said to me. "Awful ballet, lousy, rotten. No good. I hate it. Old-fashioned. Terrible ballet. Don't do it. Do something else."

But I pleaded with him. I said, "It'll be wonderful, Mr. B. They really want it, and I would really like to do it with them." I made my case for over twenty minutes.

Finally, he sighed and looked at me kindly.

"Okay, dear. You know, ballet is like old coat between old friends. I lend you old coat."

211

FIFTEEN

Jerome Robbins joined the New York City Ballet in 1950 as a dancer/choreographer and associate director. In the 1950s, he also choreographed and directed some of the greatest musicals in Broadway history—*West Side Story* and *Gypsy*. In 1959, he left the company to work exclusively in the theater. But early in 1969, we heard that he was coming back to create a new ballet. His timing couldn't have been better, and we were all excited. Balanchine needed a splash of new energy. He was about to turn sixty-five, and he seemed to be feeling less vigorous, less fiery, less enthusiastic. His administrative burdens, the bane of every artist's existence, had greatly increased in the years since the New York City Ballet had moved to Lincoln Center. There were now close to eighty dancers in the company, and enrollment in SAB had tripled since the Ford Foundation grants.

It also seemed as if Balanchine needed a creative break. He had to have some relief from the pressure of having to produce new ballets season after season. The most recent work he created for me was a pas de deux I danced with Patty, "Divertimento Brillante," the final movement of a new ballet called *Glinkiana,* a suite of dances to four pieces of music by the Russian composer Mikhail Glinka.

"Divertimento Brillante" was full of intricate beats and ports de bras; it was very classical, elegant, and understated—

212

and difficult to dance. Glinkiana may not have been top-drawer Balanchine, but it was head and shoulders above most other ballets. The critics were lukewarm to it, and it took on the aura of a flop. Two other Balanchine ballets from this period, *Metastaseis and Pithoprakta* and a revival of *Slaughter on Tenth Avenue,* a ballet he'd originally made for the Rodgers and Hart musical *On Your Toes,* seemed like novelties. *La Source,* also from this time, is one of those works whose virtues are not immediately apparent and takes a while to find a place in the repertory. Now it's a great favorite, but in 1968 it didn't look as if it would last.

Some critics were hinting that Balanchine was losing his touch. Mr. B, who never paid any attention to what the critics said, redoubled his indifference. He was always waiting for the critics to catch up with him, and after a while they usually did. John Martin, the *Times* reviewer, had been highly critical of Balanchine in the 1930s. He wrote that *Serenade* lacked spontaneity and was "decadent." But by the time the New York City Ballet was formed in 1948, he was proclaiming Balanchine's greatness along with everyone else. Balanchine still occasionally received negative criticism. *Jewels* was a big success and was packing houses, but many critics thought that "Diamonds" was flawed and "Emeralds" a little dull. Only "Rubies" seemed to be an unqualified hit. The overriding problem was that people had come to expect so much from Balanchine that they were often disappointed no matter what he did. Those of us who worked with Mr. B were not worried about his ability to choreograph; we were concerned for him personally. Suddenly he seemed human, vulnerable, emotionally exhausted. His relations with Suzanne were troubled. She had married Paul Mejia, and Balanchine had taken it badly. He was obviously upset, brooding about his rejection. Tensions mounted between Suzanne and Balanchine. It seemed to some of us that he had lost all sense of distance from her. He seemed to have been completely engulfed by his obsession.

He needed a helping hand. Most people believed that Jerry Robbins alone had the stature and the talent for the job, and his return lifted everyone's morale. Most of us talked of little else. Those who'd worked with him before remembered that he was a perfectionist, a taskmaster who drove dancers hard. But

213

everyone was looking forward to rehearsing with him. Different stories circulated about what he was going to do, and I became excited when I heard that his new work was a pas de deux for Patty and me, set to music by Chopin. No one said anything to either of us directly, and it wasn't until the ballet was officially announced that Patty and I were called to rehearsal.

I had, of course, worked with Jerry on *Afternoon of a Faun* during my first season in the company. We'd remained casual acquaintances. I knew that working with him on a new ballet was going to be very different from working with Balanchine. And I was excited. I wanted to do a good job, and I intended to be perfectly warmed up beforehand, ready to do the steps full out because I knew that I wouldn't be able to mark them in rehearsal. Jerry would need to see if I could do what he wanted, if the steps fit the music, and if they proceeded logically and smoothly, one after the next.

I said to Patty, "You know, I'm going to prepare for this session so I'm really in shape when he arrives. He's been away for so many years. I think we should make him as comfortable as we can."

Patty agreed. The day of the first rehearsal, I warmed up alone in a small studio, then went over to the Main Hall where we were going to work. The rehearsal of another ballet was finishing up, and I was standing quietly at the barre doing a few simple battements tendus when Jerry walked in. His hair had gotten a little gray, but he looked fit and spry as always. But on his face was the most terrified expression I had ever seen on a choreographer. He barely said hello. Nervous tension had stiffened his body, and his eyes were darting around in his head.

He went straight over to the piano and buried himself in the score. Every now and then he looked up, but it was as if he were hiding, not daring to come out into the studio. How unusual, I thought, to see the great man of Broadway and ballet, the winner of so many Tony Awards, and an Oscar, one of the world's most acclaimed choreographers, looking so vulnerable and insecure. I suddenly remembered our first *Faun* rehearsal all those years before. I had found Jerry then sitting alone at the piano fingering the keys, plucking out notes. He looked up shyly when he saw me as if he'd been caught at

214

something shameful and said, "I'm just learning how to play." I thought that it was admirable for a person in his forties to be taking piano lessons, and I felt an instant warmth and affection for the man.

Now here he was returning for the first time in ten years to these so-called hallowed halls to work with the most accomplished ballet company in the world. What's more, these were dancers who were used to working with Balanchine. I was always intimidated whenever I had to choreograph anything on City Ballet dancers for television appearances, lecture demonstrations, or concert tours. If I didn't now what I was doing or got stuck on a combination for a minute or so, the dancers would throw up their hands in exasperation or tap their feet impatiently. It was done good-naturedly, but I knew that Balanchine never got stuck. Whatever he came up with, even on the spur of the moment, was almost always inspired.

Patty arrived a few minutes later, and I caught her eye and waved her over.

"He's very uncomfortable," I whispered. "I guess he doesn't know what to expect. Let's make it easy for him."

We both walked to the piano, and I shook Jerry's hand.

"I'd really like to welcome you. I'm delighted to have the opportunity of working with you," I said. It sounded a little stiff, and I think he thought I was just being polite. But I meant it from my heart. Then Patty also told him how glad she was to see him, and she kissed him on the cheek. It's hard to resist Patty. She's so charming and direct, and I could see him relax a little. I think he felt our sincerity. The room had emptied now, and except for Gordon Boelzner, our pianist, we were alone.

Jerry started to work very tentatively. He showed us a few steps and we picked them up fairly quickly. Still, he didn't seem like himself. He laughed nervously and tried to act casual but there seemed to be a wall around him. We kept working, absorbed in what we were doing. Then, after I demonstrated a step to his satisfaction, I noticed that Jerry's shoulders suddenly relaxed. He no longer seemed uptight. The wall had disappeared, and his movements were more natural. After twenty minutes or so, he asked us to dance from start to finish what he had given us, and he seemed satisfied by what he saw.

215

During the last quarter hour, the session really took off. By the time the rehearsal ended, the ice had been completely broken. It was more than that—we felt we'd accomplished something. Patty and I were both drained and worn out, and we were unsettled because we were both scheduled to dance that evening. Yet it was great to have Jerry back, and we were elated. From that day on a great deal of energy and enthusiasm was generated in every rehearsal, and the pas de deux worked out beautifully.

As I had anticipated, working with Jerry was very different from rehearsing with Balanchine. Balanchine usually chose a dancer for a new role because that dancer epitomized an idea that he had in relation to the music; he was going to showcase that dancer's unique qualities and abilities, his technical talents, his musicality and his temperament. When the session began, Mr. B was satisfied if the dancer was able to pick up what he wanted. But if a dancer couldn't, that was fine, too. He'd change it. Jerry didn't work this way at all. He might have been choreographing with a specific dancer in mind, but he tried to bend the dancer to his vision.

Jerry's background as a theatrical director played a large part in the way he used dancers. He was far more detailed in his instructions than Balanchine. He often came up with four or five versions of a step or a sequence, and then he'd select the one he liked best. He imposed his vision on us, but he was also testing himself to see what he could come up with. He talked very specifically about what he wanted, and in great detail. He'd dissect the movement and give us images to work with. On the other hand, Balanchine sketched out an overall structure and allowed us a lot of freedom and flexibility within it as long as we didn't violate his vision or misunderstand the style. Once Balanchine felt a dancer understood the essence of what he wanted, he let the dancer "go."

Balanchine believed that if what he had choreographed didn't feel natural, he was at fault, not the dancer. With Jerry, if the dancer didn't do exactly what he wanted, he tended to hold the dancer responsible. Jerry had difficulty instilling confidence in people because dancers could never entirely please him: it was never "right" enough. And if the movement he gave us didn't feel natural, he didn't concern himself. The danc-

216

ers had to adjust. For the most part, however, it wasn't difficult doing what he wanted. Instinctively he came up with things that suited us, things that taught us something about movement and our own potential. So it was an odd kind of collaboration. Jerry was a dictator of sorts, but we could move comfortably within the confines of what had been laid out. He made us stretch ourselves, and it was important to be open to his process. Working this way was valuable. In one way, New York City Ballet dancers had been spoiled by working with Balanchine because he was so flexible.

When he had first been asked to return, Jerry wasn't sure if coming back to a ballet company was the next logical step in his career. He decided to experiment by working on a small scale and doing a pas de deux. If it went well, then he'd see what else he could create. Now, because he was so pleased with our progress, he called in other dancers and started working on additional choreography. After a while, he asked Balanchine to come to the studio to look at what he had done. Jerry asked him if he thought it was okay. Mr. B was entranced.

"Wonderful," he said. "Don't stop. Do more. Make it more, make it more."

Jerry was delighted. He expanded the concept of the ballet and turned it into an ensemble piece for five couples he called *Dances at a Gathering*.

The return of his self-confidence revealed Jerry's manner of working more clearly. It was along the lines of more is better: the more dancers he had to work with and the more versions of a particular dance he came up with, the better it was for him. His concentration was more focused, his stamina increased, and he expected us to match his intensity. Rehearsal time also expanded, radically. We began working six hours a day, six days a week. This turned into a problem for me. I was dancing one or two ballets a program, eight times a week, and I had to rehearse these ballets as well. In addition to my NYCB work load, I was making various concert appearances, and my time and energy were committed to these performances, too. My body began to rebel. On top of this, my personal life was beginning to unravel. Janet and I either fought fiercely or ignored each other. We lived in the same house but we were strangers.

217

EDWARD VILLELLA

The next dance Jerry made as we worked was a solo for me that turned out to be the second variation I perform in the final version of *Dances*. Very striking, it had been influenced by ballet films that he had been running backward at the time. After analyzing the film, he'd then set the movements on me in the studio. He told me the variation had also been inspired by my performance in *Harlequinade*—Harlequin from the point of view of Chopin. After this variation was completed, however, he said that he wanted to do another one for me, something original and unexpected, and was looking for appropriate music.

"I see something in you no one has used yet," he said, "but the music has to be just right."

He tried one or two selections, but they didn't work. He didn't give up. Finally he came bounding into the studio one day saying, "I found it, I found it!"

The music was a Chopin mazurka, Opus 63, No. 3, and on the spot he started choreographing the variation.

"I feel that there's a romantic side to you that people don't see because they don't look beyond your pyrotechnical ability, the physical, athletic feats you do, all your jumping and your speed," he said. "I'm going to try to express this romantic side in this dance. This variation is very introspective. It's as if you're looking inside of yourself."

The choreography contained jumps and turns, but it wasn't really bravura or pyrotechnical. It reflected the contemplative state Jerry had described, and he gave me very specific directions about the mood he wanted me to project.

"When you walk out onstage, you're actually beginning the ballet. You look around. It's as if it's the last time you'll ever dance in this theater, in this space. And this is your home, the place you know. It's familiar, and I don't want to overstate it, but it's almost as if the atom bomb is going to fall. Everything is going to change."

In fact, the variation opened *Dances at a Gathering* and was essential in establishing its mood. The curtain rises on an empty stage. The piano is offstage right, visible to the audience on a platform at the far end of the orchestra pit. I enter downstage left, my back in three-quarter profile to the audience. I begin to walk, but not a note is played. On my third step, the music

218

starts, and I dance. There was no doubt in my mind once it was completed that Jerry had created what had to be one of the most beautiful solo male variations ever choreographed. I felt so emotional after dancing it that some nights I wanted to go home immediately—it seemed as if I should leave the theater at once. Often it was hard for me to get back onstage for the rest of the ballet.

Rehearsals continued on *Dances at a Gathering,* and everyone was happy with the way the ballet was coming together. Jerry seemed glad to be back. In the ten years that he had been away, New York City Ballet had evolved and developed on every level, and he could see the difference. The New York State Theater was the envy of dance troupes all over the world. The company's costume and scenic designers, the stagehands and the technical crew, were the best in ballet. And the orchestra, under Robert Irving's direction, was acclaimed in its own right and had made several recordings. Hugo Fiorato, the principal conductor, was also responsible for the excellence of this ensemble.

But despite the level of accomplishment, Jerry still couldn't have some things to his exact specifications. He had been used to working in the commercial theater with performers who were engaged in nothing but the project at hand. Extended rehearsal periods and out-of-town tryouts were part of the process. At New York City Ballet we had a large, active repertory to perform night after night, and this had to be taken into consideration no matter what new works were being created. The old ballets still had to be rehearsed and performed, and rehearsal time in the company was at a premium. Once a new ballet had been completed and was about to premiere, it usually had to make do with a couple of run-throughs in the studio and on the stage, a technical and dress rehearsal, and then the premiere. Two orchestra rehearsals were considered a luxury. Sometimes the regular repertory was put on with much less than that. It was far from ideal, but given the enormous number of ballets we performed, it was the best we could do.

Jerry needed more time. He liked to see things over and over, and he'd tailor his choreography, snipping and cutting, adjusting it here and there. I sometimes thought that he rehearsed passages to the point of taking the life out of them. He'd work on some things until they hit the peak of perfection, but then because of the repetition, they threatened to become stale. Jerry made profound demands on our energy, our time, our physicality, our attention, our stamina. Because most of us were performing so intensely night after night, we had just so much energy available for rehearsals. And because he wasn't always easy to please, some dancers became frustrated. Sometimes Jerry sensed the frustration and became impatient. Rehearsals could become very tense.

One problem for most of us was that Jerry choreographed so many different versions of particular sequences, and we never knew which version he was going to include in the end. What was even more irksome was that he often taught the same variation or role to several different dancers before deciding which person was actually going to perform it. We felt we were constantly auditioning. We weren't used to working like this and it undermined us. It didn't seem fair to have to learn so much when we had such a big load to carry in our normal repertory. At one point this situation precipitated an incident between Jerry and me.

I knew that two other dancers were understudying my role, and as we went along, they were busy learning the material Jerry was creating for me. At one point during rehearsals, I missed a few because of a television appearance I made. When I returned, Jerry wanted to work on the opening variation. "Okay, let's see it," he said to me.

I got up and stepped into position. I was about to start dancing when in the mirror I saw seven people behind me also getting ready to rehearse. I did a double take. It took me a second to believe my eyes. I didn't like the fact that so many other dancers had learned the steps and were going to dance it with me, but what really bothered me was that he had also taught the variation to a woman and she was also about to try it out with us. I found this disturbing. I couldn't understand what he wanted from the variation. I took a breath, grabbed on to the bar, swung myself underneath it, and sat down.

"What are you doing? Get up and do the variation," Jerry said, obviously annoyed.

"Do you think I know this variation, Jerry?"

220

"Yes, of course. But I have to see it, I need to see it."

"But do you know who's going to dance it?"

He looked startled.

"I have three ballets to dance tonight," I continued, "and I need to conserve my energy. I'll be happy to dance. You decide whether or not you want a woman or a man to dance it, and then I'll do it. In the meantime, let them do it without me. I know the steps."

He told everyone else to sit down. I danced the variation alone, and the rehearsal continued.

Dances at a Gathering was going to be premiered at the annual Spring Gala, a yearly ritual that had become a fund-raiser for the company and attracted New York's most glittering society. The casting sheet for that evening contained information that unnerved me: I was scheduled to appear in third movement *Symphony in C* as well as in *Dances at a Gathering*. I didn't think I could do both, and I wanted to bow out of "Bizet," which is how company members refer to *Symphony in C*. This presented the administration with a major problem. My understudy for the ballet was Paul Mejia, Suzanne's husband. Balanchine was reeling, and the situation was about to explode. After she'd married, Mr. B let Suzanne dance all her roles, but he took his wounded feelings and his rage out on Paul. He wouldn't cast him in any solos, and he surely didn't want him to appear in *Symphony in C*. Suzanne delivered an ultimatum: if I bowed out of that ballet that night because of *Dances* and Balanchine didn't cast Paul in my place, she was going to leave the company. My decision to drop out of "Bizet" may have sparked the final showdown between Mr. B and Suzanne, but I was really unaware of all that was happening. I was focused on the premiere of *Dances* and what it meant for me.

In order to avoid a confrontation Balanchine suggested that *Stars and Stripes* be substituted for "Bizet." This idea wasn't entirely acceptable because expensive tickets had been sold to an audience who expected to see the other ballet. No one wanted to disappoint them. But after much discussion it was decided at the last minute to perform *Stars*. Suzanne and Paul left the company the next day. Everyone was stunned. The

221

months that followed were difficult ones for Balanchine, and for Suzanne and Paul. Eventually she joined Maurice Béjart's Ballets du XXe Siècle in Brussels and danced there for five years before her problems with Balanchine were resolved. She rejoined the company in 1975. Paul never returned. Balanchine, Suzanne, and Paul may never have recovered from the pain of those years, but that night in 1969 everyone else's anxieties and hopes were centered on *Dances*.

Jerry had been backstage before the curtain went up. He was dressed in dinner clothes, his face was flushed, and he was wishing everyone *merde*. It means shit, which is how French performers wish each other luck. Then he went outside to watch from the audience. Excitement was building backstage, and presumably out front. I collected myself, continued to warm up and focus my concentration. The curtain rose, I walked out onstage and danced the first variation. I felt that I had never done it as well and came offstage in a little bit of a daze. I could hear the applause in the wings. Backstage everything was spinning. People were clustering around congratulating me, but I wasn't even aware whom I was talking to. Suddenly an image floated before my eyes, a head, a man's bearded face. It looked like Jerry, but it couldn't be. He was out front. I tried to blink the image away, but it wouldn't move. Then my hand was being grasped and I was startled to see it *was* Jerry. His eyes were open wide and he was breathless.

"I've never done this before. I never left the audience while a ballet was going on in the middle of a premiere, but I had to come back and tell you. You danced so beautifully. I was so impressed that I couldn't wait in my seat. I had to come back to see you now."

He embraced me quickly, turned around, and disappeared. At first I was stunned and walked around aimlessly letting what he had said settle in. I was deeply appreciative. It felt like the time Balanchine had complimented me on my performance as Oberon, and I knew then it was something I was never going to forget.

Dances at a Gathering was a phenomenal success. *Dance Magazine* said, "By common consent it's a masterpiece." Critics talked about the glowing comradeship of the participants and the folk elements in the choreography. Jerry told

222

Edwin Denby, the famous dance writer, that when he had me touch the floor with my hand in the final moments of the ballet, he was thinking of the dancer's world—the floor below, the space around and above. The ballet was a triumph that marked the formal return to the company of Jerome Robbins, who would remain there as a ballet master for the next twenty years.

As challenging and demanding as rehearsing *Dances at a Gathering* had been for me, my energies at the time were consumed by problems outside the theater. Janet and I were breaking up. This, one of the most painful periods of my life, was made even more painful because I was still grieving over the death of my mother.

In the mid-1960s, my father and mother made plans to retire to Florida. They sold their house in Bayside and bought a new one in a retirement community in Orange City, Florida, filling it with new furniture. They also bought a new car and were about to drive south when a routine physical exam revealed that my mother had bone cancer. The news was devastating, but they went ahead with their plans to start a new life, no matter how brief.

In Florida, my mother's condition deteriorated, and she suffered terribly. I tried to do everything I could to help. I convinced her to consult with doctors at New York Hospital and brought her north. There was nothing they could do. It was just a matter of where she wanted to be when she died. I'll never forget the moment—it seemed to knock the life out of me. But I didn't let her see how upset I was. She returned to Orange City, and whenever I could arrange time, I flew down.

As time was running out for my mother, I thought it was important that she and my sister try to reconcile. Carol had been out of touch with my parents for years, and at first she didn't want to make contact with them again. She felt the breach between my mother and her could never be healed. My father was less of a problem, and she agreed to see him. I told Carol that if she didn't see my mother before she died, she would regret it for the rest of her life.

"At some point you might feel differently about her," I said.

Finally she gave in. She flew to Orange City with her two

223

children. There was still strain between Carol and my mother, but I thought the gesture my sister made meant a great deal to both of them.

As my mother's death approached, I tried to spend as much time as I could at her bedside, and I'd stop over in Orange City after every concert appearance I made. I slept on the sofa and tried to help my father. Since little could be done for my mother at the hospital, she was being treated at home. The doctors had wanted to amputate her arm to stop the spread of the disease, but she wouldn't agree to it. She was in excruciating pain and wouldn't let anybody touch her but my father. He fed her, bathed her, lifting her out of bed. My father's gentleness, his compassion and his great love for my mother, amazed me and touched me profoundly.

As she weakened, the doctors advised admitting her to a hospital, but at first she wouldn't go. My father pleaded with her, but she wouldn't change her mind. I was appearing in Houston and had planned to stop in Orange City on my way back to New York. When my mother heard that I was coming to visit, she agreed to be hospitalized, but not until I arrived. She wanted to see me at home. I spent a few hours with her in the house until it was time for her to go. It was a terribly painful moment. Although she asked me not to, I accompanied her to the hospital. She knew that she was never going to return, that she was leaving her home for the last time, but she faced her fate bravely.

I flew back to New York to dance, then I traveled to Florida for one more visit. I was in New York when my father telephoned to say that she had died. Once again, I flew to Florida, this time to help my father arrange for her body to be shipped to New York for burial. I was scheduled to dance "Rubies" the night I returned, and although everyone in the company would have understood, I decided not cancel. My mother had never seen me dance that ballet, and that night I danced it for her.

Not long after my mother died, Janet became pregnant, and our son, Roddy, was born on June 28, 1969. I resolved to be a good and loving father, but fatherhood left me with a welter of conflicting emotions because it seemed clear that my

224

relationship with Janet was over. We could no longer agree about anything. Every time I entered the house, Janet would pick a fight with me that would build into a major brawl.

One night when I returned from a concert appearance in Kansas City, I let myself in at three A.M. Habitually, I washed and dried my practice clothes before I went to bed to have them ready for the next day. No matter the hour I returned home, I did the laundry. The ritual was comforting. I was loading the washer that night when Janet came flying down the stairs in a rage and stormed into the kitchen. She accused me of disturbing her sleep by coming home so late. I was tired and worn out and only wanted to finish what I was doing. But she kept arguing. Finally she went back to bed.

I plotted some petty revenge. Janet was not accustomed to cooking for dinner parties, but every day she made two perfect soft-boiled eggs for breakfast. She took great pride in it. Her morning routine was to talk on the phone and read the *New York Times* in the kitchen while she ate the eggs. Angry and frustrated, I reached into the refrigerator and took out the carton of eggs. Then I filled a big pot with water and, one by one, carefully placed the eggs inside. I cooked them for twenty-five minutes until I was sure they were hard-boiled. Then I replaced them in the carton, put them back in the refrigerator, cleaned the pot, put it away, and went to bed.

At eight-thirty the following morning, I was awakened by a cry of rage. Janet had discovered what I had done and carried on about it. It was something she never forgot.

The years that saw the end of my marriage to Janet were the most traumatic of my life and took a psychological toll on me. I was unable to sleep; no matter what time I went to bed, I'd fall off at five A.M. and I'd wake at nine. Four hours of sleep was not enough for my body to recover from the day's work —my muscles needed time to recuperate and regenerate—and dancing a full repertory and rehearsing for the premiere of *Dances at a Gathering* felt like more than I could handle. I was under duress, aching, overworked, and exhausted. My body was a tightly strung instrument, and my strings were near to snapping. I felt like the walking wounded. Rehearsing for *Dances* gave me something to focus on outside my personal anguish. The relief of dancing became so palpable that it was

225

almost like taking medicine, a painkiller that relieves a migraine. The opening variation, in particular, used to give me a great deal of solace, and I was very grateful at the time. Yet in my mind the music from the ballet became so associated with my personal problems that it eventually caused trouble for me.

Sometime not long after the premiere of *Dances,* Balanchine knocked on my dressing room door one afternoon and asked me to do him a favor. He wanted to know if I wouldn't mind partnering Gelsey Kirkland, a gifted young principal dancer, in a performance of *The Nutcracker.* The young man she was scheduled to go with was having problems partnering her and needed to be replaced.

"Of course, I will," I answered. I was sympathetic to the situation. My own problems with partnering were still fresh in my memory, and I was delighted now to be considered a capable enough partner to help out in a pinch. And it was nice of Mr. B to ask me personally. I appreciated the courtesy. He could just as easily have put my name down on the casting sheet without saying a word.

Gelsey Kirkland was something of a prodigy, an immensely talented teenager who was already a leading ballerina. She had the appearance of someone who was soft and easy, but in fact she generated a great deal of tension when she danced, and she was rather insecure. She'd clutch at her partner, lunge for his hand, and grasp it in a way that restricted his movement. She was very particular about what she intended to do onstage. She'd examine the tilt of every finger in relation to her head and her body and was very precise about what she wanted her partner to do for her. She wanted me to hold her at a particular spot on her hips and on her back, neither too high or too low but exactly right, and she even told me the precise length of time she wanted to be supported for each balance, the exact manner in which I was to turn, lift, and move her across the stage.

I didn't say much at first. The partner is supposed to serve and I wanted to be agreeable, but after a while my patience wore thin. I started to object when she began to change the counts in a particular piece of choreography.

"You know, Gelsey," I said, "this isn't the way this step is done."

226

"Well, that's the way I learned it," she said. She had a bit of a chip on her shoulder. I had danced the role many times with many different partners and felt I knew it, but I wanted to avoid a confrontation and so I just put up with her demands. But as we went along, these demands became increasingly picky and somewhat ridiculous. It seemed unprofessional to break down a performance so minutely and compulsively. That kind of overinvestigation takes the life out of the choreography and results in a stilted performance.

Finally, in the middle of a complaint about something or other, I stopped the rehearsal in its tracks.

"Gelsey," I said, "I'll see you at the performance." And I turned and walked offstage.

I didn't see her again until we were in the wings just before we went out to dance the performance. She couldn't have been more pleasant, and the pas de deux went smoothly. Gelsey's technique was remarkable. Her insecurities made her intent on overinvestigating everything she did, and she impeded her progress, but classical ballet came naturally to her. Watching her dance was a pleasure. She had an amazing purity. She was youthful, but her style and phrasing was sophisticated. It seemed she could do anything, and it looked as if she'd have an important career.

In 1970, Balanchine decided to revive *Theme and Variations* as the final section of a new ballet he was going to choreograph to the remaining movements from Tchaikovsky's beautiful score. The new ballet was called *Tchaikovsky Suite No. 3* after the music, and Gelsey and I were to dance the leads in the *Theme and Variations* section. Ten years earlier I had replaced Erik Bruhn in *Theme* opposite Violette, but that version never entered the repertory. Now I was pleased to be part of the first cast in a new staging of a ballet that called for the purest classical technique.

For this revival, Balanchine altered some of the choreography for the ballerina. Utilizing Gelsey's extraordinary technique, her speed, and her lightness of movement, he made the role even more demanding. The choreography for the man was as challenging as it had ever been, but I had much more confidence in myself now. I was a better dancer, a more classical dancer than I had been ten years before, and I felt equal to the

227

task. Rehearsals went smoothly, and Gelsey and I soon learned to work well together.

My only difficulty had to do with my private life. I was divorced and living alone, and one night I was gripped by a compulsion. I bought a large supply of cleaning liquid and began mopping down the house from top to bottom. I was sure that I was symbolically taking possession of my home— and myself—again. The house was mine alone now.

But I got carried away. I lugged the mop and pail up and down the stairs, and because I cleaned and scrubbed every surface so vigorously, I threw my back out. This was the day before the premiere of *Tchaikovsky Suite No. 3,* my second debut in *Theme.* The following morning I woke up in a lot of pain. I could hardly move, but I had no intention of canceling the performance. I struggled through the day, had a massage, and went to see Dr. Carnival. I returned to the theater, warmed up as best I could, and went out onstage. When the lights come up on *Theme,* the ballerina and her partner are standing in a beautiful classical pose, pulled up and straight, in fifth position with precise port de bras. Stanley told me that when he saw me, he burst out laughing.

"I felt so sorry for you," he said. "You were tilted over on a complete angle. You looked as if you were going to topple over onto the floor."

I was glad I didn't have to see what I looked like, but I managed to get through the performance.

A pile of fan mail was often waiting for me at the State Theater, and I usually tried—and failed—to make the time to answer it. After the "Man Who Dances" special was aired on the "Bell Telephone Hour," an avalanche of extra mail poured in. A young man who was friendly with people in the company and who was a fan of mine asked if he could help with it. He was so efficient that as time went by I began to rely on his services. I started paying him a modest salary and asked if he'd also go through my personal papers and put them in order. He said yes and took them to his apartment. I gave him extra money for the job.

Later I suggested we get together so that I could sort out the papers with him. He made dinner, and we watched televi-

228

sion. But when I wanted to get down to work, he stalled. He wanted to do it another night. For a while I had suspected he was developing an emotional attachment to me. Now it was obvious, and it made me uncomfortable. I asked him to return the papers, but he refused. He finally gave them up with the greatest reluctance.

Then letters from him began arriving at my house that were suggestive and embarrassing. They contained sexual innuendos, and in one he accused me outright of leading him on, of having kissed him. In my position it wasn't unusual for people to become infatuated with me, but this man's imagination seemed to be running away with itself. I thought about taking legal action, but my lawyer advised me against it. He thought it would only provide further stimulation.

The letters grew more heated and impassioned, and I decided to confront him directly to try to put an end to them. I went up to him in a bar in Saratoga where the company was dancing during the summer season and asked him to step into the street. I told him we had to talk. He was very haughty, but he came outside with me.

"I'm telling you straight off," I said. "Stop harassing me. Stop writing these letters."

He was antagonistic and he baited me. I grew furious and lost my temper. I hauled off and whacked him, striking a few blows to his stomach before I got ahold of myself. I didn't want to hurt him physically. After that, matters only got worse, his letters more farfetched and upsetting. Before he was through I had received close to two hundred.

Eventually they stopped, until some years later when he wrote one more. This letter contained a profuse apology and an explanation. He said he had been abusing alcohol and drugs for years and asked for my understanding. I tried to understand, but the episode left me uneasy. I consider myself a tolerant and sympathetic individual, however, with limitations, and in retrospect I regretted letting him get close to me. I knew in the future that I had to be more wary of people whatever their sexual orientation. I had to take people's hidden motives into consideration before opening up and letting them into my life.

229

EDWARD VILLELLA

SIXTEEN

Dances at a Gathering was one of the biggest hits in the history of the New York City Ballet, but despite the success, the company was "in crisis." Balanchine was still suffering from the break with Suzanne, despondent and inconsolable. His creative power seemed exhausted. We all had known what Suzanne meant to him, and now we all felt his pain and anguish. A bond existed between all of us and Mr. B, a blood tie. No matter what else we felt about him, we were connected to him in ways that were, and still are, hard to articulate. We had danced his moods, his doubts, his joys. As time went by, we also became more concerned about the state of the company; the future seemed unclear and uncertain. In the past Balanchine had been the center. Everything flowed from him. Now, unbelievably, he had nothing to give.

Suzanne's departure had one positive effect: the other ballerinas felt better, less threatened. Many returned to old, favorite roles, and opportunities were plentiful now for a new generation of ballerinas. Balanchine was hardly idle. He forced himself to work. His gloom lifted. He created a major new ballet to Gershwin songs he called *Who Cares?* It contained smashing roles for three ballerinas, and a role for Jacques. Patty scored a great triumph in the piece. Many of us thought the title was an ironic comment on his feelings about Suzanne, and

230

the new choreography he created for *Tchaikovsky Suite No. 3*
also seemed to contain obvious references to her. In the opening
section, "Élégie," the ballerina appears as an elusive, shadowy
figure, and as the section comes to a close, the man is left alone
onstage, his head bowed in despair and resignation.

I could easily identify with Balanchine's feelings of des-
pondency. I had hardly recovered from my divorce. In the past,
dancing had always been an escape from personal problems.
Being onstage made me feel as if I were in command of my
life. Maybe because I was getting older, the richness of my
work seemed a sad comparison to my personal life. Suddenly
my emotions began to intrude upon performances, and I had a
great deal of trouble appearing in *Dances at a Gathering*. Just
listening to the music could throw me into feelings of loss and
sorrow. My life was empty; I had no real family. I had lived, I
realized, for myself, my career, my great hopes. What was I
missing? Would my life offstage ever catch up to my life as a
performer? Every time I stepped out onstage to do the opening
variation, I'd feel a pang, a pulling at my heart and soul. I was
drained before I danced a single step.

After dancing the ballet for close to two years, I thought
the time had come to give it up. I decided to speak to Jerry
about it. I was sure he'd be angry, but instead he complimented
me. He said he didn't think he could see anybody else in the
role—he didn't want the ballet to "go" without me. Because I
loved the work and because Jerry, perhaps self-servingly, had
flattered my ego, I decided that I owed it to him to stay in the
ballet. I didn't want it to disappear. But the problems remained.
It drained me. A few months later I decided to broach the
subject again, and I talked to Jerry in Saratoga, during our
three-week summer season when everyone tended to be more
relaxed. This time he didn't bother to manipulate me. Irritation
flashed in his eyes. He paced the ground. I pleaded my case. I
knew the request was unusual, but I needed to get away from
the role to restore my emotional equilibrium. Things got tense.

Finally, I said, "Jerry, do another ballet for me."

"No," he shot back. "I can't trust you. I can't invest any
more time in you."

I told him I was sorry. We shrugged our shoulders, and
the conversation was over. Tension between us lingered for the

231

EDWARD VILLELLA

next few months until one day Jerry telephoned me at home in New York. He asked me to come into the rehearsal studio because he had an idea for a new ballet. He wasn't sure if I'd be able to do it, or even if he was interested in having me do it, but he wanted to discuss the possibility. When I got to the studio, he explained his idea. It was highly original, experimental. It might not work, but he wanted to try it. I listened intently, fascinated by the concept, which was heavily influenced by Eastern philosophy. Basically, a sort of Everyman contemplated his past. It was as much a theater piece as a ballet and was going to be performed to specially commissioned music by a Japanese composer. We tried out a few of Jerry's ideas, and by end of the session both of us felt that the concept had promise.

We shook hands and I left for another rehearsal. A few days later, he left a message with my answering service. He said that he wanted to move ahead on this ballet—he couldn't imagine it with anybody but me. He said my work in the studio demonstrated exactly what he wanted the ballet to be, and he asked if I was willing to continue. I was relieved that he felt that he could work with me and didn't hold any grudges. It had never been my intention to insult him. I understood that I had a responsibility to the company, its resident choreographers, and the repertory. I knew that my personal problems had to be kept separate and distinct from my professional priorities. This discipline was second nature to me. But *Dances* haunted me. I had to let go of it.

As soon as rehearsals got under way, I saw that *Watermill* was going to be extraordinary—and controversial. Working on it became a process of elimination, a paring down. The collaboration between Jerry and me was intense and satisfying. He never minced words and was never less than completely honest. Because of this, I felt I could open myself. He would rein me in if I went too far. I wasn't concerned about my lack of experience with the style. It was a departure for everyone.

Jerry demonstrated what he wanted and this time allowed me to play with it. It felt as if everything were being created on the spot, and not only the movement. The composer, Teiji Ito, and his musicians, attended rehearsals, and the score, which was played on Japanese instruments, was written as we worked. For me, it was a new kind of working relationship

232

with musicians, and during performances of the ballet I found that I sometimes took cues from the instrumentalists and they sometimes took cues from me. That was fascinating because it meant staying in touch with them rather than the audience.

The ballet was influenced by Japanese Noh drama and Kabuki, but stylistically it had nothing to do with *Bugaku*. It was going to be a long ballet, running for over an hour, but there were no virtuoso steps in it. In fact, it hardly contained steps in the conventional sense. I moved very, very slowly, almost in slow motion. Rehearsing it was not the physical experience of rehearsing, say, *Dances at a Gathering;* but because my concentration had to be so intense, it was draining nonetheless. But it was easy for me to warm up for another rehearsal or for a ballet I had to dance in the evening, so preparing *Watermill* didn't interfere with my other roles.

Watermill gave me a chance to explore things I had never contemplated before. I was expressing my physicality in an incredibly subtle way. I had to control the stage, rivet the audience's attention by barely moving at all, and this was a new kind of challenge. The irony was that I probably wouldn't have been able to do the ballet if I hadn't been an en l'air dancer, comfortable with pyrotechnics.

The ballet slowly assumed its shape. Themes emerged, ideas having to do with the passage of time, the nature of time itself, and the seasons or stages of a man's life as they are marked by the phases of the moon.

As the style of the ballet became clear, people in the company quickly formed opinions about it. I found this unproductive. For the first time in my career I didn't allow myself to judge a new work because I thought it would be detrimental to the characterization. Analyzing the quality of a new ballet is the job of the critic or reviewer, not the dancer, I told myself. The fear that the ballet was a little pretentious flickered at the edge of my mind, but I quashed the feeling and developed a totally neutral attitude. When people began to express opinions as we worked, I just walked away. Some people felt the pace of the ballet was too slow. I didn't because so much was going on inside me during it. Everything had to appear as a single gesture. But it was unorthodox in that there were no favorite moments.

My approach to *Watermill* was to adapt my concentration   233 to the time frame of the piece. When we rehearsed, Jerry always told me, "Take *your* time." The stress was on the *your*. If I was comfortable with my inner rhythm, the movements would flow. Although the ballet was steeped in the philosophy of Zen Buddhism and Taoism, I didn't investigate its background the way I had with the biblical themes in *Prodigal* and with the Gagaku in *Bugaku*. *Watermill* is a highly personal abstraction. I had the sense that the most important aspect of my work was that what I was doing should feel right to me, and to the choreographer.

The *Watermill* setting contributed much. The exquisite scenery and lighting, which Jerry created with David Reppa, was probably its most successful element. Patricia Zipprodt's costumes were also evocative. The stage picture resembled an Oriental master painting, and I could quickly fall into its dreamlike setting. The setting framed and supported me. It communicated a clear sense of place to me, and I used some of the ballet's props to help me make my effects. I'd watch the play of light off the reeds, stare at them shifting in the breeze that gently wafted across the stage. And I'd gaze into the key lights. The glare made my eyes tear, but that seemed somehow appropriate.

When the curtain goes up on the ballet, I'm clad in a beautiful cloak, enfolded in it, and its weight gives me a sense of being connected to the floor. As the action progresses, I remove the cloak along with the simple, shapeless top and trousers I wear, and for most of the ballet I'm in only a dance belt. I felt that I was as naked as I could be on the stage and still perform in public. My instinct was that I should have performed the ballet completely in the nude, and I tried to feel as if I were, as if I were clothed in my nakedness. I made connections in my mind between this ballet and the way I was stripped of all my possessions and clothing in *Prodigal Son*. There were other similarities between the two works, connections in the pared-down movements of the two protagonists, especially the movements in the last few scenes of *Prodigal*.

On the opening night of *Watermill,* I knew five minutes into the ballet that a challenge lay ahead of me. Almost immediately I could feel tension building in the house because of the unfamiliar style. Because of my reputation as a bravura dancer,

234

people were waiting for a variation. The static pace was interrupted only by the entrance of a group of runners who jog back and forth across the stage a number of times before dispersing. Stirred by the memory or the sight of the runners, I too sprint across the stage, tracing the pattern of a figure eight on the floor before returning to my position downstage left. These are the "biggest" moves I make.

At the premiere, the audience began coughing and murmuring, and I could hear muffled laughter. For one moment my concentration wavered, but I recovered quickly. I think some people needed to express themselves because the ballet made them uncomfortable. When the curtain came down there were shouts of approval, but there were also boos and hisses. I knew the piece was very different from what anyone expected from the New York City Ballet, that this Eastern heartbeat was not necessarily compatible with our Western attitudes. I had anticipated a certain amount of surprise, maybe even controversy, but I didn't expect the amount of disapproval. I had expected audiences at least to respect it for its originality. There were those who were entranced by it. The audience seemed equally divided. I think Jerry was shocked by the reception. When he came onstage for his bow, his eyes were wide open, but he wasn't seeing. I was relieved that when I took my solo bow, I received cheers. Two good friends who were also fans, Trumbull (Tug) Barton and John McHugh, hosted a black tie dinner after the opening. Margot Fonteyn sat next to me. She praised my performance and explained to Tug and John that what I had done was equal to the challenge of a bravura part. When the reviews came out, some of the critics compared the role to Hamlet.

In June 1972 the New York City Ballet staged a Stravinsky Festival, a celebration of the great composer, who had died the year before. It made history.

Stravinsky was unquestionably the greatest ballet composer of the twentieth century, arguably the century's greatest composer. His connection to New York City Ballet was such that a company festival in his honor seemed inevitable. In a press conference announcing the event, Balanchine said of Stravinsky, "He was like Einstein—nobody like him. He made 235 *musique dansante.* There have only been three who could do it. Delibes, Tchaikovsky, Stravinsky. They made music for the body to dance to. They invented the floor for dancers to walk on. We can't make time. Maybe not even space . . . but Stravinsky made time."

Balanchine conceived the festival and billed it as a "Presentation of Thirty-one Ballets to Music by Stravinsky, Twenty-one Made for the Occasion." The remaining ten were already in the repertory. There had been several other festivals dedicated to Stravinsky, even while he was alive, but these were modest in scope compared to ours, and none really involved original works. They were usually productions of Stravinsky's most famous ballet scores, *Firebird, Petrouchka,* and *The Rite of Spring.* Nowhere had anything been done on this grand scale, and I believe that NYCB was the only company in the world that could have managed it with such a high level of artistic understanding, integrity, and commitment.

The company had to mobilize all its forces to undertake an enterprise of such proportions, and the festival seemed to mark the return of Balanchine's creative fire. He was scheduled to choreograph eight new ballets, as well as collaborate with Jerry on one more, a new production of *Pulcinella.* I was cast in the title role and in another new ballet Balanchine was creating for the occasion, *Symphony in Three Movements.* This ballet turned out to be one of the festival's biggest hits, an enduring masterpiece still in the repertory today.

Symphony in Three Movements is the single most complicated score I had ever danced to. It brought back the problems I had had years before with *Agon.* During the rehearsals, despite all my experience dancing Stravinsky, I couldn't really hear the music and couldn't count it. To this day I have trouble with this music. As always, we rehearsed the ballet to a piano reduction Balanchine had made himself, and just as in the old days, it was difficult making the transition from the piano to the full orchestra. I had to adjust to the color and shading of the orchestrations, to the full dimension and the rhythmic complexity of the music. Dancing to the opening movement of that score was the biggest musical challenge that I ever faced, and I don't think I ever performed it successfully, or at least to my own satisfaction.

236

Stravinsky was inspired to write the symphony after seeing Nazi brownshirt officers rough up bystanders at a rally, and the score is driving, hard-edged, a little heartless. The visual equivalent Balanchine came up with for the opening of the ballet was a line of women stretched across the stage on a diagonal. The women look Amazonian, ferocious and powerful. But they also have the benign air of cheerleaders, and a sense of energy and of ambiguity characterized the section. I entered leading a group of boys, not unlike the boys who chased me around the stage in "Rubies."

I danced the pas de deux in the ballet opposite Sara (Sally) Leland, and the tone in this section was completely different from the other movements. The music sounds exotic and foreign, not exactly Western. Balanchine had a terrific time choreographing this pas de deux. He viewed it as a witty, inside joke and came up with extraordinary invention for Sally and me. Every now and then he offered a few words of explanation. At one point when he was fixing our arms into somewhat contorted positions, he said, "Balinese," and the word conjured up exactly what he wanted: Asian gods with many arms and legs.

At one point in the pas de deux the ballerina stands in front of her partner looking out at the audience. She crouches down and moves her outstretched arms in a circular pattern. The man stands at his full height and moves his outstretched arms in the same way on a different count. Then as the woman rises up, he begins to crouch, but their arms are still moving. Balanchine said to us, "Helicopter," and somehow the movements do conjure up the whirling of a helicopter's propeller action. He also had us crook our heads as we danced, look over at each other like wild creatures, stare like big birds, and then run away. We stand, and stop and look, and then run.

The Amazonian/automaton motif returns in the final section. The movement for everyone here is aggressive, mysterious, and frightening. The patterns suggested by Balanchine summon up images of Nuremberg rallies. But the finale also contains strict dance passages that are witty and sharp, like those in the pas de deux. Some of us had trouble with these steps during rehearsals, and Balanchine would show us what he wanted.

237

EDWARD VILLELLA

"You know, dear," he said to me, "you go around in a circle and move your feet like this and that. You go—you know. The Boston shag."

I couldn't believe it. It was the Boston shag! He had actually worked popular dance steps into some of the most intricate choreography he had ever devised.

All through the rehearsals I was very aware that my choreography didn't really call for a bravura technique. But I was beginning to welcome these new roles, such as the one in *Watermill,* which called on another aspect of my artistry. In former days I might have worried and said to myself, oh, God, Mr. B thinks I don't have a bravura technique, he doesn't think I'm a classical dancer. But now I could see that he was not only using my physicality in these ballets, he was drawing on my experience, my understanding of style. He knew I could give him what he wanted once he had demonstrated it, and I was grateful for his confidence.

I was particularly excited about the role of Pulcinella. I'd never worked with Balanchine and Robbins in tandem on a new work. Janet Roberts summed it up: "You've reached the point when you've got two geniuses making one role for you."

Balanchine began *Pulcinella* by demonstrating the appropriate movements. He had already explained to me the differences in the various commedia styles when we were working on *Harlequinade.* Now he was going to coach us in the finer points of Italian commedia. It was always thrilling to watch Balanchine perform a dance style, and as he showed me what he wanted, he turned into Pulcinella before my eyes.

I could make out the differences in the two commedia styles immediately. Pulcinella was not at all like Harlequin—he was no premier danseur. Balanchine confirmed my impressions when he said to me, "You know, dear, this guy Pulcinella, he likes to look under girls' skirts." He had summed up in one sentence everything I needed to know about what I was doing —it provided me with the framework to create the character.

Once I began to work I was grateful to have already performed French commedia, but here I could be much freer, wilder, raunchier—vulgar. The challenge was to maintain the essence of the broad comedy without degenerating into slap-

238

stick, no mugging. Stravinsky's score was based on music by the Neapolitan composer Pergolesi, and for all the story's raucousness, the score is elegant and refined. The more I worked, the more the essence of the challenge revealed itself to me: to be both broad and restrained at the same time, to be economic in my means and make the raunchy and ridiculous exist within the boundaries of good taste. Pulcinella was ridiculous—a character who thought he was a great lover but who was really a buffoon. He never really admitted it to himself, vain fool that he was. Jerry expanded on these themes in an interview.

"The story is mostly George's," he said. "His Pulcinella combines the traditional commedia dell'arte with Goethe's *Faust*. He's a terrible, stupid man with a marvelous voracity for life. He steals and gives his loot away. He beats up people and becomes a victim. He has a great instinct for survival."

Each time we rehearsed, I found myself mesmerized by Balanchine. I often felt that I was his audience. Work became entertainment. But I also knew that I was going to learn exactly what to do by watching him. There was no way I would have been able to do the ballet without that experience. It confirmed what I had realized years before when he demonstrated the role of Apollo for me: Balanchine was probably the greatest single dancer I had ever seen in my life. He didn't do tricks, fast turns, or jumps, of course, but what he did was real dancing.

As he often did when he worked, Balanchine took breaks, sitting around and reminiscing about the past. He talked about his days in the Soviet Union right after the Revolution. As a young man working in his spare time with a group of Imperial Ballet dancers he called his Young Ballet, he had originally set dances to sections of this music. He told us he was only seventeen years old when he first looked at Stravinsky's score.

"We didn't have much to dance those days," he said. "Minkus, Fritz Kreisler. I also made waltz to Ravel. And I composed music myself for pas de deux."

After Balanchine's initial sessions, Jerry came in and started working on the crowd scenes. He was absolutely terrific at this. It wasn't terribly different from numbers he might have staged on Broadway, and his expertise was impressive. He could get the maximum effect from a group of people with a minimum of effort. Ordinarily I would have expected him to

239

coach me in the small details of characterization that he did so well, but naturally enough, he wasn't as familiar with the style of the ballet as Balanchine. But having both of them on hand added to my confidence.

They usually worked separately, dividing the ballet between them and choreographing sections individually. Sometimes they showed up for the same rehearsal and each man contributed to whatever was going on; sometimes their sessions overlapped. When we put the scenes together, however, we saw that the sections the two worked on individually didn't always mesh. The ballet suffered from an embarrassment of riches. What it needed, I thought, was one of these masters to create a coherent scenario, to edit the material, shape it from a single point of view. The ballet felt episodic. It seemed to lack a dramatic continuity linking the high points of the action.

In time this might have occurred naturally. As it was, time was in short supply and the ballet was never completed to everyone's satisfaction. So many other ballets were being created for the festival, some technically and musically infinitely more complicated, that Balanchine's energies, and Jerry's, too, were taken up with those works. Who could complain? Works such as *Symphony in Three Movements* or *Violin Concerto* might ordinarily have taken a full season or more to premiere.

I can't ever remember such a concerted expenditure of energy in all my performing career than the Stravinsky Festival. Preparing all these ballets and dancing a full season meant that the studios were buzzing with activity from morning until night. We'd start rehearsing at ten A.M., and some rehearsals lasted until close to midnight. A dancer might work all day, appear in the first ballet on the evening's program, and then have to rehearse for two more hours. And the choreographers and ballet masters were pressed into service above and beyond the call of duty. Of course no one worked harder than Balanchine. We all experienced an extra rush of adrenaline and exulted in the excitement of what we were doing. We all were high. Naturally enough, some works couldn't be fully realized under such circumstances, and *Pulcinella* was one of them.

At one point during rehearsals, Eugene Berman visited the studio. A great artist and distinguished costume designer, Berman had been commissioned by Balanchine to create lavish scenery and costumes for this new production. He based his

240

sketches on Pulcinella drawings by the younger Tiepolo, and he surpassed himself. The costumes were as imaginative and inventive as the choreography, and utterly charming. When we started to rehearse, we all wore practice clothes, but Balanchine described some of the costumes to me and eventually Mr. Berman showed me some sketches. It was then that I saw the problems I was going to have.

Two major difficulties faced me. The first was that the costumes were going to swallow me up, almost bury me. Pulcinella's clothes are baggy; pantaloons are part of his identity. The second problem was related to the first and was just as severe. I had to wear a mask during the whole of the ballet, a covering that extended from my forehead to my mouth. Its most prominent feature was a huge, pointy nose. Up to this point, my facial expressions had been a major part of my characterization. In effect, I'd been speaking with my face. Now I had to reconceive everything I had been doing.

It wasn't clear just how radical the change was going to be until days before the premiere when the costumes arrived with the masks. The mask completely concealed my face, and the costumes made any attempt at characterization even more difficult. Dressed in pantaloons, I felt as if I were trapped in a bulky, uncooperative blanket, but I struggled. Quickly, as I tried to investigate my options, I came up with ways in which a characterization could emerge. My stance, the angle of my frame, and my posture had to communicate who I was and what I was feeling to the audience in lieu of facial gestures. My hands could serve as instruments of expression. If I made a fist and used one finger, it meant one thing. Using a fist with three fingers extended meant something else. And having the fingers of one hand clenched in a fist while the fingers of my other hand were free enabled me to express a variety of complex emotions.

I also realized that standing absolutely still could convey a wealth of information. I could silence my body, so to speak, in relation to a lively piece of music by not moving. In this way, I spoke volumes. My head movements also became very expressive, and the huge nose attached to the mask had its own energy and momentum. It created comic effects. I used the nose of the mask as if it were my eyes.

I found a way to use basic classical steps to articulate char-

241

acter. A chassé is a simple movement where each foot alternately brushes the floor. It's similar to the lateral movements of a tennis player. One foot reaches out and the other chases it as the body moves. In ballet, however, a dancer can chassé forward and back as well as to the sides. As Pulcinella, I would chassé rather than walk. I'd raise my hand above my head and execute this classical step, distorted but not unrecognizable, all bent over to the point where my nose was practically touching the floor. And I hunched my back as I moved around, isolating my shoulders and using each one separately, so that if I lifted my right shoulder, I'd also move my head to the right to make a point. It might have been grotesque, but it grabbed everyone's attention. I worried at first that I looked a little bit like Groucho Marx, the problem in *Harlequinade,* but Balanchine assured me that loping around the stage like Groucho was perfectly appropriate here. I began to relax. I was having the time of my life.

Violette danced opposite me in *Pulcinella* and the experience was a trial for her. She played my girlfriend, the girlfriend of a buffoon, and she had to function within the conventions of the style. This went completely against her personality. An elegant, musical, refined performer, she was not comfortable with the pratfalls and slapstick in this ballet. The story calls for me to treat her badly, to kick and slap her. It was certainly not a role that she wanted, but given the exigencies of the festival, she was going to be a good sport about things and dance what she was given. But I could see that she was suffering.

Her variation was long, difficult, and in the end thankless. It comes at the end of the story, and because it is so classical, it seems to stand apart from the rest of the ballet. Violette was wearing an elaborate heavy costume with fringes and baubles, and a hat, and had to perform some difficult steps on a floor cloth that was draped over the stage during much of the action. I think the variation was physically painful for her, and there was no payoff to boot. The audience barely applauded when it was over. It wasn't that she was poor or that the choreography was mediocre. It was just that the audience wasn't motivated to applaud. As always Balanchine choreographed the piece strictly to the music and let that define the structure, and because the music was extended and tended to drift away, the

242

variation didn't have much impact. Mr. B tried to adjust it and make it work for Violette, but somehow nothing he did ever improved it, though she struggled bravely with this role.

I also had physical problems in the ballet—there was absolutely no time to rest. From start to finish I was hunched over, running, jumping, turning, lifting, falling, being slapped and generally manhandled. There were times I thought I would suffocate. Only my wrists, my chin, and my hands were exposed. Even my neck was covered up, and my lungs were compressed because of my posture. It wasn't easy to breathe. Whenever I stood still, I was aware that I was soaking with sweat, aching for breath. Near the end of the ballet, I'd rush offstage for a costume change, but this change was so intricate that I barely had time to breathe. Two dressers tore at me, stripped me down to my dance belt, shoes, and socks, and covered me up again in a new costume. More often than not they didn't work quickly enough, and I'd be a few beats late for my next entrance. It wasn't all that complicated an entrance, but being off the music disturbed me, and it always took a few long seconds before I was able to get back in step for the finale.

Pulcinella absolutely exhausted me, but when I thought about it, I realized that there were few ballets that didn't tire me out. I attribute this to my personality, to the fact that I am an athletic dancer, that I use every ounce of energy at my disposal for the ballet.

One of the highlights of the ballet was that Mr. B and Jerry appeared in it at the premiere playing beggars. Dressed up in their tattered costumes, they did an enchanting dance, leaping and stumbling around, hitting each other with canes. The audience loved it, and so did the dancers. Seeing Jerry and Mr. B. onstage was a thrill.

I received two great compliments on my performance in *Pulcinella*. The first was from Eugene Berman. He autographed one of his designs and inscribed it "To Edward Villella, the great Pulcinella (truly great), with admiration and friendship." He also told me I was the best Pulcinella he had ever seen. I was embarrassed but happy to hear it.

After the performance I received another compliment. Stanley was outside my dressing room door. He had been a great character dancer, and as soon as he saw me, he began to

243

imitate my movements as Pulcinella as I came along the corridor. He didn't say a word, but he was telling me with his body just how much he thought I had achieved.

Their praise was deeply satisfying and meaningful to me, and I cherished it, but something had occurred during the curtain call that had made me reel and I was still feeling the effect. I had gone out in front of the curtain for a call with Jerry and Mr. B. I was holding my mask in my hand. Suddenly, as we were bowing in front of the curtain, Balanchine turned to me. He reached over and kissed me on the cheek in front of the audience.

In 1972, I traveled with the company for a return visit to the Soviet Union. I had little interest in making the trip, but I felt obliged to join the tour. Jerry had asked me personally to appear in *Dances at a Gathering* there, and I didn't want to turn him down. However, in his usual way, shortly after we arrived, he began casting Helgi Tomasson in my role. You can imagine how happy that made me.

I was miserable in the Soviet Union; nothing had changed since my last dreary visit. I felt like a veteran returning to an old battlefield.

In Leningrad, a young Russian boy of sixteen attached himself to the company. I can't remember his name, and I never knew much about him, but he seemed like a normal teenager. He spoke only a few words of English, but made himself helpful to us running errands. He took us to restaurants that foreigners didn't know about and showed us where to buy fresh produce without waiting on line. A devoted ballet fan, he loved hanging around the theater, fraternizing with the dancers. He watched rehearsals and attended every performance. But the Soviet authorities felt he was becoming too friendly with us and warned him repeatedly to stay away.

At the start of the tour, Gelsey and I and a few other dancers decided to pay a visit to Valery Panov, the Jewish dancer who'd been forced out of the Kirov Ballet because of his activities as a dissident. He was relegated by the government to the status of a nonperson. An international committee of concerned citizens, including dance writers and critics, was attempting to secure Panov's exit visa, and Panov was eager to

244

meet with us. He wanted to maintain visibility in the West: he was afraid he was going to be forgotten outside the USSR. He took a few of us back to his tiny apartment, which was not much bigger than a walk-in closet. Ballet barres lined the walls of the room so he and his wife, Galina, could give themselves class, and this makeshift studio was one of the most distressing sights I'd ever seen.

As we had arrived at the apartment building, I had noticed that we were under surveillance. A man wearing a leather trench coat stood at one end of the corridor and watched us go up the stairs. Inside the flat, Panov showed us the bug in his telephone. Gelsey and I and the other visitors gave him a few gifts, a bottle of scotch, a nylon shirt, everyday items hard to come by in Russia. A record album was still worth a lot of money in the Soviet Union, and the whiskey could buy enough rubles on the black market for a person to live on for a month.

Panov came to the theater to watch me dance, and we agreed to meet during the intermission. The custom in Leningrad is to promenade during intervals. People strolled around the theater, and Panov and I walked about together.

"Aren't you concerned about being seen with me?" I asked.

"I want to be seen," he said. "It keeps me alive."

More than ever, the country seemed like a prison. At close range I was watching someone be systematically terrorized, and it had a demoralizing effect on me. I thought about Panov constantly, but felt there was little I could do.

One afternoon after a rehearsal at the theater, I climbed onto the bus that was waiting to take us to the hotel and stretched out across the backseat. I was exhausted, about to doze off. Then I heard a commotion outside: the sound of cars screeching to a standstill. I got up and looked out the window. Scores of policemen, the army, and the militia in brown and blue uniforms were converging on the square, piling into every entrance of the theater. Then a large unmarked truck with bars across its windows careened to a halt in the street. The back door opened and a half dozen burly men poured out. They were dressed in leather coats or jackets and had crew cuts. As they made their way to the theater, each man was putting on a pair of leather gloves.

245

EDWARD VILLELLA

For a few minutes nothing happened. All of us were confused, but suddenly the group of men in the leather jackets came out with the sixteen-year-old boy who had befriended us. He had been hiding somewhere in the bowels of the theater, and they found him. He was being dragged to the truck, but his feet barely touched the ground. His face was beet red, and he was wailing. Right below us outside the bus they began beating him below his shoulders, and then they threw him bodily into the back of the truck. From inside the bus I could see through the barred windows. The kid was being bounced off the walls, jerked back and forth and up and down, and he was doubled over in pain. It was a horrible scene to witness, and I had nightmares about it every night for the next two weeks.

In a rage, I started to scream out a protest. I slammed my arm against the back window of the bus, trying to bash it open, but I only succeeded in raising a welt on my forearm that ran from my elbow to my wrist. Within seconds it began to swell. Some of the other dancers tried to pull me away. Now the interpreters assigned to the company piled onto the bus, and they tried to calm me down.

"You see, he violated a rule of the theater. You're never supposed to be on the stage," one of them said.

"Nonsense," I shouted. "A sixteen-year-old kid, and you call out the army and the secret police because he's watching a rehearsal!"

"You don't understand—"

"This is nonsense!"

It took me hours to calm down. Back in my room, I was heartsick. I felt that I didn't want to stay in the country a minute longer, and I said to myself, I'm getting out of here. That's what I'm going go do. I'm going to leave! The first people I notified were the interpreters, and they tried to dissuade me. But you haven't been to Moscow yet. They remember you there from ten years ago, everyone is talking about seeing you again. That encore, they said. They went on like this endlessly, but I couldn't be persuaded. I told them, I won't go there. I won't dance in this country.

Then I went to see Balanchine. I told him how I felt, what I wanted to do. I said, "This country horrifies me. I can't stay in a place where they treat people this way." I don't know how

246

persuasive I was. I was just pleading with him, saying, get me out of here. I want to get out of here. He listened intently, and he wasn't pleased. I'm sure like everyone else he thought I was being overemotional and hysterical.

After a moment he said, "If you feel you have to go, go."

I thanked him and left. As soon as I could, I contacted the American embassy representative who had been assigned to us and asked her to return my passport. The woman was unsympathetic and refused to help me. "We're not going to give you your passport back," she said.

"You can't keep me here against my will, you have no right to retain my passport," I shouted at her, and threatened to make an international fuss and embarrass the embassy staff. I presume she discussed it with her superior because a few hours later she met with me and told me I could have my passport, but said that the embassy would not aid in my departure. I thought, the hell with you. I'll get out myself.

I tried to make my own arrangements to return to New York and became ensnarled in Soviet red tape. I was told it was impossible to get on a flight, but that I was to wait in my room for a phone call in case of a cancellation. I waited for three days. Nothing happened. I decided to change my strategy—and my itinerary. I knew that Stanley was guest-teaching at Stockholm's Royal Theater, and I decided to visit him. Instead of hassling with airline officials on the telephone, I checked out of my hotel, traveled out to the airport, and tried to get on the first flight to Sweden.

The SAS desk was manned by a suspicious Russian who searched for my reservation with a skeptical air. I repeated my name over and over, hoping to bluff my way into a seat, but of course he couldn't find my reservation and told me there was no room on the plane. I threw a fit and started shouting that I had an engagement to dance in Sweden, that I was going to lose money if I didn't show up. I demanded to get on a flight. The agent turned to an airline employee for help, and this man inspected my passport and my visa. By a miracle, he found a seat on a plane that was going to leave in a few hours. I was instructed where to place my luggage for customs inspection and directed into a room for passport control. I couldn't believe I'd pulled it off.

The windows of passport control were barred, and the   247

immigration officers were surrounded by armed guards. I broke into a cold sweat. But my passport was stamped and I was told to return to the waiting room. I felt some relief and tried to calm down, but after a few moments I heard my name being paged. I was escorted back into the room with the barred windows and surrounded by four men in jackboots. My luggage was inside.

"Is that yours?" I was asked.

"Yes."

"'Why did you place it on that bin?"

"I was told to."

"You placed it in the wrong bin," the official barked at me. "Open it, please."

They examined the contents of my suitcases, took everything out, and emptied the pockets of my clothes. They acted as if I were smuggling something out of the country. I didn't think they would let me leave. I could see I was being intentionally terrorized, interrogated like a political prisoner. I felt unprotected, lost, and scared to death.

"Listen, I'm a citizen of the United States," I finally said. "You can't do this to me. I'm a principal dancer with the New York City Ballet—"

"Balletski?" One of the officers smiled. They seemed a little more respectful and sympathetic but continued to go through my belongings. At last they let me go. This time I carried my luggage with me and gave it to an airline attendant to be checked. My heart was beating, and I waited for my flight to be announced.

I boarded a bus that took passengers onto the tarmac. On the top of the staircase at the entrance door of the plane stood an armed soldier. One by one passengers mounted the stairs and displayed their passports and visas. The soldier compared each visa and passport photo against photos he had in his possession and only then let the travelers board the aircraft. Having gone through customs, immigration and passport control, passengers were subjected to one final humiliating inspection.

On the plane I began to relax, but I wasn't comfortable until we taxied onto the runway, took off, and left Soviet airspace. I was happy to be out of that country, so giddy with joy that I concocted a silly practical joke to play on Stanley.

248

At the airport in Stockholm I cleared customs, hailed a cab, tossed my luggage onto the backseat, and told the driver to wait. I knew the hotel Stanley was staying in and I telephoned his room.

"Stanley, it's me!" I cried, pretending to be scared. I guess I wanted him to know how frightened I had been at the Russian airport. "Whatever you do, don't hang up, just don't hang up! I'm in Leningrad. You can't believe what I've been going through, it's the most incredible nightmare. But if anything happens, if we get disconnected, don't hang up. It's harassment and they'll reconnect the line. Don't hang up!"

I didn't give him a chance to say a word, and I put down the phone. I raced to the taxi, gave the driver the address of Stanley's hotel, and told him to drive as quickly as he could. I assumed that the city was only fifteen minutes from the airport, but I was mistaken. It took me over an hour to get to the hotel. Stanley opened the door to his room, bleary-eyed and red-faced. He had met an old friend the day before, they'd spent the night on the town, and he'd only been asleep a few hours when he got my call. He had a tremendous hangover. The phone was still off the hook, and I think he'd been holding on all the time. Now, of course, he figured it all out. I apologized profusely, but it took him a day or two before he started speaking to me.

EDWARD VILLELLA

SEVENTEEN

I had always planned to dance until I was forty-two. I had joined the New York City Ballet when I was twenty-one, and the idea of staying with the company for twenty-one years and then retiring sometime around my forty-second birthday struck a nice balance in my mind. I liked the symmetry of it. But in 1973, at the age of thirty-six, it began to look as if I wasn't going to make it.

My bad back was growing steadily worse. The pain was never-ending. Over the years, Dr. William Hamilton, the company's orthopedic consultant, had become increasingly alarmed about my condition. At one point, he x-rayed my spine and vertebrae from various angles to see if there had been a significant deterioration in my condition. After looking at the results he called me into his office and with a somber expression told me that he was extremely unhappy with what he saw. He wanted me to curtail my New York City Ballet performances, and my concert dates. He even suggested that I think about winding down my career. He said my back couldn't endure much more strain, and he told me flat out, "Eddie, you're crazy to continue dancing. It'll be a life of nothing but pain."

Despite his prognosis, I refused to consider his option—I would not stop dancing. It was totally out of the question. I still had things left undone.

A dancer is likely to gain profound understanding and ar-

250

tistic maturity just as his physical instrument becomes less and less able to express the insight and knowledge he has attained. There is a moment, however, when a dancer's physicality and his artistic ability converge, and a kind of perfect integration occurs. I felt I was approaching that point, and I had no intention of allowing old familiar injuries put me out of commission. I decided to confront the situation head-on, embarking on a period of intensive therapy that I hoped would cure the problems with my back once and for all—or even for just a little more time. I wanted my last years to be the culmination of all the hard work I had done.

Bill Hamilton was frankly skeptical. He believed my back problems were irreversible, but I was determined. I took six months off from dancing and began a regimen based on my mother's treatment of her arthritis problems: natural foods, juices, and megadoses of vitamins. I soaked in kosher-salt whirlpool baths, did Pilates exercises with a vengeance, and worked with my chiropractor. I took muscle relaxants, got a massage every day, and swam. I worked out regularly at the gym—and *never* went to ballet class! In the process I could feel my body rebuilding itself and healing. Slowly the strength returned to my back. After six months I was in good enough shape to take class again, and not long after I started going to class I felt I was ready to perform.

As soon as the new season got under way, I was cast to dance in *Agon*. Wearing my costume and makeup, I was on my way down the stairs to warm up in the wings when I saw Dr. Hamilton. He did a double take and stared at me in disbelief.

"Eddie! What are you doing here?"

"*Agon,*" I said with a grin.

"But I wrote your career off six months ago!"

"Yeah," I said. "I didn't."

He shook his head in pleasure and watched me go out onstage and perform. His pleasure was icing on the cake—I was ecstatic. I felt completely rejuvenated—at the height of my powers, dancing not only *Agon,* but "Rubies," *Brahms-Schoenberg Quartet,* and *Tchaikovsky Pas de Deux.* I never felt better in my life. I had achieved tremendous control over my body and felt that my technique had actually improved. My lifts were effortless. In fact, I raised Patty so high in the air with such

251

speed and force in the *Tchaikovsky* that I was actually able to support her with only one arm. I managed to reproduce the feat every time I danced it. I'd be running across the stage performance after performance executing one-handed lifts to my own and the audience's astonishment. I was able to lower her with one hand as well. I had a new sense of myself and for a brief time felt indestructible. My strength and power had returned and so had my enthusiasm. I resumed my usual schedule, dancing ferociously, all over the country. My back didn't give me any trouble.

Then I noticed a nagging pain, an ache and stiffness on the inside of my right thigh, and a loss of mobility in my right hip. Most of the time I could live with it. I tried not to think about it. Once I warmed up, it seemed to go away, and if necessary I could force the movement in my hip to achieve my effects. But the pain never really entirely disappeared, and it began keeping me up at night. After a while it was clear that it was getting worse and worse, and though I continued to dance, some days I couldn't move my thigh. I could barely get out of a taxi now or the backseat of a car. I couldn't really raise my leg by itself and had to grab the inside of my trouser leg to lift my limb and place my foot outside the cab on the street before I could stand on my feet to get up and out.

I assumed the discomfort I felt in my leg and my hip was a recurrence of my old back problem. I felt resigned to it and more or less learned to live with the pain. I continued dancing, but the newfound euphoria was short-lived, gone. I spent most of 1974 eliminating roles from my repertory. My City Ballet appearances were restricted to *Watermill* and *Afternoon of a Faun,* but I danced excerpts from *Apollo* in concert appearances. I was frustrated. I longed to dance "Rubies" or *Donizetti Variations,* but the risk involved was too great. I felt I was marking time until the end of my career, but Balanchine hadn't given up on me. At the end of the year I learned he was going to use me in a new ballet to music by Ravel.

Three years after the phenomenally successful New York City Ballet Stravinsky Festival, Balanchine decided to stage a tribute to the French composer Maurice Ravel, and in 1975 the company put on a Ravel Festival very much in the style of the

252

1972 Stravinsky celebration. Balanchine choreographed a number of ballets for the occasion. The new one for Kay Mazzo and me was called *Shéhérazade*. Kay Mazzo was one of Balanchine's loveliest dancers, a dark-eyed beauty, easy to work with, always good-humored. Onstage she had a Dresden-like delicacy, and she danced that way with purity and clarity.

I didn't feel that *Shéhérazade* was one of Mr. B's major efforts. In fact, I don't think the festival on the whole achieved the level of the Stravinsky enterprise, although some wonderful ballets were created for it, such as Balanchine's *Le Tombeau de Couperin* and Jerry's *In G Major*. The pain I experienced as we worked on *Shéhérazade* worried me. Dancing it was very painful. I felt agony each time I tried to move, and by the night of the second performance my hip hurt so much that I didn't think I was going to be able to dance.

I asked Peter Schaufuss, my understudy, if he could go on for me. Schaufuss, a Dane, had recently joined the company as a principal. He said he simply didn't know the ballet well enough to substitute for me. I was hurt and distressed by Schaufuss's refusal. I thought his attitude was not only ungenerous, but also unprofessional. I went on that night, but I was barely able to complete the performance. The extent of my pain acutely interfered with my ability to dance. When the curtain came down, I was worried what the performance had done to my future.

In late spring 1975, President Gerald Ford invited Violette and me to dance at the White House during a state dinner honoring the prime minister of Singapore. I had danced at the White House many times in my career and was delighted to attend. Violette and I decided to perform the pas de deux from *Le Corsaire*. We flew to Washington on the day of the event and spent most of the afternoon rehearsing. As always, we had to adapt the choreography to the peculiar dimensions of the stage in the East Room. It was hard to avoid crashing into the large, ornate crystal chandelier suspended from the ceiling right over the performing platform. All that could be done was to move around the fixture, but on more than one occasion, despite my built-in radar, I had grazed my head during a variation.

Toward the end of the rehearsal, Mrs. Ford came by to watch. She had studied modern dance before she married and

253

was interested in ballet. We did the entire pas de deux full out for her, and she applauded enthusiastically when we were done. She thanked us and told us she was also looking forward to seeing us as her guests at the dinner.

State dinners at the White House are glamorous affairs. The company always made me feel important. The food was great, but Violette and I had to excuse ourselves to put on our makeup, warm up again, get into our costumes, and deliver a performance.

I'd already done the basic warm-up at my hotel. After years of doing concert dates and guest appearances with symphony orchestras and dancing in such places as the Soviet Union where conditions are cramped and uncomfortable, I'd developed a method of warming up in my hotel room. I knew from experience that there was no space in which to prepare adequately for a performance at the White House and so had already completed my routine before leaving for dinner.

My spirits were high that night even though the pain in my thigh was bothering me. It hurt like hell, in fact. I had tried to put it out of my mind when I warmed up and while I ate, but onstage during the adagio the pain got worse. And as I took a flying leap off the stage during the coda, a sharp jab in my right hip made me gasp out loud. I doubled over in pain in the wings. I thought I was going to pass out, but the pain subsided, and I was actually able to get up, go out and bow, and then change into my clothes. Later, in spite of a burning sensation in my hip, I jitterbugged with Mrs. Ford at the reception.

Back in my hotel room, however, drying myself after a shower, I felt the sharp jab in my hip socket with a new force that took my breath away. A searing red pain shot through me, and I grabbed on to the bathroom sink to keep from falling. I tried to calm myself by inhaling deeply and moving toward the bed, but the pain was excruciating: it felt as if the bone of my leg had actually penetrated my hip socket, impaling the socket on the tip of the bone. I massaged my thigh to ease the pain, but it made no difference. The pain was beyond the reach of my hands, running up the center of my leg, inside the bone.

I took a deep breath and held it, slowly making my way to the bed where I collapsed in agony. As I tried to find a

254

comfortable position, I realized that I couldn't rotate my leg in my hip socket. The leg wouldn't move. It was as if it were locked at the hip and the pain locked inside of that. I couldn't even imagine what could cause this kind of pain—I couldn't recognize it. I lifted my leg with both hands and turned my whole body onto my side with that motion. Lying there, with Washington night noises sounding through the window, the screech of brakes and car exhausts, and late-night revelers laughing in the hotel corridor, I lay awake until dawn.

At six A.M., I pushed myself up in bed with my arms and swung my body over the side like an invalid who'd been bed-ridden for months and had lost the use of his limbs—a terrifying thought for a dancer. I sat on the edge of the mattress while a new wave of red pain swept over me. Driven by fear, I managed to dress, check out of the hotel, and hail a cab to the airport. Somehow I got myself onto the first shuttle to New York. Thinking that Bill Hamilton would surely do something to help me was the only thing that made the plane ride bearable.

By nine-thirty I was in his office. He listened intently as I described in detail what had happened. Then he took X rays. I'll never forget the look on his face when he called me into his conference room and we looked at the two sets of X rays together. He shook his head and pointed.

"See this dark area here? Those are shadows around your hip socket." He turned to face me. "Eddie, it's not good. It's the end of your career."

"What . . . ?" My first thought was that we'd been through this before. But the look on his face chilled me. He took a breath and slowly explained what was causing the pain. The head of the femur, the thigh bone, rests in the hip socket. The leg is able to rotate evenly in the socket because the socket is lined with cartilage and this cushions the bone. But either because of a congenital deformity or, more likely, because of my back injury, which had been aggravated by years of jumping and landing on hard surfaces, something had changed the angle of rotation of my leg in the socket. As I continued to dance and jump, the bone had continued to rotate unevenly, and over the years the cartilage had worn away.

Bill was certain now that the pain in my leg and hip during the last few years had been the result of the limited rotation in

255

EDWARD VILLELLA

the socket; he was sure that the last bits of cartilage had worn away in Washington, first during the pas de deux and later in the shower in my room. In fact, because of my back pain, I had been unconsciously putting more pressure on my right hip than my left one for a long time. My cartilage would have worn away even if I had retired when he told me to. The excruciating pain I was now experiencing, like a white-hot poker jamming into my hip every time I shifted my body, resulted from bone on bone—pain that was the equivalent of a broken leg. Short of surgery, little could be done about it. The bones were locked. I had no rotation in my hip, and every time I moved, the bones rubbed against each other, surfaces tearing and scraping away.

"I'm afraid you're going to have to have an operation," Bill said. "For now I'm going to start you on four Percodans a day to ease the pain."

I stared at Bill dumbly. I felt certain of one thing only. "No surgery. I'll do anything before surgery. I cured my back and I'll do something to help with this."

Bill shook his head. "I'm going to refer you to a hip specialist, a Dr. Stenchfield at Columbia Presbyterian."

He explained that Stenchfield, a leading doctor in the field, used a surgical procedure that involved cutting six to eight inches of bone off the top of the femur, and replacing it with a steel head. The hip socket is then removed, and a steel shield lined with plastic instead of cartilage is inserted in its place. The operation had been designed for the elderly.

In a daze, I made an appointment with the doctor and saw him in his office in the Atchley Pavilion. Stenchfield was remote and uncommunicative. An eminent member of the American Medical Association, a top man in his profession, he was seeing me as a favor to Bill. He looked at the X rays, and talking to me between phone calls, he bluntly stated his opinion.

"Typical halfback injury," he said. "You're going to have to find something else to do with yourself because you certainly aren't ever going to dance again."

I don't remember leaving his office. I recall that the day was gray, but even if the sun had been shining, it would have been gray. I walked along Riverside Drive dragging my leg and

256

tried to take in what he'd told me: one day I had been a world-class dancer and the next I was an invalid. I needed time to understand it, come to grips with it, time to be alone. I wished I could have walked home but that was impossible, and I didn't want to take a taxi so I boarded a bus. I didn't want to get anywhere, and certainly not fast. I sat in the back and rode all the way down the Drive. I remember watching the people around me moving with ease, taking their mobility for granted. Movement had been the most important element of my life, and now it was all over. I didn't know what to do. I was booked in advance for at least two years of concert performances.

I got to Bill's office and told him what Stenchfield had said. He was sympathetic but not surprised.

"You know, Eddie," he said. "I think we ought to tell Mr. B what has happened."

I immediately felt the wisdom of his remark; it was as if Balanchine, maker of miracles, might have a solution. I felt I couldn't face him alone and I asked Bill to accompany me. We found Mr. B at the theater and engaged him in casual conversation. He was feeling very chatty, he seemed to want just to talk. Finally Bill said, "Mr. Balanchine, we have something to tell you."

Balanchine furrowed his brow and looked at me oddly.

"Mr. B!" I blurted out. "I can't dance anymore. My career is over."

For a moment, he didn't move, and then he started to shake his head in disbelief. Bill started to explain the situation.

"No, no, no, no, no . . ." he muttered as he listened. He was visibly shaken and reached out to touch me. He had never expressed his concern for me in such human terms before. I could barely speak. He wanted to know all the technical details of my condition and what the options were. Suddenly he turned to me.

"Maybe is all for best. At least you stop when you dance well. People remember you at height of powers, at best."

What he said was tremendously painful for an instant, but as I thought about it later, it had a kind of healing effect.

After I left the theater I telephoned Janet Roberts. I wanted to make an announcement to the press that I was going to stop

257

EDWARD VILLELLA

dancing, but Janet told me to take my time, to reflect on my situation. With the painkillers that Bill was going to prescribe and rest and recuperation, she thought possibly I could function in a limited fashion and perhaps perform *Watermill* or *Afternoon of a Faun*, maybe even *Apollo*. I wasn't sure—I could barely walk—but I decided to take her advice, to slow down for the first time in my life and wait and see.

It was during this period that I also consulted a psychiatrist, not because of my physical difficulties but because of my feelings about the failure of my marriage. I also felt that I needed to learn more about myself. A friend recommended a doctor, whom I worked with over a period of months. After that length of time, I felt strong enough to try to plan the rest of my life—whatever that was going to be.

Some months after my grim consultation with Dr. Stench-field, as I rested and thought about the future, I got a letter and then a phone call from Ted Mann, a Broadway producer and the director of the Circle in the Square Theatre. He was planning a revival of Rodgers and Hart's 1940 musical *Pal Joey,* and he wanted me to play the title role.

The show has a wonderfully witty, sophisticated score and is something of a cult favorite. I was intrigued and tempted and the timing was right. I was no longer a classical dancer, but on a regimen of painkillers and with a considerable amount of effort and will, it seemed likely that I could perform the movements required for the role. Still, I had grave doubts. I was no singer. I'd always been the butt of people's jokes whenever I tried to sing, and I was self-conscious about my voice. I never even sang in the shower and had only sung professionally once before, playing a small role in a summer-stock production of the musical *Carnival*. I felt that starring as a singer in a Broadway show would be presumptuous of me. But friends encouraged me to take the part, and even Balanchine thought it was a good idea. I gave in.

Things didn't go well with the production from the start, and I realized how fortunate I had been to have spent most of my professional life in the privileged environment of the New York City Ballet. There I always had a clear sense of what I was doing and how the piece we were working on was coming

258

together. I wasn't getting that feeling with *Pal Joey*. At the first run-through it was obvious that the show wasn't working. And in fact, both Balanchine and Jerry offered to help. Mr. B actually choreographed my number that closed the first act, and Jerry spent a week staging the rest of the musical numbers. But the problems persisted. And as my concerns about the production mounted, my costar, Eleanor Parker, the Hollywood film actress, was having difficulties of her own with the show.

Pal Joey was a difficult experience for me, and I left the production before it opened. So did Eleanor Parker, Gene Palumbo—the music director—and several others. I felt that I should never have gone against my instincts by agreeing to take the part. I began to wonder what was waiting for me. Was there going to be a second life?

EDWARD VILLELLA

EIGHTEEN

After my hip gave out, I was virtually without means of earning a living. It was a disaster. I could barely walk, let alone dance a classical pas de deux or appear on television. Before the injury had gotten so bad, appearances on the "Carol Burnett Show" and the TV series "The Odd Couple" had given me extra money when I needed it for alimony and child support payments. I'd also conceived and produced a CBS television special called "Harlequin" and won an Emmy for it. But I still had to sell the stocks and bonds I owned and the various art objects I'd collected to meet my bills. I had also danced with symphony orchestras all over America and in Europe. But in 1976, the only money I had was what I was paid as a member of the New York City Ballet.

I don't think I can ever express my gratitude to the New York City Ballet for keeping me on salary for those years in the late 1970s. I will forever be indebted to Balanchine, Lincoln, and Betty Cage for their kindness and understanding. That kind of magnanimous gesture was typical of the attitude of the company toward its dancers, and it sustained me during the most difficult days of my life. The money wasn't enough to cover all of my bills, but it gave me a base from which to exist. I was able to collect some insurance money and tax rebates in order to help me live, but because of the amount I had to pay

260

out every month, I was devastated. I used to limit myself to a personal budget of five dollars a week. A bowl of soup was my main meal of the day.

I was now virtually a cripple, a physical wreck. I was close to despair. Simple acts such as walking and sitting in a chair were extremely difficult and painful for me now. In order to be comfortable sitting down, I had to hold myself at an angle so that my torso, hip, and thigh were all in a straight line. To maintain this position for any length of time was wearying. It was sometimes comfortable to stretch my left leg out, but this was awkward in restaurants because waiters and patrons could trip over it. Getting up was also a trial, and so humiliating that I desperately tried not to call attention to my struggle. I'd place my palms either on a tabletop or on the arms of a chair and push up hard enough so that I could lift my weight. Once I was on my feet, it took me a few moments to get steady, and it often seemed to me as if the process took a full ten minutes.

Walking was even more of an agony. I had to drag my right leg with me every time I took a step, and with each step searing pain shot up the length of my limb into my hip. I'd try to distance myself from the pain, but the strain showed on my face. I was worn out. I'd reached the point where I wasn't able to walk more than half a New York City block without stopping for a rest, and I couldn't get across Broadway during the time it took for a single green traffic light to lapse. I had to time my movements to make it to the other side of the street during the length of two lights, stopping to rest halfway on the tree-lined dividing mall when the light changed and the traffic flowed. I felt so humiliated. My chiropractor, Dr. Carnival, suggested that I throw my knee out ahead of me as I walked as a way of disguising the limp. Eventually I had to use a cane. Even so, walking ate up what little energy I had, and I was beat for most of the day. But I couldn't really sleep comfortably at night either and replenish myself.

As physically painful as this was, the real pain was the indignity of it all, the overwhelming sense I had that I was an invalid. People who had seen me for years bounding up Broadway and taking stairs two steps at a time now saw this pitiful figure limping and hobbling along like an aged creature. I think many people empathized with my situation, but many others

261

EDWARD VILLELLA

didn't know how to deal with it and simply decided not to see me anymore. Dragging my leg along Broadway, I'd often see people I knew. When they'd catch sight of me out of the corner of their eye, they'd either duck into a side street, cross the road, or step up their pace and pretend they didn't see me. I was embarrassed by my condition and hurt by their reaction. But I wasn't really comfortable seeing people either. At first I withdrew from the company, and then I began to retreat from the world, becoming something of a recluse.

Bill Hamilton tried to intervene. He kept insisting that I have surgery, but it sounded so primitive that I still refused.

"I'm going to try to see if I can help myself my own way," I told him.

From 1976 until 1979, I looked into every possible cure, traveling all over the country as well as to Europe to see if some help was available for me, but nothing I found seemed to work. I tried acupuncture, Rolfing, yoga, all kinds of massages. I had painkillers injected directly into the bone. One doctor came up with a novel treatment, bombarding me with massive doses of calcium by injecting me with the mineral. Then he abruptly shut off the supply by discontinuing the shots. He hoped that my body, having become used to the excess of calcium in my system and craving it, would draw on the calcium nodes that had collected on the head of my femur and were causing me such pain, thus breaking them up. This would, of course, alleviate my suffering. I never did find out if this treatment had a scientific basis, but like all the other things I tried, it was of no use.

Occasionally Bill sent information about miracle cures for arthritis in the hip and news of the latest in hip replacement operations, and I was touched by his concern. I even consulted a mystic who lived in Long Island and for two weeks walked along the beach every morning at dawn with her paying homage to the rising sun. I felt like an idiot but was willing to give anything a chance. Standing on the shore, I stretched my body skyward, but instead of feeling a connection to the cosmos, all I felt was the damn pain in my leg.

Attending a New York City Ballet performance was tremendously depressing and painful. A year went by before I was able to go. When I finally saw a performance of *Prodigal Son,* I

262

felt as if I were being eaten alive with envy. I would have been happy to appear as one of the drinking companions. In 1977 I was able to return to the stage in *Afternoon of a Faun, Watermill,* and sections of *Apollo,* but I didn't really dance these roles as much as stumble through them, disguising my inabilities. My technique was barely adequate, and the experience wasn't satisfactory from any point of view.

At the time of the injury I had been booked for a number of concert dates, and I foolhardily tried to keep one or two of them. In Houston I actually danced a performance of *Prodigal Son* after receiving seventeen injections from a local doctor to ease my pain. To this day I don't know what he gave me, but I got through the performance. It was an experience I don't ever want to repeat.

Through all of this I was desperate to hold on to the sense of myself as a dancer, and I tried to maintain my physicality. Every morning I did a barefoot barre in the dressing room of the bedroom in my brownstone in which there was a large mirror, and I'd try to work as long as I could, for more than an hour, because when I was finished, I wasn't sure of what to do next. I literally had nothing to do with myself and was desperate to fill up my day with some activity. After the *Pal Joey* experience I tried to think seriously about a new career that would appeal to me, but no matter what I decided on, I saw that it would take time to set up, and I needed something to do *now.* If I picked up a phone and said to someone, "Hey, I'd like to teach," or, "Do you know of a lecture date?" invariably people would say, "Fine, call us next season and we'll set something up."

Janet Roberts and I discussed the possibility of scheduling a special performance that would formally mark my retirement from dancing, but since I felt helpless and the object of everyone's pity as it was, I couldn't bring myself to do that. I wanted a quiet, orderly transition, a *Faun* here and another one there, and then I'd just quietly disappear.

One of the mainstays of my life at this time was the relationship I formed with Susan Hendl, who was an NYCB soloist. Balanchine was fond of her. He had respected her father, Walter Hendl, a well-known musician and conductor. Susie was one of Mr. B's "women"—tall, blond, and thin. She had

263

a "drop dead" figure. I got the feeling that Mr. B objected to my dating her, but he never told me so directly.

Susie provided me with wonderful, womanly companionship during this dark period, and I remember fondly some terrific times we had together. I owe her a continuing debt. One night Balanchine invited us to his house for dinner. This, after all the years, was the first time I'd been invited for a meal in his home. The other guests were Edward Bigelow and Karin von Aroldingen and her husband. Eddie Bigelow was a former NYCB dancer who served as a kind of general factotum for Balanchine. Mr. B made a delicious meal and served expensive red wine and Taittinger's champagne.

Balanchine had knocked down the walls in his apartment to turn his living room, dining room, and kitchen into one large space. Inside the kitchen area was a big counter at which he prepared meals for his guests. That evening, he scraped, chopped, and cooked all the ingredients as he entertained us with witty anecdotes and charming stories.

The apartment was spare, underdecorated except for basic necessities. Alongside the counter, however, was a big, round, formal dining room table where dinner was served. There was a beautiful armoire in the room, too, which Mr. B had painted himself in an Italianate, floral design. Tucked away in a closet was a large refrigerator/locker that served as a wine cellar. The locker was a gift from the company. We had all chipped in to buy it for him because we knew how much he loved good wine. Cases from Sherry-Lehmann were always being delivered; it seemed as if Mr. B had hundreds of bottles of wine in the apartment.

In 1977 I flew to England to confer with a doctor, a Greek osteopath living in London who had been able to help severely injured dancers. He'd been credited with saving Peter Schaufuss's career, and I decided to see what he had to say. I stayed in London for five weeks and worked with him.

While I was there, I received a telephone call from a television producer who was putting together a special, starring Dorothy Hamill, the Olympic ice-skating champion who was also a star of the Ice Capades. He wanted me to participate, to dance on the show. I explained that I was no longer a bravura

264

dancer and that I didn't really know anything about ice-skating. That was okay, he said, and he asked if I would be willing to choreograph the dances. I turned him down.

When I returned to New York, he called again. He told me their cameraman was a former hockey star who could skate backward and forward with equal facility and that he would be using a Steadicam to shoot the show. The Steadicam is a device used frequently in Hollywood. The camera, attached to a harness worn by the cameraman, is suspended and balanced in the air so that it remains in place no matter what jerky movements the cameraman makes. I was fascinated by the technique. It was perfect for filming on ice, and my resistance began to wear down.

I was also offered the services of an assistant on the show, a woman who had worked with Dorothy Hamill in the past, named Linda Engel. A former Canadian national figure-skating champion, she'd competed in the Olympics and had also appeared in the Ice Capades. I was still saying no, but yielded when I heard how much money they were offering. I could sustain myself for months on such a princely sum, so I agreed to meet with the producers and the woman who would become my assistant. They flew in from California.

I hadn't thought about it much, but I had expected the assistant to be an older, out-of-shape, overweight woman. I pictured her dressed in a short skating dress taken in at the waist, wearing brown woolen stockings and white gloves, and looking like an aging Sonja Henie. Engel, the woman's name, somehow contributed to this image. When I entered the room, however, I was introduced to a beautiful blonde, a petite woman who was frankly gorgeous, and my interest was immediately aroused. I almost let out a sigh.

"I'm Edward Villella," I said. "Who are you?"

"Linda Carbonetto. I'm your assistant." Engel was her married name, she said, but I soon found out she was separating from her husband.

I was immediately taken with her, and the more I got to know her as we worked together, the more things progressed. She seemed far more sensitive than anyone else I had ever met. She was smart, tenacious, honest, and open, and she didn't let anyone walk over her. We began spending more and more time

265

together, and when it came time for Linda to return to California, we were in love.

We both cried when she went home, and I felt that things couldn't have been worse. I was dead broke, a cripple, unsure of how to earn a living. We both thought we'd never see each other again. We telephoned each other constantly, and whenever I could, I flew out to L.A. I was beginning lecture dates now, and I always took a detour to visit Linda before returning to New York. Even if my fee for a lecture was only $150 plus airfare, I'd accept the engagement, say, in Dallas, fly out, deliver my talk, and then use the $150 to travel to L.A. and spend time with Linda. I did it over and over again, and we had great times together—we were deeply in love. It wasn't long before we decided that once Linda's divorce was final, we would be married.

Linda wanted me to move to Los Angeles after our wedding, but I was reluctant. I didn't think that L.A. was stimulating enough for me, and I tried to convince her to move to New York. She was against it. She was familiar only with her ex-husband's New York, which was the world of show business, and so I decided to show her mine. She flew east and we went everywhere in Manhattan. We went to the Maritime College in the Bronx and out to Bayside, and I showed her the neighborhood I had grown up in. Then I was struck with an idea.

"I'd like to show you where I first studied ballet."

We drove along Bell Boulevard and approached the building that had housed the Anne Garrison School of Dance. The first floor of the building was now occupied by a travel agent, and we went inside. The entrance to the second floor, where the ballet studio had been, seemed to have been walled up. A huge glass display case stood against what had been the old door.

I introduced myself to the people behind the desk and told them who I was. I was happy that they knew me, and they said they had often seen me dance. I told them how much I wanted to take another look at the studio where I had first taken ballet class. Was it still there? I wondered. They thought it was and were happy to help me move the display case. I pushed the door, now dusty and cracked with age, and it opened. I looked up the stairs and a shaft of sunlight was pouring through.

266

We all walked up the stairs together, Linda, the people from the travel agency, and me. At the landing was the bathroom where I used to change. To my right was the school's administrative office, and the area that had been the main studio was empty except for a radiator lying on its side on the floor. The partition that had separated the office from the studio was also lying on the floor, and we walked into the space. The floor was buckled, splintery, and the long, narrow mirrors that had lined the walls were stacked up at the far end of the room. The sight of the globelike fixtures hanging from the ceiling stirred a flood of memories. I stood quietly thinking about those days and marveled at how much smaller everything was than it had been in my memory.

Linda could see how moved I was. She hadn't realized yet how much I missed dance. She didn't really sympathize that much; her skating career had ended when she was twenty-one. But she soon came to understand my years of struggle and the disappointment. Visiting my old neighborhood helped to convince her to come to New York.

One of my worries about getting married again was that I was dead broke. I had been concerned that I wouldn't be able to support an ex-wife and a son as well as a new wife and a stepdaughter. And Linda and I were planning on having a child together as well. But we went ahead and made it legal.

Linda and I were married in New York City on May 24, 1980, in a quiet ceremony in my brownstone that was attended by family, a few friends, and Linda's five-year-old daughter, Lauren. But we threw a hell of a party afterward.

At first, Linda's father wasn't terribly enthusiastic about our getting married, and Linda told me later how vigorously he had voiced his objections about me when she first informed him of our relationship. "First a TV producer," he said to her, "and now a Ukrainian ballet dancer. What about someone normal?" "Don't worry," she answered. "He's Italian, Dad." She was trying to sell him on me, but also to tell him how compatible we were, that we were made for each other. I think it was true because all these years later, our relationship is still thriving.

Before I had gotten married again, I had decided to sue Janet for custody of Roddy. After several postponements, a

267

hearing was held and it looked as if I could win. As part of the process I consulted a psychiatrist. He told me he thought it was too late. Roddy was too old. Leaving his mother and moving into a new home wouldn't be in his best interest. I talked the situation over with my attorney Burton I. (Buddy) Monasch. Buddy represented me in my divorce and had become one of my closest friends. I agonized over my decision, but I dropped the case.

As time went by, I found it increasingly difficult to live with my physical problems. I'd been in pain for over five years, and at night I still couldn't sleep longer than two hours at a stretch. Rolling over in bed was so painful that it would wake me up, and I wouldn't fall off to sleep again for hours. It was taking a profound toll on me, and I had reached the point where I was drinking two bottles of wine a night to knock myself out. This was becoming a problem. And everything I had looked into to help me had come to nothing. I was adjusting to the fact that nothing was going to, and that I was never going to dance again, when Bill Hamilton telephoned me and told me about a new development in hip replacement surgery. He strongly recommended the operation and said the chances for success were high.

I said, "Bill, I'll tell you what. I need the operation now because I can't take the pain anymore. It's no way to live."

But something in me was still reluctant, and when Bill talked about setting up an appointment for the surgery, I told him I wanted to postpone it for a year, or at least until the surgeons had perfected the procedure even further. He thought I was mad, but went along with my decision. After I suffered for another year, hoping that the doctors would develop the next, best version of the operation, Bill called one day to say that they had. I said, "Okay, Bill. Let's do it."

The surgeons who performed the operation lived and worked in London, so I made plans to travel there and enter the hospital. I had to finance the trip by selling my car. Bill told me something about the operation that truly set my mind at ease. The New York City Ballet was going to be on a European tour performing in Copenhagen at the time of my surgery. He said he would take time off and fly to London so he could be

268

present in the operating room during the procedure. I was tremendously grateful.

Before I left for the trip I put most of my business in order, and I telephoned Roddy to tell him what was going to happen. Since he still lived with his mother, he and I hadn't had many opportunities to spend a lot of time together. It seemed as if we barely had a relationship, and the conversation started awkwardly.

"I've just got to tell you that I'm not going to be around for a while," I said. "I'm going to London to have an operation." I tried to explain to him what it was, but he was silent. Then he said, "I love you, Dad." He had never said this before.

Linda accompanied me to London for the operation, and she told me she had never seen anybody walk into a hospital for major surgery as blithely as I.

"You know, after all my reluctance," I said, "I'm kind of fatalistic. What am I going to do? It's in the hands of these professionals, and I have to believe in them."

The operation was performed in the London Clinic on Harley Street in the center of town. The procedure was a new development; the hip socket is lined with plastic and the head of the femur is shaved and a double steel cup is put over it. The way in which the head of the femur is inserted into the hip socket is crucial—it affects balance and the patient's ability to walk. Bill later told me something amusing that he had discussed with the surgeon prior to the operation regarding this step. "Now listen, when you're about to insert the bone," he said to the doctor, "why don't you give him just a little turn-out."

After surgery, as soon as I came to in the recovery room, drugged and dazed as I was, I was happy to see the faces of Linda and Bill hovering over me. In my stoned state I said to them, "I'm ready to dance 'Rubies.'" To this day they both contend that I was delirious, but I remember that I was just trying to be lighthearted.

The aftermath of the operation was brutal. My entire system shut down due to the anesthetic: I couldn't move. But the operation was deemed a success and my recovery was speedy. The day after surgery I was forced to stand on my feet and walk. I took four tiny steps, reached a wall, and passed out

269

onto the floor. The nurses lifted me up and got me back to bed, securing my leg and hip in place with a sandbag. I was then not allowed to move for five days. When I finally did move, I could tell that the inflammations had subsided because the pain in my hip had disappeared. I was overjoyed.

The English hospital staff nurses were extremely matter-of-fact, dispassionate, and cold and dry in their approach to the patient, but I have great affection for one. On the day she brought me my first meal, I sighed and made a joke. "Jesus," I said, "I'd love a beer to go with that."

"Why not?" she answered. "You certainly can have that."

"And red wine with dinner?"

"Yes, indeed," she said.

I was overcome with joy. I also loved being wheeled out on the veranda to gaze at the rooftops of London. A week or so after my surgery, a regimen of physiotherapy began. I walked around on crutches and found I was very mobile. Because my muscles were in good shape, my recovery was extremely rapid. I was released from the hospital within ten days, though I had to remain in London for three more weeks. Linda had returned to New York to be with Lauren. She was also very pregnant. After she left, I tried to enjoy myself in the city riding the underground, taking in theater, and seeing the sights.

When I returned to New York, I worked with Marika Molner, the New York City Ballet physiotherapist, who also contributed to the speed of my recovery. Today the operation that was performed on me is obsolete. At the time its positive effects were expected to last for about six years. But I'm very fortunate. More than eleven years have passed since the surgery was performed, and I still haven't had to undergo another operation.

In a short time I felt as if my recovery was complete. I could walk and move about with little pain, and I felt like my old self. I had another reason to be joyful. Linda gave birth to our daughter, Crista Francesca, on April 9, 1981, and the Sixty-ninth Street brownstone was now inhabited by a real family— Linda, Lauren, Crista, and me. My relationship with Linda gave me a firm base, and I was able to devote time now to

270

family life. I felt grown up and able to fulfill my role as a husband and a father. I was Dad for Lauren and Crista and I wanted to be a real father for Roddy.

As happy as I was, I continued to dwell on the end of my career and the romantic notion of privately saying good-bye to each of my roles. In one way I was lucky. If it hadn't been for my hip, I might have dragged myself around the stage like some of my colleagues, long, long after the time had come to gracefully give it up. I fully understand their desire and their passion, but I think they often do a disservice to the art form. Nonetheless, I wanted a private ritual that would mark the end of my career, and I started to take class again. Eventually Bill Hamilton found out about it and objected in the strongest terms possible. I told him not to worry, that I wouldn't be working for long.

In 1979 I had met Marcia Preiss, a talented arts organizer who began to book lecture demonstration dates for me across the country. She was also able to arrange master classes I conducted at several universities, and in 1981, she secured an engagement for me in the Hansher Auditorium at the University of Iowa. I would dance two performances of *Afternoon of a Faun* and *Apollo* with Gelsey Kirkland. As it happened, Gelsey dropped out a week before the scheduled dates, and New York City Ballet principal Heather Watts graciously filled in. These performances on November 13 and 14, 1981, formally marked the end of my life as a dancer (or so I thought at the time), for after those two appearances, taking off my makeup in front of the mirror, I looked myself in the eye and said, "Edward, you old son of a bitch, you're retired."

271

EDWARD VILLELLA

NINETEEN

My new family made developing a new career even more essential. I had grown as a man since stepping away from ballet. For the first time, really, my life was about other people and their needs. I wasn't living just for ballet anymore. I went through a long period of thinking about myself—my drive to dance, my need for approval and acclaim. I thought about Janet and whether our failed marriage stemmed from my single-mindedness. I still missed dancing desperately, but even more I wanted to make my new family and my new life work. Even with my commitment to them and having finally, I thought, grown up, I knew I needed something challenging to absorb my energy, passion, and attention.

I contemplated my options. In many ways, my career in the New York City Ballet had been like a fantasy. How was I going to match the experience of working with the best, of being applauded and admired? Who was I, if I wasn't a dancer? Whom was I supposed to please, if not George Balanchine? I didn't want to live in the past. I decided to look into teaching, lecturing, and coaching and try to learn more about them. By investigating all these areas at the same time, I thought I might be able to create a new career, a blend of things that really fitted me. I knew it wasn't going to be easy, and I didn't know exactly where to start. Then something happened.

In 1978, the big news in ballet was that Mikhail Baryshni-

272

kov was leaving American Ballet Theatre to join City Ballet. He had been dancing at ABT since he had defected from the Kirov Ballet in 1974. Misha was eager to work with Balanchine and dance in his ballets, and as soon as he became a member of the company, Balanchine cast him in many of the roles that were closely associated with me: "Rubies," *Prodigal Son,* Oberon, and *Harlequinade.* Misha was going to have to perform an entirely new repertory, and I was called to rehearsals to offer whatever assistance I could.

At the time Misha's fame was phenomenal, as it is today. He had been celebrated in the Soviet Union before his defection as the greatest living technician in ballet, and if anything, his reputation had been enhanced by his dancing in the West. He was the epitome of the Soviet classical style, yet he was willing to take on a new, difficult repertory in which he might be ill at ease. Guiding him along was a fascinating opportunity for me. I remembered what it had been like learning the roles without much instruction. I can't say that I wasn't acutely aware that this man was taking on *my* roles. I can't say that didn't sting like hell. But I wanted my roles to continue to be performed— for Balanchine and, in a way, for me. Whatever I had brought to them as a dancer was now, I realized, part of the life of the ballet. Misha would step into pieces that I had helped form.

Baryshnikov arrived to work on "Rubies" cloaked in his premier danseur identity. He was proud. There was a certain aloofness about him, a reserve and distance, but I understood the reason for it and wasn't offended. I knew I had something important to offer. I had performed "Rubies" very differently at the end of my career because I had learned more and more about it with every performance. It was the same with all the roles in my repertory. I had explored every facet, every tiny detail and nuance of the choreography, and now I wanted badly to pass on what I had discovered.

As soon as we began working, I could see that Misha was uncomfortable with the choreography. He understood that he had to learn a whole new approach, but the neoclassical style didn't come naturally to him. I thought about how to approach my task and decided that I wouldn't try to get him to imitate what I had done, but try to give him a sense of the overall structure of the role and a sense of the style.

As I had suspected, the speed at which the ballet is danced 273 presented him with the greatest challenge. He was very much used to taking a long, deep plié; he wasn't accustomed to landing and using the landing as the position from which to attack the next step. Now as he worked, he took his time doing the plié. I showed him how I thought it should be done, but I didn't insist on anything. It was a delicate matter. Balanchine was the artistic director of the New York City Ballet, and it was up to him to tell an artist he had cast how he wanted the role danced. But I wondered if Misha was going to be able to perform the ballet at its usual pace. I was curious about who was going to set the tempo.

Despite these questions and the slight tension, working with Misha was fun, though he never let down his guard, never opened up. *Harlequinade* was easier for him than "Rubies." He had a point of view from which to approach this role, and that added to his confidence. The Russians bring a distinctive manner and style to commedia ballets: it's part of their tradition and very different from ours. Misha's characterization of Harlequin seemed to derive more from mime than from dancing. It didn't seem to grow out of the music and the French commedia spirit. His manner didn't seem as light and frothy as Balanchine had originally conceived the role. But Balanchine had been working with Villella and this was Baryshnikov.

I tried to understand his position. Here was Baryshnikov, one of the supreme masters of that old-world, nineteenth-century style, having to abandon it, having to put aside his security blanket, so to speak, in order to assimilate Balanchine's modern developments. He was one of the greatest technicians in the history of dance, but he had a hard time learning how to articulate the Balanchine style. I confess to taking pleasure as I watched him struggle to conquer roles that were choreographed for me, just as I had had to struggle to conquer the roles of the nineteenth century.

Marcia Preiss, meanwhile, had arranged various master classes for me to teach at several universities in New York State. They turned out so well that my services were soon in demand at universities and regional theaters across the country. I devised several different programs to present at these lecture performances as we now called them, programs that grew out

274

of the lecture demonstrations I had taken part in at the New York City Ballet during the 1960s and 70s. With Marcia's help I seemed to be taking the first step toward a new career.

The evenings were billed as "Edward Villella and Dancers" or "Edward Villella and the Art of Balanchine," and they included my introductory comments as well as a demonstration at the barre by me and the other dancers of the basic points of classical technique and the Balanchine style. We then presented excerpts from ballets performed by the dancers (who were members of the various companies I was associated with), excerpts that included *Tarantella,* the second movement pas de deux from *Concerto Barocco,* the *Minkus Pas de Trois, Agon, Swan Lake,* the pas de deux from Bournonville's *Flower Festival at Genzano,* and *Shenandoah,* a pas de deux I choreographed to traditional American folk music.

My contract stated that I wasn't going to dance. But I often asked the audience's indulgence, as I put it, to visit an old friend, and I passed through the male variation from *Apollo.* Dancing again was like a powerful drug. Oh, how I missed it. My muscles would come alive and my body tingle. I felt like an old fighter giving an exhibition bout. I got high, and the audience would respond with a roar.

The evenings were generally well-received, and when I think of the places we appeared, a map of the United States surfaces in my mind: Akron, Ohio; Albany, New York; Buffalo, New York; San Diego, California; Colorado Springs, Colorado; Las Vegas, Nevada; River Grove, Illinois; Chattanooga, Tennessee; Marietta, Georgia; Athens, Georgia; Easton, Pennsylvania; Cleveland, Ohio; Winston-Salem, North Carolina; Glassboro, New Jersey; and many, many other towns and cities. I even gave a lecture performance in Monte Carlo, Monaco, under the auspices of the IBM Corporation, and another with Allegra Kent at Harvard University sponsored by Time, Inc. I was beginning to earn a living from this work, traveling the country and spreading the word about Balanchine.

The master classes I conducted at universities across the country were also popular. In 1981 I served for a year as visiting artist at the U.S. Military Academy at West Point. The response there was as enthusiastic as anyplace I had ever talked. I had been invited to West Point by the Cadet Fine Arts Forum,   275 and I asked Arlene Croce to accompany me on the day of the first session. Arlene is the respected dance critic for *The New Yorker,* and I was pleased that she was interested in observing the lecture. But I had no idea how complicated the first day was going to be.

At the time, I was also producing a gala ballet performance billed as "A Night of Stars" at Robin Hood Dell, an outdoor theater in Philadelphia. Natalia Makarova (another great defector from the Kirov), Gelsey Kirkland, Patrick Bissell, Yanis Pikieris, and Marielena Mencia were among the artists taking part in the event, and the opening night had been a great success. Another performance was scheduled for the following evening, which was the day of my initial West Point class. My plan was to leave Philadelphia early in the morning, drive to West Point, deliver my lecture, and be back in time for the evening performance.

At six in the morning I was heading for my car in the garage when I was greeted at the hotel entrance by the sight of an ambulance, a police car, and my production liaison. This man frantically waved me over and told me that we had a major problem. It seemed that after the performance the night before, Gelsey and Patrick Bissell had remained in their dressing room for hours finishing off a bottle of vodka and various other controlled substances they had in their possession. When they had run out of alcohol, they broke into the theater owner's office and helped themselves to his vodka.

At one A.M., Gelsey had finally emerged from the stage door. She had ample assistance; basically she was carried out. After more or less greeting her fans who were still waiting to see her, she had taken a waiting limousine back to New York. Patrick had gone out on the town, drinking some more on his own. He returned to the hotel at four in the morning and when he couldn't find Gelsey, began breaking up his room and threatening suicide. Someone had called the police and he was now being taken to the hospital. It wasn't clear to anyone what kind of condition he was in.

Although I knew I had to resolve this crisis at once, I felt that I couldn't cancel my first West Point lecture at such short notice. I set off in my car leaving my production associate in charge. On the way, I stopped every half hour to phone Phila-

276

delphia to keep tabs on the situation and inquire about Patrick's condition. If he had really done damage to himself, in addition to all the problems this would cause for him personally, we'd have to find someone in a matter of hours to replace him in the evening.

As soon as I arrived at West Point, I met Arlene and we were taken to a huge gymnasium where I was to address both the football and lacrosse teams. I delivered the lecture that I had polished during the past two years. As I spoke, I showed exactly how ballet movements are related to the movements of athletes, and then I proceeded to put these tall, vigorous, hulking athletic cadets at the barre in first and second positions. Before the session was out, I had them doing pirouettes, jetés, changements, and passés, and everyone seemed to be having a hell of a time. When the lecture was over, however, I couldn't bask in my success. I had to take off at once for Philadelphia. As far as I knew, nothing had been resolved, but I had learned that Patrick hadn't seriously hurt himself.

I arrived in Philadelphia at seven in the evening, drove straight to the theater, and walked out onto the stage. Gelsey and Patrick were at the barre warming up. Patrick was wearing a sheepish expression, and small strips of gauze and adhesive on his wrists, but he had recovered. He and Gelsey went on that night as scheduled, and they danced beautifully. The episode had been an isolated incident, no more than an inconvenience for me, but it left me feeling sad and depressed about these talented young artists. Living on the edge had become a way of life for both. Patrick died of a drug overdose in 1988 at the age of thirty.

Teaching at West Point turned out to be a lot more rewarding than I had expected, and the rest of my tenure there was a success. The athletes who had taken part in the first session spread the word that there was nothing painful or embarrassing about the ballet class; they said it was a blast, exhilarating. All my subsequent lectures were crammed. As well as basic ballet movements, I demonstrated exercises that stretched and strengthened backs and tendons, exercises that were later incorporated by the strength coach into the football team's regular workout. I also worked with gymnasts and with cadets from the English and drama departments, lecturing the latter 277 on characterization and movements for the stage as well as exercising them at the barre and in the center of the gym. The senior officers at the school told me they were delighted with the work I had done, and an article on the lectures appeared in *Time* magazine. CBS's "Sunday Morning" also filmed a news report on my activities at the school.

At the end of the academic year, an exhibition of photographs highlighting my career was held in Eisenhower Hall. Marcia Preiss had researched and gathered the photographs from sources all over the country and curated the retrospective, and Arlene wrote an introduction for the catalogue. She called her essay "Edward Villella: A Man and His Roles" and wrote: "If Villella's art was reflected in *Apollo,* his life was reflected in *Prodigal Son.* Villella had emerged during the period of Rebels Without Causes in America and Angry Young Men in England, and made his first major debut on the brink of a turbulent decade. . . . When the final tally is taken and it shows American ballet in our time to have been largely a Balanchine production, there will be the honor roll of Balanchine dancers, name upon name. All those girls—and Edward Villella."

I delivered my final lecture at the Military Academy to two thousand cadets. When I finished speaking, they cheered and tossed their caps high into the air.

I was branching out professionally. I was appointed by Mayor Koch and served a partial term as chairman of New York City's Commission for Cultural Affairs, drawing on my previous experience as a member of the National Council on the Arts as well as on my term on the National Endowment's dance panel. In the late 1970s, I hosted a "Dance in America" series on public television devoted to Balanchine ballets, and a few years later a Bolshoi Ballet performance of *Giselle* starring Natalya Bessmertnova and Mikhail Lavrovsky that was aired on NBC-TV. In 1981, I signed on with PBS as a producer/director and made my debut directing a broadcast of "Bournonville Dances" for "Dance in America" that Stanley had staged for the City Ballet repertory. Merrill Ashley, Darci Kistler, Heather Watts, Peter Martins, Ib Andersen, and Helgi Tomasson and various other NYCB members danced on the program.

278   I approached this assignment with a measure of real excite-

ment. It was a chance to direct members of the company I had belonged to in a ballet staged by one of my closest friends and collaborators. At the same time, I was slightly unsure about the project. I knew that I had a lot to learn. Although I had appeared on TV innumerable times and was an Emmy winner, I had never had sole responsibility before for every aspect of a broadcast.

My main question was: How can dance be presented on television so that the essence of a work comes across to the viewers? I knew I had to vary the way each pas de deux in "Bournonville" was presented in order to keep the broadcast from becoming static. It was necessary, of course, to open with a master shot, a wide angle that showed the structure of the choreography and the space in which the ballet was going to be danced. Then, according to the way each section unfolded, I made my decisions about the various angles and cuts I had to make.

What became clear to me as I worked was that if I followed the line of the choreography, if I understood the choreographer's purpose for each section and for the movements of the principals, soloists, and corps—as well as for the way in which the corps was used to support the principals—then the ballet would come across coherently on the screen.

I learned a great deal from working on the broadcast with a brilliant editor, Garish Bhargava. Garish had served as editor for Emile Ardolino and Merrill Brockway, two of the most respected dance directors in television, founders of the "Dance in America" series. Emile Ardolino would later achieve success as the director of the movie *Dirty Dancing*. Needless to say, I made some mistakes as we went along, and Garish was always there to save the day and I'm indebted to him.

Over the years I was aware that even though Balanchine and Lincoln were always on good terms, they were basically reserved with one another. Temperamentally they were very different, and they were not really pals. As Violette once put it, "Balanchine was a Francophile and Lincoln an Anglophile." They held opposing opinions on many subjects. Their values and their points of view were often opposite as well, and most of the time they acted as very separate entities.

In the late 1960s, Lincoln had suffered a heart attack, and   279 he asked me to visit him in the hospital while he was recuperating. When I arrived in his room, Philip Johnson, the architect, was getting ready to leave. Once he was gone, Lincoln revealed what was on his mind. He told me that if something happened to him and he wasn't able to continue as the general director of New York City Ballet, he wanted me to replace him. He told me that he wanted me to become more involved in company operations, and he asked me in what area I thought I could be useful.

As everyone knew, Balanchine was far more interested in developing the women in the company than the men. It was also true that, except for Balanchine's invaluable coaching, New York City Ballet had no formal training or instruction. I hoped to work with the men in the corps de ballet and coach them. From what I could see, no one really communicated with these guys. I could fill a void. Lincoln agreed.

A week or two later, I met with Barbara Horgan. I thought Lincoln and Balanchine had probably mentioned the new setup to her and I wanted to work out the details. I was stunned by the look of total shock on her face when I told her what was on my mind. I vividly remember the curt tone of her voice when she said, "Mr. Balanchine doesn't like anyone interfering with *his* dancers."

There was another incident a couple of years later, this time in Munich where the company was dancing during the 1972 Olympics. Lincoln and Norman Singer, the head of the City Center for Music and Drama, asked me to lunch. They were interested in setting up a second company, a New York City Ballet II, just as the Joffrey Ballet had a Joffrey II, a small junior troupe. They wanted to know if I was interested in becoming the head of such a project. Lincoln told me Balanchine had said I was the only person to do it. When I expressed not only interest but excitement, they asked me to work up a budget and to think about the troupe's artistic policy and how such a company could be structured.

I set about the task with a great deal of enthusiasm, but as time went by, I heard nothing more about it. Soon enough I realized that nothing *was* going to come of it. I imagined that Balanchine had had second thoughts about me given my reputation as a "difficult" person who had locked horns with him.

280

Balanchine's resentment of my relationship with Stanley Williams was never really resolved, and I didn't want Mr. B to get the idea that I was trying to intrude on his company. I was disappointed but not surprised.

In a way I think I was being manipulated in these situations by Lincoln, who saw himself as a latter-day Diaghilev. Diaghilev had been Balanchine's first boss in the West. He had given Mr. B his first opportunities when he was just starting out as a young choreographer and had told him what to do. Lincoln would probably have liked to have had more artistic input in the New York City Ballet. I was beginning to feel like a pawn in a game, a contest of wills between these two giants.

In the 1960s and 70s, the question of Balanchine's successor in the company was often discussed. Jacques D'Amboise supported the rumor that he was the heir apparent. Occasionally, however, a concerned party would let me know that he or she thought I was the natural candidate for the post. I was flattered, but I told them, and I meant it, that I didn't want to be caught between Lincoln and Jerry. I didn't want to be ensnared in NYCB politics. But the job was never offered.

By 1980, it was clear to me that what appealed to me was a job that encompassed all of the activities in which I had recently been involved, a job that I had been becoming more and more interested in all along: I wanted to be the artistic director of a ballet company. I had the energy for it, the appetite, and the interest in learning as much as I could about how it was done. In fact I had had some experience functioning in this capacity as the director of the small, quickly assembled ballet troupes I danced with around the country. But to be the artistic director of a major company would be a new goal to shoot for.

A number of large companies expressed interest in talking to me, but I wasn't really sure of the direction I wanted to go. I thought that rather than becoming involved with an established ballet troupe, I would profit most from becoming associated with a second-rank company that had problems and needed help. The André Eglevsky company fit the bill, and I was tempted when the board approached me and asked if I was interested in running the company.

The situation appealed to me for many reasons. The troupe was artistically impoverished. The repertory consisted of me-

281

diocre productions of classical ballets such as *The Nutcracker,* *Cinderella,* and *Coppélia* that reflected André's eclectic and vaguely vulgar aesthetic. The scenery and costumes for these productions were inappropriate and the dancing was inconsistent. I thought I could help improve the quality of the productions and raise the level of the dancing. The company was in total disarray since André's death, and I was drawn to another part of the repertory, a core of Balanchine ballets. This was a real attraction for me. There was another factor. Although the company performed in Long Island, rehearsals were held in New York City and that suited me, too. I wanted to spend time with my family. I took the job.

Running the Eglevsky Ballet was my first experience in turning around a disastrous situation. I eliminated what I thought was most unsatisfactory in the repertory and tried to inject some life into the productions I kept. I worked with the dancers on matters of style and musicality. I was warned that the subscribers were used to the corny, old-fashioned, adulterated productions the company had been staging and that many of them might refuse to renew. This was a risk I had no trouble taking. There were people in the company, and in the audience, who were interested in quality and who respected the art of ballet and wanted a change. I tried to instill a coherent artistic vision on an operation that from the start had been put together in an improvised and haphazard way. I often got the impression that the company hadn't been set up by professional, competent staff members but rather the mothers of the dancers who had been infatuated with André.

I stayed with the company for four years. I think both the repertory and the dancing improved a great measure. And I profited as well. I learned about the financial side of running a company, budgets and contracts and public relations and marketing. But this was not the New York City Ballet: I encountered characters with petty ambitions who had their own agendas for being involved in the ballet company. Driven by politics, they moved in devious ways. They were people whose word had very little meaning.

During this period I also became the artistic adviser to Ballet Oklahoma as well as to the New Jersey Ballet. My association with both these organizations radically increased my

282

knowledge of the day-to-day problems involved in running a company, and in a relatively short time I gained a great deal of experience.

Before long, however, a serious clash developed between George Dempster, the chairman of the Eglevsky board, and me, a conflict that resulted in litigation and a great deal of unfavorable publicity.

At the time I was scrapping with the Eglevsky board, Balanchine became gravely ill. His health had been deteriorating for some time. In March 1978 he had suffered a serious heart attack, but instead of being upset about it, it was said that he was actually somewhat relieved. He'd been feeling fatigued and had been suffering from dizzy spells; now it seemed as if his condition had finally been diagnosed. Most of us in the New York City Ballet had been alarmed and concerned about the state of his health, and we somehow felt that the real details of his illness were being kept from us. Balanchine was a very private man. He never discussed his personal life with anyone outside a small, select group of intimates.

It had made me profoundly uneasy to think of Balanchine ill. He was a man of great energy. He loved to be around youthful people. His eye had a mischievous glint and he always seemed young and snappy. He himself never talked about getting old and always predicted that he would live a long time. He pointed out that he was Georgian, and some Georgians had lived to the age of 130. We all believed him. We took him at his word and imagined he'd be around forever. And he encouraged us. He never talked about slowing down. If anyone asked him if he ever thought of retiring, he'd say, "Oh, no. I'm not going to retire. I'm going to *die*. I'm going to die in harness. I'll keep doing what I'm doing now until I'm no more."

After his heart attack, however, his health continued to trouble him. His recovery was slow and he developed cataracts and glaucoma. He also endured bouts of angina so severe that eventually he had to undergo a triple bypass operation, which was a success. Then sometime in 1981 neurological problems began to plague him; he was beginning to lose his balance. He was terrified; imagine the idea of a master choreographer losing his balance. Gradually his situation grew worse, and as the year progressed, he seemed to go into a serious decline. 283

EDWARD VILLELLA

Since a second NYCB Stravinsky Festival in 1982 it had been obvious that something was drastically wrong with Mr. B. I had had the feeling for some time before that that he had been trying desperately to finish the new ballets he was choreographing for the festival, and I was shocked when I saw *Perséphone*. The cast didn't dance; they just sort of promenaded across the stage. I assumed that because Mr. B could no longer demonstrate what he wanted, he wasn't able to devise steps.

After the festival, Mr. B's condition grew rapidly worse. Soon he was unable to come to the theater, and after taking a few spills in his apartment, first breaking his wrist and then a few ribs, he was hospitalized. Tests were performed, and although it was clear he was failing, his actual condition could not be diagnosed.

I had decided to visit him in the hospital but was concerned about when. We were told he had good and bad days. Certain days he couldn't recognize people and only spoke Russian. Some days he was completely disoriented. I didn't want my visit to come during a bad period. I didn't want to embarrass the master, and I didn't want to remember him as a sick old man. Despite my fears, I called and made an appointment. Linda and I went to Roosevelt Hospital and to our relief found Mr. B cogent and in wonderful spirits. I had brought him some bottles of Guinness Stout.

He was charming and flirted shamelessly with Linda. She had always been at ease with Balanchine. Most people clammed up when they were introduced to him, but Linda was always herself with him—easy, warm, and natural. Balanchine was crazy about her and went out of his way to engage her. I was delighted that I had finally done something offstage of which he approved.

He patted the side of his bed and told Linda to sit there, and then pointed me to a chair at the foot of the bed. I was thinking even now he's still "giving it" to me, defining our relationship. No matter what, he wasn't going to miss an opportunity to needle me a little bit. He told charming stories, laughing merrily, performing for us. After an hour and a half he began to tire. He thanked us for coming and asked us to leave. I will forever remember his naked arm reaching out from his hospital gown as he hauled himself up in bed into a sitting position to say good-bye. On his wrist was the turquoise brace-let he always wore. The sight of the bracelet and his bare arm was unbearably poignant. I knew that this was the last time I was ever going to see him.

Balanchine died on April 30, 1983, a Saturday. He was seventy-nine. An autopsy revealed that he had been suffering from Creutzfeldt-Jakob disease, a rare virus that attacks the brain. His funeral was held at the Russian Orthodox Church where he worshiped. The church filled with dancers, associates, and members of his audience—people who loved him. There was a tremendous sadness and love. Everyone held thin yellow candles with wax guards on them, and each mourner stood during the long Orthodox ceremony filled with pageant and music—the pageant of his origins. When the service was con-cluded, mourners filed past his casket. Many of the Russians kissed him. I touched his forehead.

Outside the church, television cameras and reporters had assembled inside the courtyard at the bottom of the entrance staircase. Many mourners stood about, but I found that I could not. I had to get away. I was holding my emotions barely in check and was close to tears. Linda and I walked along Ninety-third Street, and suddenly I couldn't go any farther. I leaned against the side wall of the church that bordered the sidewalk. I just stood there. I didn't know what to do. I didn't want to stay and I couldn't leave. Eventually I went home, where I'm not ashamed to say that I broke down and wept for several days.

At the time of my involvement with the Eglevsky Ballet, Linda was becoming increasingly distressed—offended really —by my association with organizations that didn't measure up to my background and experience. She wanted me to recon-sider some of the companies I had decided to work with. But I felt that by becoming involved in worst-case situations I would be prepared for almost anything if, one day, I ran a company of my own. The work I had been doing seemed to me like the equivalent of earning a bachelor of science degree in being an artistic director.

In 1985, I was in Florida giving a lecture demonstration under the auspices of the Dance Umbrella of the Gusman The-

285

ater in downtown Miami. The Dance Umbrella was run by David Eden, an arts organizer. David had recommended me to two local residents who were eager to talk. At the conclusion of the lecture, he introduced me to them. A Rockefeller Institute study on the cultural climate in southern Florida indicated that a real need for a professional classical ballet company existed in the state. These residents were interested in starting one in Miami, but they hadn't the slightest idea how to go about it. They wanted my counsel and advice, and I was happy to give it. Eventually they hoped I might serve as artistic adviser.

I didn't hold out much hope for the project. I thought that these were well-meaning people who had romantic notions but no real idea about what it took to create a ballet company. But I met with Toby Lerner Ansin and her friends, Barbara Singer, an attorney, and Robin Reiter, a banker, at Toby's home and explained my ideas about starting a ballet company. Most people think it begins by hiring a guest star and raising money to stage an opulent spectacle. People dress up for opening night, and presto, there's the ballet company. It doesn't work like that at all, I said, not for a serious troupe.

Time is the first requirement, I said. I suggested it would take a minimum of ten years to create a first-rate ballet company. It would take no less than a year and a half from inception of the company to the initial performances. I also said that an institution presenting old-fashioned nineteenth-century ballets exclusively didn't interest me and that I would want to devise a repertory for a new company based on the best of the masterworks created in the twentieth century. The core of the repertory should, of course, be Balanchine ballets.

Balanchine ballets train dancers in a particular style, creating performers who move in a fresh and exciting way. Few areas in this country have been exposed to Balanchine ballets as they were originally intended. But I envisioned even more, new ballets and works by such choreographers as Antony Tudor and Jerry Robbins, even works by Paul Taylor and José Limón. As I talked, I became increasingly excited. Suddenly, the idea of starting a company in Miami seemed like a real possibility.

286   Sitting at Toby's dining room table I outlined an eleven-

and-a-half-year plan for creating such a company. The plan was comprehensive, detailed, and precise, and Toby wrote it all down in longhand. The paper still exists today. The more we spoke the more I realized that she and Barbara were serious about the project. After Toby introduced me to other members of the community I was convinced of the viability of the plan. I was impressed by everyone I met. I liked them all and I liked the community, and when I returned to New York, I did research of my own on the project.

The population of Florida was growing by almost one thousand new residents daily, and most of these immigrants had come from large cities where they were used to seeing opera, ballet, and symphony orchestras. All the major dance and musical attractions that played New York also came to Miami. The city was part of a densely populated urban area that stretched along the coast to Fort Lauderdale and also embraced other cities such as Palm Beach, where the New York City Ballet had previously performed. These communities were isolated from one another, and basically competitive; each one had a superior sense of itself in relation to the other. But they represented a vast audience, and it occurred to me that a company that was based in Miami could with little difficulty have a minimum of three home cities. When I spoke to them again, Toby and her friends listened attentively. They were with me all the way, and they assured me that a functioning board of directors could be formed readily. Toby was true to her word; in no time at all a board was being assembled.

I was excited. Many ballet professionals and several colleagues in New York warned me against the project. Florida is a cultural wasteland, don't get stuck in Miami, they cautioned. But my research and my initial experience left me with a different impression. The audience there was knowledgeable and sophisticated. I was beginning to think that creating a ballet company was not only logical but practical—it was beginning to look like a great idea.

Meeting again with Toby and other interested people, I explained that I would head such a company only if I could guide every aspect of it: the artistic policy, the repertory, the decisions about advertising and marketing. They offered me the job on the spot, and I felt a debt of gratitude to the Eglevsky

287

troupe and to Ballet Oklahoma, for even though my association with these organizations had been painful, they provided me with a thorough education. A contract was drawn up. I was to spend six months of each year in Miami, leaving me time to pursue other projects.

Linda and I talked at great length about the project in Miami. She responded to my enthusiasm and listened to my plans. She knew better than anyone how much running around I had been doing because of the projects I'd been involved with and said, "You're the last one to know it, but you really don't live in New York anymore. If you feel strongly about this, I think we should move there permanently."

I agreed. It was time to move on.

After giving the matter a great deal of thought, I decided to commit fully to the project. Once I signed the contract to become the artistic director of the Miami City Ballet, I moved my family to Florida. Stuart Danoff, the president of the board, Toby, and Barbara Singer were astonished when they first heard of my decision. Eglevsky board chairman George Dempster and his associate Pepe Semler had bad-mouthed me so thoroughly that people in Miami thought they'd be lucky if they saw me six months a year. They were thrilled when I became a legal resident of the state. Given the breadth of what I wanted to accomplish, Linda was right, there was no other way for it to be done. For I envisioned a Miami City Ballet not as a New York City Ballet South, but as an original entity: it would be a classical company that would present as its foundation the great ballets that Balanchine and other choreographers had created in the twentieth century. But it would also be a company that would take part in the next evolution in the art form as it occurred. I could barely contain my excitement about getting this company going. I saw that I had an opportunity to pass on Balanchine's legacy, not only the ballets themselves but the elements necessary for performing them, the approach to technique, to phrasing, and to music.

288

TWENTY

I wanted to make the Miami City Ballet into an instrument that would be true to Balanchinian aesthetics, but not a duplicate of the New York City Ballet. My strategy was twofold. First, I had to select ballets for a young company that would appeal to a new audience, ballets that would point the way to even more sophisticated and complex works.

The first ballet I staged was *Allegro Brillante,* which Balanchine choreographed in 1956 to music by Tchaikovsky. This ballet made a statement. It told the world that we were a classical company with the energy of the twentieth century but with respect for nineteenth-century tradition. Balanchine said of *Allegro Brillante,* "[It] contains everything I know about the classical ballet—in thirteen minutes." The creation of the ballet was a gesture of homage on the part of a twentieth-century genius to his most cherished tradition, and it suited us marvelously. Other works I scheduled for our first seasons were *Apollo, Prodigal Son, Concerto Barocco, Square Dance,* and *Tarantella,* ballets that showed the audience the progression of neoclassicism. For the most part, they were works I had danced in, and my knowledge of their background, my experience in rehearsing them with Balanchine and performing them under his watchful eye, were still vivid in my mind.

To be sure, the majority of ballets we danced were going

289

to be Balanchine's, but I wanted the repertory to consist of ballets by other choreographers in other styles as well, for I believed that this would enrich the lives of both the dancers and the audience. So while setting up the Balanchine repertory, I decided to bring in a resident choreographer who would create original ballets for us. I hired Jimmy Gamonet de los Heros, my first choice for the job, a talented man I had worked with in Oklahoma. Jimmy's ballets for Miami City Ballet, among them *Transtangos* and *Nous Sommes,* have proven to be great successes, and they have contributed mightily to the company's achievement.

But repertory can't exist without dancers. The second part of my strategy was to create a company of dancers who would be able to dance these ballets. I had to have good dancers, the best, and once I had them, they had to perform these works on a very high level. Even though we were going to dance ballets by other great choreographers, such as Bournonville and Petipa, I knew that for Miami City Ballet to move into the twenty-first century with a viable identity as a major ballet troupe, we had to understand and assimilate all I had experienced with Balanchine during those golden years in New York. This was possible, but only if we, the dancers and I, worked on a daily basis. I knew that not every dancer was suitable to the task. What I did ultimately was to hire dancers who could move instinctively in a way that showed me their potential for neoclassicism, dancers who were innately musical and who would be suited to the repertory.

I had worked out a very definite approach that was different in many respects from Balanchine's. He had the time to start from scratch. Balanchine wanted a uniform look, and he had a large pool of dancers to choose from. He founded a school in which the training of his dancers began when they were young children. By necessity I had to be satisfied with a variety of types, but what I was interested in was a uniform quality of movement, a developed musical understanding. I was more restricted because I was working with dancers who had already been trained, and I had to force them to change. To do so, I had to go all the way back to the beginning with them, to the basics.

290   In class I started working with dancers in the very first

position at the barre, heels together, feet turned outward in a straight line. That's turnout, and turnout is really what this technique is based on. It's crucial, essential. We are opening our bodies outward to the left and to the right. Turnout is a rotation and its great effect is in the hips, but it really starts in the arch of the foot. From the very first movement, the arch is lifted and rotated outward and upward, and that places the balance of the leg over the toe. As the arch is lifted, the heel of the foot is brought forward, and the rotation of the calf, the knee, and the inside of the thigh begins. The movement then naturally extends to the inside of the buttock, which moves forward, and it then passes through the rib cage, the chest, and the shoulders. The movement has flowed smoothly from the foot through the leg, upward through the entire body. And this upward, outward rotation occurs simultaneously in the left and right sides of the body.

Turning out, the dancer is no longer standing flat on his feet. His weight is off the floor and he has a lightness, an airiness, an ability to move without tension. As the dancer rotates, he isn't really executing a gesture complete unto itself. He is letting go of the gesture, so to speak, letting it go upward and outward. It's a release. This is a most basic idea, but it's very rare that it is ever discussed or explained in class. So I begin every class by insisting on turnout, by telling the dancers, "Lift the arches, upward, forward, and out, upward, forward, and out."

I watch carefully to make certain that the dancers are working on this principle. If a dancer fails to turn out as soon as he begins to dance, he will land on his feet, flat on his heels. He will then have to stop and pull himself up over his balance to make the next gesture, and this will give the impression of lumbering. But if a dancer turns out at once and rotates, he's always up over his balance going forward all the time, going up and out. In a sense turning out and extending the gesture is the primary act that creates the movement. It's really the most simple and basic fact of life, essential in order to perform neoclassical choreography (but again, I know from experience that this, too, is rarely, if ever, discussed).

The dancer's understanding of musicality is another crucial element in this repertory and style, and my approach to it is 291 very calculated. I begin with a square, straightforward tempo and then I change it. Stravinsky will often begin a phrase in one meter and then switch to a different meter for three or four bars before returning to his original count. Therefore I'll start with a phrase in one tempo, break it down, and subdivide it. If it's a phrase with a count of eight, I'll subdivide it by one count of four and two counts of two. But within the two counts of two, I'll ask for a different accent. I won't ask for simply one, two, one, two. What I want is *One,* two, *one,* two. The attack is on one; the other foot is brought in on two.

When I give the dancers this kind of exercise in relation to music, they have to connect the music to the step, they have to make a conscious choice of how to move. And once I have given them the basic exercise, I ask for longer combinations that require the dancers to move quickly in relation to the music but also to change direction. But during the change of direction, they must still execute syncopated movements underneath the overall movement. I force the dancers to move within a different time frame from the one they're used to.

Sometimes within one single exercise I will give three different syncopated rhythms, and unless the dancer is thinking about what he is doing, is utterly conscious of every movement, the third rhythm will elude him, he won't be able to express it in his body. I proceeded like this on a daily basis, repeating what I wanted, giving these important exercises over and over, and even those dancers who initially resisted what I asked for caught on after a while. By working hard they're able to understand what I want.

This all took time. It was three years before I got the eclectic group that formed the Miami City Ballet to move in a similar fashion the way I wanted, as if to sing with one voice. The bodies are different in size and shape, yet because they all move together in the same way in relation to the music, a pleasing look of uniformity is communicated that's expressive of the heart of the ballets they dance.

Once they reached this level, I was then able to delve into the complexities of Balanchine's style. I told my dancers that they must know how to get from step to step when they dance Balanchine. Most dancers are never exposed to this concept.

292

Teachers don't concentrate on how a dancer moves from position to position but only on the positions themselves. In a sense, students are taught positions the way children are taught the alphabet and vocabulary. Yet is it our purpose to teach only alphabet and vocabulary to dancers as if they were children but not to teach dancers to express the poetry of gesture and movement?

One of the keys to enable a dancer to move from position to position, from step to step, so that the dancing comes alive, is to make the dancer aware of his second leg. Dancers have two legs to work with, I always say, but many of them concentrate only on the leg that moves first, the leg that attacks the step initially. The second, "lazy" leg gets forgotten and consequently it often drags. I tell my dancers that they must be aware of it even as they are concentrating intently on the first leg. A gesture must not be divided into two separate parts for the two different legs, but rather the front and back legs must be used together as part of the one gesture. Working in this way unites a dancer to the music, it helps create speed, and it enables the dancer to achieve positions with clarity. Momentum is created so that a dancer never stops moving.

Of course the first thing that happens to most dancers when they start moving at the high speed necessary for Balanchine is that the positions become blurred. I deal with this problem in an unorthodox fashion. Rather than concentrating on achieving the position, I work on how the position is completed. I make the dancer aware not only of the attack but of how to finish what he has begun. I tell the dancers not how to get out of the position quickly so they can rush to the next step, but rather teach them how to make the time to finish the position and then go to the next position, and I explain that only by moving deliberately, by finishing the position carefully, will they be able to move quickly. Once again it is a question of slower is faster. Speed is created by taking the time to finish the position.

I work on this in class at the barre, doing the most simple basic exercise, battement tendu, starting first with the accent out. The dancer moves his leg in, *out,* in, *out.* Then I change it so that the emphasis is on the movement in, that is, *in,* out, *in,* out. The dancer now becomes aware of both parts of the move-

293

EDWARD VILLELLA

ment. His mind becomes conscious of what his foot is doing while the gesture itself trains and tones the muscles in the foot to execute the subtleties inherent in the step. The muscles in the feet are all-important because the quickness of the feet is a major component of this kind of dancing. Strong, quick feet are basic to the Balanchine approach. When a dancer jumps, it's the speed and strength in his feet as well as in his legs that give him power and propel him aloft, so these simple, basic ballet exercises are crucial. Balanchine knew it and had complimented me years ago by simply saying, "You can do battement tendu."

In these complex, advanced classes I also discuss how my philosophy of movement is manifested in the landing from a jump, and I explain how jumping and landing must be connected, that "down" is really only a means of going "up." The difference between "down" leading to "up" and "down" as an end unto itself is the difference between the drop of a ball and the thud of a stone. The stone ends its trajectory with a thud. On the other hand, the ball rebounds from the surface, launching into another arc just as a dancer should. This concept is particularly alien to many Soviet-trained dancers and to dancers brought up in the traditional nineteenth-century style, as I saw firsthand when I watched Baryshnikov struggle to master "Rubies" and Oberon. The speed and propulsion of Balanchine's choreography were beyond him.

Above all else, however, I point out it's this quality of movement allied to music that imbues steps with their classic form, and that such a relationship to the music is basic. In spite of the fact that I give exercises every day designed to help dancers master the sophisticated musical phrasing necessary for Balanchine, many dancers still have problems with the combination of high speed and complex musical phrasing that comes with this territory. I'm sympathetic. I recall that even in the New York City Ballet, many times during rehearsals with Balanchine some dancer or other might say, "Oh, Mr. B, I just can't dance this step so quickly."

"But that's the way it's written," he'd answer. If the dancer persisted and worked hard, he'd eventually be able to do what Balanchine wanted. Unfortunately if he resisted, he didn't get anywhere at all.

•

I was going to allow five years for the Miami City Ballet to reach the point at which I might be able to stage such sophisticated Balanchine ballets as "Rubies" and *Raymonda Variations,* but we were able to get there in half the time. It wasn't only our leading dancers, Yanis Pikieris, Marielena Mencia, Iliana Lopez, and Franklin Gamero, and all the other members of the company who gave their all and worked hard. The talents and professionalism of our choreographer, Jimmy Gamonet de los Heros, his unique way of setting gesture to music, was another important factor in our progress. I was fortunate in hiring Elyse Borne as my ballet mistress. A former New York City Ballet soloist, Elyse has an intimate understanding of the Balanchine style and the brilliant ability to pass on her knowledge.

I also had the good luck to put together a remarkable administrative team. The depth of experience of Timothy Duncan, my executive director; the intelligence and sensitivity of Pam Miller, my executive assistant; the creativity of Haydée Morales, my costume designer; and music director Ottavio Da Rosa and scenic designer Carlos Arditti—each is responsible in some way for our success.

It had always seemed natural for Marcia Preiss to do the booking for the company as she had done for me for many years, securing engagements for us all over the country as well as internationally. In the earliest days of the Miami City Ballet, when we only had a staff of three professionals, Marcia became a de facto consultant. Her guidance and wisdom have been essential to the company's development.

I must also comment on Tobin Lerner Ansin's involvement in our progress. Toby's the perfect board member. She has grown and developed in all of her capacities as the Miami City Ballet has also grown and developed. And Barbara Singer and Robin Reiter are our unsung heroes. Barbara has donated time, money, and her legal expertise to the company, and Robin has used her knowledge of finance to help us develop programs for raising money.

By 1990, the company had over 13,000 subscribers and was being heralded in Europe and the U.S. for the purity and precision with which it danced Balanchine. It was the only American classical ballet company to be invited to the 1990

295

Lyons Festival. England's major dance critics heaped praise on us. Clement Crisp wrote in the *Financial Times:* "What Miami has done is to extend the significance and potential of Balanchine's view of American classicism." Mary Clarke pointed out in the *Guardian* "the brightness of attack and scrupulous attention to detail" of the dancers, and the *Telegraph*'s Nicholas Dromgoole wrote that "it is arguable that were Balanchine alive, he might be as happy with Miami's fledgling company of thirty dancers as with the larger, grander NYCB."

Nineteen ninety marked the first full-length ballet we staged for the company, Balanchine's *Nutcracker,* which was also greeted with great success throughout the state, and we're planning a new production of *Jewels* in the future. The Balanchine Trust has sent us people such as Karin von Aroldingen, Victoria Simon, and Richard Tanner, whose knowledge of Balanchine ballets is invaluable. And so the work continues. I can only hope that Mr. B would have been pleased by all of this. He would have appreciated that I have a former New York City Ballet dancer such as Elyse as ballet mistress for my company, and that I brought Allegra Kent to Miami to coach the ballerina role in *Bugakau,* which, of course, was made on her. And I think he'd also appreciate that the ballets are being presented with their original intent, with their format intact, and that his legacy was being passed on in this manner.

Nineteen ninety was noteworthy for another reason. The Eglevsky case was finally resolved in my favor and I felt vindicated. I received a cash settlement and a formal apology I reproduce here: "The Eglevsky Ballet acknowledges that at all times, while in its employ, Mr. Villella acted in a professional manner consistent with his duties and responsibilities to the Company. The Eglevsky regrets any statements ever made on its behalf which were inconsistent with the foregoing."

TWENTY-ONE

I was always immensely proud to be a Balanchine dancer. It always seemed to me that dancing in a Balanchine ballet was to step into the minds of great men, geniuses—Balanchine, Stravinsky, Tchaikovsky, Brahms, Mendelssohn, and others. When I started up in Miami, I knew it was crucial to reflect on these minds, Balanchine's particularly.

In the New York City Ballet a dancer was constantly challenged to be the raw material for genius. I had always struggled to meet this test. No matter what I was given to do in Balanchine's company, I did it. I translated and articulated it according to my understanding, then gave it back, always remaining within Balanchine's guidelines. I left my impression on his works, made my own comment on them, and this gave me tremendous confidence. Learning to understand the complexities and nuances of the roles I danced, the Prodigal Son, Apollo, Oberon, the protagonists in *Bugaku, Agon, Tchaikovsky Pas de Deux, Brahms-Schoenberg Quartet, Donizetti Variations,* and "Rubies," developed me as an artist.

Balanchine dancers are a breed apart. They are not only highly accomplished technical wonders. They have a calling, and they are asked to participate in an almost sacred way of life. That was the Balanchine ideal. He wanted all of us to be a part of a religious order of which he was the leader. He was not a

297

despot or a false god and it wasn't just a matter of authority or ego. Balanchine understood that he was the equivalent of a Mozart or a Shakespeare. But he understood that his genius had been conferred on him, he had been ordained by God. He used to say that only God was a creator. He preferred to think of himself as a craftsman and compared the art of choreography to the art of cooking, gardening, cabinetry. He had no great airs.

Balanchine was a deeply religious man—his spiritual life was important to him. And this was why, despite the times he was petty or perverse, he always forgave his dancers when they disappointed or offended him. Another man might have fired me unceremoniously or ignored me for refusing to attend his class or for failing to rehearse in the manner he requested.

I occasionally rattled the gates of Balanchine's world. I had been too much a part of real, practical life to cloister myself completely in the hermetic environment of ballet. But somehow I always returned. I realized that starting my own company, a company in which I put into practice what I had learned from Balanchine, was another return. This time I didn't return alone. My dancers understand what Balanchine is all about, and they dance the ballets in a way that I think would please him.

Balanchine ballets are unique—phenomenal. Sophisticated writers, critics, students, and highly educated balletomanes watch these ballets over and over and derive the greatest pleasure and intellectual stimulation from them. But a person can be completely uninitiated in the art of classical dance, attending the ballet for the first time and knowing nothing about it, and still be greatly entertained by them. Balanchine's ballets are built on the tradition of Marius Petipa, the great nineteenth-century choreographer and ballet master to the Imperial Ballet in St. Petersburg. Balanchine adapted Petipa's style to the twentieth century and expanded it. His style was the next profound link in the evolution of the art form after Petipa, and in order for this evolution to continue as we prepare to enter the twenty-first century, we mustn't lose what Balanchine taught us. Yet at times this evolution seems stalled; worse, it's as if we've come to the edge of a precipice, with two hands pressed to our backs about to push us into the abyss.

298   In many ways I think of ballet as an art form that's lost its

conscience. Artistic directors are presently so concerned with financial considerations, fund-raising, recalcitrant, uninformed boards, and other problems that artistic vision often goes by the wayside. And in this environment dancers look out for themselves. They switch companies or dance where they can earn the most. This is not always best for the ballets they dance and the company they're part of. In such an atmosphere Balanchine ballets are an endangered species. Lincoln said that when Balanchine first came to America he remarked, *"La danse, c'est une question morale."* He meant that morality as much as talent is crucial to this art form; and in fact, it was in a profoundly moral as well as creative atmosphere that Balanchine choreographed his great ballets.

Ballet is a human art form—it's passed on from body to body, mind to mind, and yet today the majority of the dancers in the New York City Ballet and nearly all the students at SAB never knew Balanchine personally and never worked with him. Many of those who did work with him are now retired or working in other cities or countries. Their knowledge would be invaluable if it could be tapped, but they are dispersed. There is no one to replace Balanchine. How could there be? Therefore, as I see it, it's up to those of us who were associated with him on a long-term basis, those who worked with him directly, day in and day out, to pass on to young dancers our intimate knowledge of him and his aesthetics. We who have had the privilege of that kind of experience owe a debt to this man (who was a great creator no matter how he protested) and a debt to the art form. If ballet is to flourish in the twenty-first century, Balanchine's aesthetics and his legacy must be kept alive so they can be absorbed and understood by future generations. Today choreographers are forced to create "breakthrough" ballets that reflect what is fashionable and faddish in the dance world. Classicism is under duress. There's a dearth of choreographers working in the classical tradition trying to extend it. We now have a New Wave, Next Wave, Make Your Own Tradition, Virtuosity Is a Dirty Word, and the "Me" Generation Who Know More Than a Genius. Are we now involved in an era of disposable art?

Balanchine ballets are now preserved on videotape. Ballet masters and their dancers watch tapes that were sometimes

299

EDWARD VILLELLA

made six months before of ballets that were choreographed twenty, thirty, even forty years ago. But a recent video can't possibly do the job. No one knows for sure what's been omitted from the particular performance. Steps, even whole sequences, are invariably lost. Details and nuances are smudged or distorted. Ballet masters and dancers are working from a copy of a copy. It's as if a Rembrandt whose colors have faded because it's been left lying out in the sun for decades were suddenly hung up and exhibited as an authentic, unadulterated representation of the master's work.

This is often the feeling I get watching some Soviet superstars dance Balanchine. And I have also watched performances not only by regional companies but also by the New York City Ballet of works that had been made on me whose dimensions have flattened, whose colors have dulled, ballets that no longer represent Balanchine's mind. I'm always disturbed by the experience of watching such performances. Balanchine said his ballets were only alive when they were being danced, but are they really alive when they are danced by people who don't understand their inner meanings, when the subtleties are absent? Videotape and film, not to mention dance notation, can certainly help in mounting these great masterpieces, but they can't do the job alone. They can show us the structure of a ballet, the mechanics, its skeleton. They're aids to memory basically, and memory is the connecting link. But we need the essence, the pumping heart, the blood, the vital organs, the intelligence of the ballet, in order to know it. Intimate contact between people and minds is essential for the ballets to be presented in this living, breathing state.

Some of these works no longer have mystery. Mystery is a reflection of the ballet's inner content. If it is absent, it is often because understanding is lacking.

For those of us who really got inside them, these ballets are like human beings. They *are* alive, they *do* breathe, and they possess a spirit, a soul, and an independent intelligence. A dancer can have an intimate rapport with these ballets. He can speak to them and they'll speak back. If a dancer treats them well, they'll treat him wonderfully well in return. It may sound corny, even ridiculous, but it's true. It's the nature of masterworks. I feel a profound debt to Balanchine's ballets. They are

300

directly responsible for making me more of a dancer than I would ever have been without them. They are friends who guided me, developed me, and nourished me, and I feel a personal responsibility for them. They took care of me, now I am taking care of them. They *are* my friends, and they're in serious trouble. I feel that I have to intervene. I can't let these ballets become invalids.

When I first considered moving to Florida and starting the Miami City Ballet, an aspect of the plan that appealed to me was that I'd be nearer to my father, who was in his mideighties, and have the chance to see him more often. In Florida, with the geographical distance between our homes reduced, I thought I'd be in a better position to keep an eye on him, and he was reaching that stage in life where he needed looking after. My father still lived in the Orange City house he and my mother had bought when they retired, and he was leading a quiet existence. Over the years he'd grown increasingly introspective. Most of the time he rarely spoke, so that when he did occasionally decide to open up and let me in on his feelings, the depth of his intelligence and his sensitivity still came as a surprise to me. Indeed, my father had opinions about almost everything in the world and could be somewhat ornery or overbearing when it came to expressing them. I saw myself in him occasionally.

For some time I had been concerned about him. He had succeeded in narrowing his social circle and his daily routine to the barest minimum. These limitations even extended to his physical activities and his diet. He didn't get any exercise at all, and he'd eat the same thing every day, eggs, a mixture of yogurt and ice cream, and little else. He was also a chain smoker and drank gallons of coffee. He refused to break any of his habits no matter how much I protested. Every time I visited him in Orange City I tried to encourage him to be more outgoing because he was almost always alone. I also tried to hire a maid to cook and clean for him, but he wouldn't hear of it. As it was, he barely tolerated visits from the various neighbors I had asked to keep an eye on him.

Once I settled in Miami, however, I discovered to my surprise that it was almost as hard to visit my father on a regular   301 basis from there as it had been when I lived in Manhattan. In New York, I used to hop on a plane at La Guardia, fly to Orlando, rent a car, drive to Orange City, and spend the weekend with him. But Orange City was a six-hour drive from Miami, and I soon found out that flying there from my new home was almost as time-consuming as from New York. And the visits were as frustrating as ever. My father seemed to be aging rapidly, and he looked distressingly unable to care for himself. Whereas he used to shave only once a week when he was younger, he now refused to shave at all and sported an enormous, scraggly beard. And no matter how I tried, I couldn't get him to vary his routine. I tried to engage him in what I was doing or in sports or in his neighbors, but it was hard to arouse his interest in anything. I repeatedly invited him to visit us in Miami for as long as he wanted to stay, but he was reluctant, although occasionally he'd come for a week or so. He adored his granddaughter Crista. She is a friendly child and she loved him. Seeing her was an incentive for him to make the trip.

One weekend when the Miami City Ballet was performing in Key West, I received an emergency call from Linda's mother, who had been staying with us. A neighbor of my father's from Orange City had telephoned to say that my father had had an accident, a fainting spell that might have been a minor stroke. He'd passed out on the kitchen floor and lain there for over an hour before he was able to summon this neighbor whom I'd asked to look after him. I asked the neighbor to telephone emergency services to take my father to the local hospital, but within an hour the man called back. The service refused to drive him without a thousand-dollar cash deposit. Because of his appearance the ambulance attendants mistook my father for a homeless man. They wanted some kind of security, but they wouldn't accept my credit card as payment. How could I raise a thousand dollars cash over the phone on a Saturday night? It was days before my father could get the proper treatment. I felt far away from him in Key West and after this incident resolved to convince him to move to Miami.

It wasn't easy, and it had to be accomplished in stages. I'd persuade him to visit for a week or two, and then after a while I arranged for him to give up the house in Orange City and

302

move permanently into a kind of retirement complex on Biscayne Boulevard, a converted motel located twenty-five miles away from our house. Really like a country club, it was pleasant for the residents. Although my father seemed happy enough there, he refused to mingle with the others, preferring to remain by himself except for his meals. He seemed to become more and more cranky and completely antisocial as time went by, and on those occasions when he did venture into the communal dining room, he'd be so argumentative and obstreperous that eventually he was barred from entering it.

The situation was difficult and disturbing, and my father now suffered from severe memory lapses and often repeated himself. Sometimes his mind was lucid and he seemed alert and clearheaded, but other days it was as if he were in a fog. He was never quite sure why I was in Miami and seemed to be under the impression that I was running a school. He might have been suffering from the early stages of Alzheimer's disease or senility, but his condition was never properly diagnosed.

I visited my father regularly in the retirement home, and although he repeatedly refused to let anybody do anything for him, he allowed me to bathe and shave him on the days I came to visit. The first time I shaved him it took me almost an hour and a half to get rid of his beard. On every visit I would change his clothes and tidy his room, and as I worked, I felt our roles had become reversed. The child was now the parent. I was amazed by my father's compliant behavior. He had resisted letting me take care of him for so long, but now he gave in to it willingly. Certainly others at the residence would have performed these services for him, but I saw that he was grateful for—he expected—this attention from me. He never questioned it. It was part of our bond, our heritage.

My father died in September 1988 at the age of eighty-nine, and at his funeral I kissed his forehead just as some of the mourners had kissed Balanchine's forehead at his funeral service. While I was writing this book, I often thought about my father, about our relationship and about my love for him. I remembered all our old times together, happy and sad, and remembered in particular the day in 1953 when he drove me from Queens to the Maritime College in the Bronx. The drive was agony for me. Entering the school was, up to that point,

303

the most painful and unhappy moment of my life, and I was suffering, but for my father it was without a doubt the proudest moment of his existence. His son was going to be the first member of the family to earn a college degree, and it gave him tremendous satisfaction.

At the time I couldn't empathize with him or understand what he was feeling. I was a kid, and the thing I wanted most was being taken away from me. But now, so many years later, I can understand what he was feeling that day. My experience as a father has helped me to understand him. For there is no doubt that one of the proudest moments in my life occurred last June when my son, Roddy, graduated from Union College in Schenectady, New York. Roddy is a dean's list student, a three-time New York State private-school wrestling champion, and a downhill skier—a healthy, solid, gentle person.

Roddy's childhood wasn't easy. He lived through family conflicts and upheavals. He saw the worst of both his parents and he dealt with it. He survived and has already made a success of his young life. I basked in his success at his graduation and had to give Janet credit for turning out such a terrific kid. Janet's married now to a businessman, Terry Martin, and they were both at the graduation.

What made me especially happy about Roddy's day was that I participated in it as more than just a spectator. The school bestowed an honorary doctorate degree on me. I was being honored for my career as a dancer and artistic director, even as an advocate of Balanchine. But I was also being acknowledged as a loving father, a man who had accomplished something in life and reached a state of maturity. I was a very lucky man.

As I thought about my family at Roddy's graduation, different parts of my life became clear to me. The death of my father five years after the death of Balanchine brought everything full circle. My father and my artistic father are both gone, and by some miracle I am now in their place. I am the father now, not only to my son with whom I'm reunited, to my stepdaughter, Lauren, and my daughter, Crista; I am also the father for my extended family, which is the Miami City Ballet, whose dancers and staff members also sit at my table. This is more than a figure of speech. Like my grandfather and Balan-

304

chine, I love to entertain. Like them, I love to open the bottle of wine and pass it around to my guests and to my friends. It symbolizes to me that I am now the giver, the provider, the teacher, the man who sits at the head of the table. Like my grandfather, I am the padrone.

I often think about the reasons for my contentment now, and I understand that my life experience has prepared me for the role I play today. I sacrificed my first forty years to dancing. I had been devoted to my career. When I stopped dancing, I felt empty. I wanted more. Balanchine had made dancing the sum of his life, and I followed his example. But then I questioned the way he lived his private life. I realized that I no longer wanted to imitate him. I no longer needed to seek his approval. I wanted something for myself. I wanted to be more than just a dancer.

I know that much of my happiness springs from my relationship with Linda. She is the partner I will dance the rest of my life with. She's been crucial in my development as a mature man. Because of Linda's values, I'm able to understand what a real family is.

When Crista was still a toddler and I was looking around for suitable work, Linda traveled to Riverdale by subway to give ice-skating lessons. We needed the money to pay our bills, and she took Crista because she didn't want to hire a babysitter. (She has always helped me in my work; as I was learning how to become an artistic director, she was learning about everything.) To Linda, however, her role as a mother always comes first. She's always there for her children anytime they need her. And she has always supported me in the same way. I realize how much I owe her. She's my wife, but she's also my mentor.

As I dwell on my life with Linda, I often think of Balanchine. I miss my artistic father no less than I miss my flesh-and-blood father and feel a real debt of gratitude to him. It did not escape my notice that he did not bequeath his ballets to the New York City Ballet, to that impersonal monolith "the company," but rather to individuals who he knew would exercise their proprietary interests in these works. With constant changes in personnel, how is anyone to know what direction a company will take? I think Mr. B left his ballets to specific people, mostly to the ballerinas who inspired him and a few to   305

Lincoln and Eddie Bigelow, because he knew that people take pride in ownership and will protect what is theirs.

Returning to Balanchine's theater to dance *Watermill* in 1990 was a very emotional experience for me, my final appearance with the New York City Ballet. Writing in the *New York Times,* Anna Kisselgoff said, *"Watermill* remains inseparable from Mr. Villella's overwhelmingly focused stage presence . . . it is the integrity of [his] performance that anchors the seriousness of the entire endeavor. Standing with his back to the audience at first, he commands the stage from the moment he looks over his shoulder; a thousand sorrows are written on his face."

Standing on that stage I understood that I spent most of my career on the outs with Mr. B. I had always wanted more from him personally than he was capable of giving. Once and for all, I saw that some of us got his love and some of us didn't.

Perhaps I was naive to think that time can heal old wounds. I had seen that Balanchine liked to dominate the lives of his dancers and control things, and I had stood up to him. From his point of view that was inexcusable, and most of the time I was banished from his thoughts. Perhaps I hurt him, and he just couldn't forgive me.

But he never let his resentment interfere in our work. Even when we fought, he never denied me any artistic opportunity. It was as a dancer that he loved me and as a dancer that I received his priceless legacy. I was a boxer. I still know how to come back from a punch, stand on my feet, and deliver. Of course, Balanchine didn't leave me anything in the legal sense, but as a dancer his ballets belong to me. In my company, we treat these ballets as if they are ours, and that is how I continue to serve my artistic father.

INDEX

Adams, Diana, 19, 42, 56, 77–78, 167
  as Siren, 82–84, 206
Afternoon of a Faun, 46–48, 59, 116, 214, 252, 263
Agon, 40, 42, 44, 48–50, 58, 77, 116, 123, 236, 251, 275
Allegro Brillante, 40, 289
Allen, Chris, 96, 109
American Ballet Theatre (ABT), 18, 109, 157, 158, 273
Andersen, Ib, 278
Annie Get Your Gun, 51
Ansin, Tobin Lerner, 286–87, 288, 295
Apollo, 40, 42, 69, 192–93, 263, 289
  EV in, 10, 144–48, 150, 252, 275, 278
Aragno, Anna, 140, 185
Arditti, Carlos, 295
Ardolino, Emile, 279
Arpino, Gerald, 20
Arshansky, Misha, 106, 209
art, Soviet, 119–20
Arthur (club), 169–70
Ashley, Merrill, 172, 278
Australia, NYCB in, 54–56

Balanchine, George:
  aging of, 212

apartment of, 64, 264
appearance of, 20, 41, 108, 145, 284–85
ballet transformed by, 10–11, 50, 72–73
casting decisions made by, 55–58, 62, 64, 67, 68, 101
as choreographer, 10–11, 19, 25–26, 40–42, 44–45, 49, 58, 74, 79, 87, 102–4, 106, 129, 135–137, 140–43, 167–168, 170, 180, 190–92, 212–213, 216, 227, 230–31, 235–240, 242–43, 252–53, 284, 294; *see also specific works*
commercial entertainment as viewed by, 65–66, 154–55
confidence of, 73, 102
control exercised by, 73–76, 124–125, 134, 140, 161, 284, 306
critics' views of, 213
as dancer, 10–11, 124, 140, 145–146, 163, 243
distance maintained by, 43, 73, 178
EV's assessment of, 297–301, 304–6
EV's career end announced to, 257
EV's compliment from, 109, 151, 222

307

309

310

311

313

.314

315

316

INDEX

317

About the Authors

EDWARD VILLELLA is America's most celebrated male dancer. The artistry and virility he exhibited during his long career with the New York City Ballet and in concert appearances across the United States and Europe and on television did much to popularize the role of the male in dance.

Villella is associated with many of the greatest roles in the New York City Ballet repertory including *Prodigal Son, Tarantella,* Oberon in *A Midsummer Night's Dream,* the "Rubies" section of *Jewels, Dances at a Gathering,* and many others.

A leading advocate for the arts in America and winner of the thirty-eighth annual Capezio Dance Award, he serves on the National Endowment for the Arts Dance Advisory Panel. In 1985, Villella became the founding artistic director of the Miami City Ballet, which has won worldwide acclaim under his direction.

LARRY KAPLAN coauthored *Dancing for Balanchine* with Merrill Ashley. He is a frequent contributor to *Ballet Review,* has published articles on dance in *Connoisseur* and *Vanity Fair,* and has written fiction for *The New Yorker.*